Write in Style

A guide to good English

Richard Palmer

Head of English
Bedford School

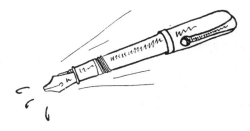

E & FN SPON

An Imprint of Chapman & Hall

London · Glasgow · Weinheim · New York · Tokyo · Melbourne · Madras

Published by E & FN Spon, an imprint of Chapman & Hall,
2-6 Boundary Row, London SE1 8HN, UK

Chapman & Hall, 2-6 Boundary Row, London SE1 8HN, UK

Blackie Academic & Professional, Wester Cleddens Road, Bishopbriggs, Glasgow G64 2NZ, UK

Chapman & Hall GmbH, Pappelallee 3, 69469 Weinheim, Germany

Chapman & Hall USA., One Penn Plaza, 41st Floor, New York, NY10119, USA

Chapman & Hall Japan, ITP-Japan, Kyowa Building, 3F, 2-2-1 Hirakawacho, Chiyoda-ku, Tokyo 102, Japan

Chapman & Hall Australia, Thomas Nelson Australia, 102 Dodds Street, South Melbourne, Victoria 3205, Australia

Chapman & Hall India, R. Seshadri, 32 Second Main Road, CIT East, Madras 600 035, India

First edition 1993
Reprinted 1994, 1995

© 1993 Richard Palmer

Typeset in 10/12 by Falcon Typographic Art Ltd, Fife, Scotland
Printed in Great Britain by Page Bros Ltd, Norwich

ISBN 0 419 14640 7

A Catalogue record for this book is available from the British Library

Library of Congress Cataloging-in-Publication Data available

For Annie, as always;
and for my father, Tony Palmer

CONTENTS

LIST OF EXERCISES

ACKNOWLEDGEMENTS

Countless people have helped me with this book – those who taught me, whom I have taught with, and whom I have taught.

It was my great good fortune as a sixth former at Dulwich College to be taught by Raymond Wilson, then Head of English, later Professor of Education at Reading University; it was he who kindled – indeed ignited – my life-long love of English, and of teaching also. Peter Clayton and Christopher Rowe were enormously helpful in my time as a student teacher at King Edward VI School, Norwich; I am also deeply grateful to former colleagues Reggie Watters and Edward Baines for their wise expertise and generosity, and to all members, past and present, of my Department at Bedford School. And I am no less indebted to my many thousands of students over the years: they have constantly stimulated and increased my interest in all things literary and linguistic, and I hope they all enjoyed my classes as much as I did.

I would also like to thank Tim Kirkup, Sarah Dixon, Michael Tucker, Roger Allen, John Fleming, Robert Kapadia, Paddy Grove and, especially, Louise Berridge, whose detailed criticisms and suggestions have been invaluable; Madeleine Metcalfe, my long-suffering editor; John Penny for his wonderful illustrations; and finally my wife and daughters for their love and patience while the book was being written.

PREFACE

THE PLEASURE PRINCIPLE AND THE WORK ETHIC

We put our love where we have put our labour.

Ralph Waldo Emerson

When work is a pleasure, life is a joy. When work is a duty, life is slavery.

Maxim Gorky

Men seldom give pleasure when they are not pleased themselves.

Samuel Johnson

The Kingman Report into the learning and teaching of English was published in 1988. Reviewing it in a leading article*, *The Guardian* assumed as a proven fact that there are two extreme factions in the English teaching profession. One is characterized by a 'yearning for more learning by rote' and a 'return to traditional grammar lessons'; the other is distinguished by its 'belief that rules should not be taught but absorbed'.

The editorial went on mildly to berate Kingman for steering a timid course between those extremes. Yet it was itself remarkably indecisive. It scoffed at the notion of 'learning by osmosis', but was also certain that 'a return to traditional grammar lessons would not raise standards'. Not only did it fail to supply the answers it found absent in the Report: it seemed to accept that one must be 'for creativity' or 'for accuracy' – that the controlling emphasis must fall **either** on enjoyment and pleasurable absorption **or** on discipline and earned knowledge.

I found this puzzling then, and I continue to do so now. Surely it is not a question of **either/or** but of **both/and**?

It is doubly wrong to reject learning by osmosis on the one hand and direct grammatical training on the other. Both are essential; both can be made pleasurable and productive; each complements the other without being enough on its own.

It is incorrect to assume that no effective learning can be achieved by

---

* *The Guardian*, April 30, 1988, p. 18.

osmosis – that is, through a process of absorption. Children become fluent in their native tongue by the age of four or five, without any formal training or conceptual understanding of the structures they employ. Later on they become competent in reading, an activity that self-evidently depends upon absorption. And this 'absorption' operates in two ways, signalled by the two separate applications of that word. 'To absorb' means to soak up, to take in fully; but we also regularly speak of being absorbed **in** an activity – captivated by it, lost in concentrated attention and wonder. In sum: 'absorption' involves profound pleasure as well as assimilation of knowledge. It is a truism that reading is one of life's great pleasures: my point here is that pleasure brings not only its own reward but a lot of other ones too. It is both fun and instructive.

Nevertheless, it is perfectly absurd to claim that you can master all English skills and requirements solely by osmosis. No one can master anything in such a way. You cannot become a competent pianist just by listening to Vladimir Ashkenazy or Oscar Peterson: you've got to do a lot of active work as well, starting with learning the notes and how to get your fingers to manipulate them accurately and pleasingly. Nor can you become a good cook just by watching someone else prepare a succulent meal. The modish phrase 'hands-on experience' describes the position very well: everyone needs direct practical involvement to become accomplished at anything. That includes the use of language.

Grammar teaching got a bad name some thirty-five years ago, through being carried out in a dry and unpleasurable way. Those who dislike the

Figure 1. 'Dry and unpleasurable'.

prospect of reviving it do so, I suspect, because they confuse **content** with the **methods** they remember from their own schooldays. But there is no reason why learning grammar cannot be fun, even exciting. Most people enjoy learning about how things work; why should language be any different? Moreover, since language is common to us all, something we use virtually all the time, finding out how it works should be especially rewarding.

Bernard Levin has suggested that the English language is the greatest work of art that the human species has yet produced. One of the chief purposes of a work of art is to stimulate pleasure – so there is no reason why mastering a language should be dull or merely hard work. Indeed, I would argue that mastery – of anything – is impossible under such arid conditions. The range of skills involved in becoming an accomplished writer and speaker means that care, discipline and concentration are always necessary; but these qualities can and must be accompanied by a sense of pleasure. There are many kinds of good writing, and many different ways in which one can write well; all are nevertheless characterized by the delight in words they both take and communicate.

Fun is an essential requirement, then. But so is skill – the ability to apply knowledge in a precise and effective way. For those who remain unconvinced that a spirited interest in how language works is fundamental to truly accomplished writing, I would offer two crisp quotations. The first is a remark made by Eddie 'Lockjaw' Davis, a superb tenor saxophonist who chose to spend a period of his career away from the bandstand, working as a booking agent and band manager. When he later resumed playing, he maintained that his time away made him a better player and a more fully-rounded man, saying

The better he knows the product, the better the salesman.

The analogy is telling: the better you know how language operates, the better you'll be able to 'sell' it – and yourself – when writing.

The advice given by Artemus Ward is much more peremptory:

A writer who can't write in a grammarly manner better shut up shop.

Anyone who thinks that the conventions and rules of English don't matter is not going to get very far as a writer, no matter how modest his or her goals. Without a working knowledge of how the signals and structures of language operate and an understanding of why they have been agreed, you are most unlikely to communicate what you might imagine you're saying.

It takes time to acquire the kind of confidence whereby one looks forward to writing as a source of delight rather than as a forbidding task or chore. But it can be done: and one of the better ways is to go back to that time when the magic of words first strikes us – childhood. Charles Baudelaire defined 'genius' as 'childhood recaptured at will' and while genius is beyond the scope of most of us, we will still benefit enormously if we can invest adult activity with the fresh excitement that distinguishes childhood pursuits. Of course, very young writers have many limitations: I am not advocating a return to 'the cat sat on the mat' practice! But young children embody in their use of language two qualities that older writers forget at their peril: they have a clear idea of what they want to say and a pleasure-based verve in the way they say it.

My aim is therefore twofold. Naturally, I want to be helpfully instructive, enabling you to write with confidence and clarity. The tasks, techniques and skills this book explores are many and wide-ranging, and I hope its advice contains something of value to all writers of fifteen years and above, whatever their particular needs. But I also want you to enjoy yourself while reading the material and, perhaps, attempting some of the exercises I include. I am convinced that students – of any age or ability – learn faster and better if they have a good time while they work, which is why the host of examples are designed to give pleasure as well as instruction. The combination of absorbed amusement and challenging work has rarely had other than a successful outcome. And what better way to start than to have some undemanding but illuminating fun at someone else's expense?

ENGAGE BRAIN
AND EAR
BEFORE WRITING

PART ONE

Figure 2. 'Engage brain and ear'.

DISASTERS 1

Troubles hurt the most when they prove self-inflicted.
Sophocles, Oedipus Rex

Destructive criticism is one of life's great pleasures, and a seriously undervalued one. As we grow up, we are often brainwashed into thinking that the only reputable type of criticism is 'constructive' – that is, essentially admiring but containing some suggestions as to how what has been done could be made even better. But when something is awful, why not say so? Children do; maybe that's why they have so much fun, and embarrass po-faced adults so often! So let's take an enjoyable look at four passages that turned out rather less well than their authors intended.

1. In this set of instructions the writer gets into a hilarious mess through not thinking clearly or 'hearing' the words.

> When feeding the baby with a bottle, it must be held at a steep angle with the bottom tilted up and the neck held firmly down, otherwise an air-bubble will form in the neck. Do not allow the baby to drink all the feed at once, but give it a rest sometimes so that it can get the wind up. Finally, when the baby has finished the bottle, place it under the tap straight away, or allow it to soak in a mild solution of Milton, to prevent infection. If the baby does not thrive on fresh milk it should be powdered or boiled.

A formal analysis of why this goes wrong would show that the loose use of pronouns sets up a farcical ambiguity. But a simpler explanation is that the writer is **lazy**. There has been no attempt to imagine how the words will 'sound', how they will affect the reader. Given that the passage is instructional, presumably intended to assist an inexperienced parent, that is a severe fault.

Exercise 1
Rewrite the above passage so that it makes clear and uncomical sense. You'll find my suggested version in the Appendix.

---

2. The next extract, taken from an A level English examination script, suffers from inadequate thought too, though in a different way.

> Fielding, having once been a playwrite [sic]*, moved into novels. In this novel he was not merely trying to parody *Pamela*, by Richardson, but his was make [sic] some clear social comments. To do this he had to use caricatures and situations, and this obviously could lead to a certain amount of disconnection of events.

Even if we ignore the spelling mistake and the brief dive into illiteracy in the third line, this is an unholy mess. The candidate is not stupid, and underneath the drivel there is a sense of some useful points trying to emerge. But they are all jumbled together, linked by a 'logic' presumed to be adequate but which in fact is non-existent. The writer needed to be aware of a very valuable principle:

Never begin a sentence until you are sure of what you want to say in it *and* of how it will end.

If obeying that principle means that you write shorter sentences for a while, never mind. Better that than to land yourself in the kind of quagmire we've just waded through.

3. The next example is clear enough, maybe, but it still won't do. It appeared in *The Daily Express* over twenty years ago, but you'll come across plenty of similar stuff today.

> *Danger Waits For The Boy Born To Rule*
> The podgy fingers of a prince clasp a dagger. A dagger stained by history.
> Once it belonged to his great-grandfather, King Abdullah.
> And he was killed by an assassin.
> But to 17-month-old Crown Prince Abdullah the dangers of ruling troubled Jordan are unknown.
> One day he will understand what his father, King Hussein, has to face.
> Today, the crown prince just plays at being king – his bearing proud and regal.
> Right now, he is looking forward to having a playmate.
> His mother, 22-year-old Princess Muna – Toni Gardner from England – is expecting a second child in October.

For a start, there are two wonderful inanities here. The idea of any

---

* 'Sic' means 'thus': it is used when quoting a passage containing grammatical errors, so that the reader will realize that the original writer committed the error, not the quoter. 'Sic' is therefore a splendidly economical way of saying, 'Yes, he/she really did write it this way!'

baby of seventeen months having a 'bearing' that is 'proud and regal' is preposterous; and how many infants know enough about human reproduction to be aware that in a few months 'a playmate' will arrive? But there are less engaging flaws as well.

Passage 1 was guilty of paying inadequate attention to its audience; this one is guilty of insufficient respect. The tone is both patronizing and gormless; the text is set out on the apparent principle that its readers will not be able to cope with more than a dozen words at a time before needing a rest. Such scorn and slush reduce a potentially interesting observation about Middle East danger to a maudlin wreck.

4. At the other end of the scale, we now encounter a writer who does not patronize his readers so much as ignore them completely. The suffering narrator here is Bertie Wooster, struggling with a work of philosophy his fiancée has thrust upon him to improve his mind: the passage comes from P. G. Wodehouse's story *Jeeves Takes Charge*.

'I opened *Types Of Ethical Theory*, and I give you my honest word this was what hit me:

'Of the two antithetic terms in the Greek philosophy one only was real and self-subsisting; and that one was Ideal Thought as opposed to that which it has to penetrate and mould. The other, corresponding to our Nature, was in itself phenomenal, unreal, without any permanent footing, having no predicates that held true for two moments together; in short, redeemed from negation only by including indwelling realities appearing through.'

Well, I mean to say, what?'

Bertie may be a 'silly ass' [Jeeves, his manservant, describes him elsewhere as 'mentally negligible'] but his reaction is a model for all put-upon readers. Equally unanswerable is Ernest Hemingway's

Figure 3. 'Never begin a sentence until you are sure how it will end'.

observation that a writer's greatest gift – and, by association, a reader's too – is 'a built-in, shock-proof shit detector'. In Bertie's position we might urge the author to call in Dyno-Rod as soon as possible.

Readers must be prepared to do some work from time to time, naturally, but they also have the right to expect that things are not made needlessly difficult for them. No subject is so elusive or challenging that it cannot be rendered reasonably clear and enjoyable for an audience. The failure to do so means only one thing, ultimately: the writer doesn't care about his audience, being enclosed in a mere ego-trip.

I've entitled this section 'Disasters'. A racier term defining such embarrassing incompetence has been coined by *Private Eye* – 'Coleman-balls', originally inspired by the daft remarks of television commentator David Coleman but subsequently extended to include any and all verbal gaffes. As a final look for the time being at incompetent use of language, here are a few of my favourite 'Colemanballs'; after that you might like to try the exercise based on others.

We are not prepared to stand idly by and be murdered in our beds.

The Reverend Ian Paisley

If Tchaikovsky were alive today he'd be turning in his grave.

Radio 1

We're waiting for the pole-vault over the satellite.

David Coleman

Exercise 2
Ten comically inadequate remarks follow. In each case:

(a) Work out **why** it fails/is ridiculous
(b) Rewrite it so that it is clear and not able to be laughed at. Keep as close as you can to the original idea and wording.

1. **With the very last kick of the game, McDonald scored with a header.**
   Alan Parry

2. **We thought this story incredible – very convincing.**
   Lord Asa Briggs

3. **The Channel Tunnel project seems to be getting off the ground again.**
   Sir Alistair Burnett

4. **Here we are in the Holy Land of Israel – a Mecca for tourists.**
   David Vine

5. **She really set the pool alight tonight.**
   Anita Lonsborough, talking about a swimmer

6. **To win a Gold Medal, you've got to come first.**
   David Coleman

7. **I thought 2–0 was an accurate reflection of the scoreline.**
   John Toshack

8. **Tell me, what's your gut feeling in your heart of hearts?**
   Radio 4's *Today* programme

9. **Obviously you do other things as well as dedicating your life 24 hours a day to ballet.**
   Mike Read

10. **The atmosphere is amazing: you could cut the tension with a cricket stump.**
    Murray Walker

My suggested answers are on page 343.

Figure 4. 'The Holy Land – a Mecca for tourists'.

TRIUMPHS

2

Style is a magic wand, and turns to gold everything
it touches.

Logan Pearsall Smith

We've just looked at various examples of how not to write. Now
let's redress the balance by considering some admirable passages.
My illustrations have been chosen to match the types of writing
included in the previous section: a passage of instructional prose;
the beginning of a student essay; a newspaper article; an advanced
philosophical discourse.

1. Taken from Sir Izaak Walton's masterpiece, *The Compleat Angler*.

How To Dress A Chub For Table

First scale him, and then wash him clean, and then take out his
guts; and to that end make the hole as little and as near to his gills
as you may conveniently, and especially make clean his throat from
the grass and weeds that are usually in it, for if that be not very clean,
it will make him to taste very sour; having so done, put some sweet
herbs into his belly, and then tie him with two or three splinters to
a spit, and roast him, basted often with vinegar, or rather verjuice*
and butter, and with a good store of salt mixed with it.

If he is thus dressed, you will find him a much better dish of meat
than you, or most folk, even the Anglers themselves do imagine; for
this dries up the fluid watery humour with which all Chubs do
abound.

This has considerable charm and it flows easily. Its chief quality,
however, is its *clarity*: the careful organization and precise detail create
a foolproof guide.

2. The start of an A Level essay on *As I Lay Dying*, a novel by William
Faulkner.

As the title so bluntly suggests, the novel is concerned wholly with
death. It is void of any romanticism, and death itself is treated with
little religious significance; it is the finality of death in a world

---

* 'Verjuice' is the juice of an unripe fruit.

ruled by nature and the unforgiving gods of ancient times that we are shown. This, indeed, is a radical and epic treatment of life's most important event, but the epic nature of the book is constantly undermined: the single most important sentence in the novel confirms my opening statement in its grotesque simplicity – 'My father used to say that the reason for living was to get ready to stay dead a long time.' The triviality of life: the finality of death without salvation or damnation.

Those that do not know Faulkner's novel will have to take my word for it that the content here is first class. But I hope any reader will appreciate the quality of its **style**. The concepts are large and the argument ambitious; yet notice how straightforward and logical the thinking and writing are. The first sentence sets up everything with fierce clarity, and then all the major implications are pursued with vigorous, stark persuasiveness. Finally, it is an excellent introduction as well as very fine in its own right: one would want to read on, avidly.

3. An extract from one of Alistair Cooke's *Letters From America*, part of an appreciation of US Chief Justice Earl Warren, who died in July 1974.

I'd always taken for granted that the ultimate truth about old people had been spoken by Aristotle twenty-three hundred years ago. Which is: 'Unlike the young, the old have lived long' – nobody like Aristotle for getting down to fundamentals – 'they have often been deceived, they have made many mistakes of their own, they have seen the pain caused by positive men, and so they are positive about nothing. And when they err, they err in all things by extreme moderation.'

As time went on, and I was able to watch young politicians age and mellow and grow positive about nothing, I noticed that very rarely there was a man who mellowed, like over-ripe fruit, into acidity. They were usually men who'd seemed to be committed all their lives to a bland, comfortable conservatism. And then something happened, something unexplained by the geriatric experts. It wasn't that they grew into a familiar type of the peppery conservative but that they grew at once more mellow and more radical.

Both comfortable to read and fascinating, the writing is masterly in its apparent effortlessness. In fact, it is very shrewdly crafted for all its air of spontaneity. Its sentences are intelligently varied in length; there are agreeable changes in tone, including one nicely understated joke; it is flawlessly punctuated (which always assists understanding). Above all, there is a central awareness of how the words will sound. That may hardly seem surprising, since the piece was conceived as a radio talk;

the crucial point is that it reads as well as it sounds, **and vice versa**. During this book I shall be stressing a great deal the importance of 'voice' in one's writing, and now seems a good time to record another fundamental principle:

All good writing *sounds* equally good when read aloud; and all good talking will *read* well if transcribed.

Sadly, the same relationship characterizes **bad** writing and talking. If you want proof, refer back to the *Daily Express* piece in the previous section (page 4): if you can read that aloud without descending into a mawkish drawl, I'll be very surprised!

4. A paragraph from 'The Vision Of A Child', one of five philosophical lectures collected in David Newsome's *Two Classes Of Men: Platonism and English Romantic Thought*.

> We may grant that distinctions of measure and discernment of categories are important to the imaginative poet as well as to the scientist. Just because he has them, the poet is a philosopher in a sense that a child can never be. Coleridge recognized this in his careful analysis of the loosing and binding power of the imagination, as we have seen, and his approval of the statement of H. S. Reimarus that 'we have no conception, not even of single objects, except by means of the similarity we perceive between them and other objects'. F. D. Maurice, likewise, pointed to the inability of a child to make refined distinctions, arising from the infant state when all men are called 'father' and all women 'mother'. But the particular genius of the child – and to Coleridge a child possesses genius rather than talent – was the combination of simplicity, innocence and sensibility which enabled it to penetrate to the essence of what it observed, without being able to explain the process in intellectual or rational terms.

Here Newsome addresses some fundamental principles and phenomena of perception, as part of a searching reappraisal of the work of a major English poet. Nobody would call the writing 'easy': such major concerns demand fierce concentration on the reader's part. But that concentration is rapidly rewarded, because the prose is both logical and vibrant, with a couple of homely examples the better to fix things in one's mind.

If you refer back to the passage Bertie Wooster had to endure (page 5), you should at once be aware of a crucial difference. The more one studies the prose there, the muddier it becomes; equivalent attention to Newsome's work quickly brings enlightenment. And Newsome's scale of reference is no smaller or less profound than that of the 'companion piece'. His ideas are large and his focus ambitious, but one senses that he is anxious to share them with us; in contrast, Bertie's tormentor seems to be indulging some private game that shuts out his audience. Huge or complex ideas need not remain inaccessible to the 'ordinary reader'. Indeed, I would argue that if those ideas cannot be expressed to the satisfaction and understanding of such a reader, they are probably not that important or worthwhile after all.

SUMMARY

Successful writing depends on a lot of things, but we have already identified three of the most important.

1. All good writing is *clear*; to achieve clarity you must work out in advance what you want to say in each sentence and each paragraph. You cannot afford to 'just write': tough-minded preliminary planning is essential if your work is to please and illuminate.

2. All good writing has a proper sense of its audience. You should assume your reader is intelligent, or not actually a moron; on the other hand, do not *over*estimate his or her abilities. At every turn you should keep your readers awake, interested, stimulated; but you should also ensure that they are comfortable, aware of what you're doing and where you're going. In short, make your reader your respected but gratified *companion*.

3. All good writing has a strong sense of 'voice'. Effective prose, no less than successful poetry, is attractive to ear and eye alike. Writing that is pleasing has a natural rhythm and melodiousness, qualities that characterize a pleasant speaking voice; in addition, the presence of good 'voice' automatically renders one's writing more personal, warmer and clearer.

With these central things firmly in mind, let us now take a close look at how language works.

FOUNDATIONS

PART TWO

INTRODUCTION 3

Style, like the human body, is especially beautiful when the veins are not prominent and the bones cannot be counted.

Tacitus

It is flesh which makes a body both beautiful and individual. Few people other than rampant ghouls find skeletons aesthetically delightful, and I've yet to find anyone who found them sensually attractive. And whereas each human body seems unique, each skeleton looks identical to all but an expert eye.

Consider what happens to the body, however, if any of its bones is deformed or deficient in some other way. Not only does the frame appear forlorn and full of pain; the flesh on it often looks comparably unhealthy. Just as good bone structure and skin tone can enhance healthy flesh and transform it into beauty, so any flaws in the body's basic structure seem eventually to infect it throughout.

It is the same with language. The ultimate aim of this book is to help you achieve an elegant, precise and individual style in all that you write – to give your writing the functional beauty that characterizes a healthy body. But that cannot be done until the skeleton is in good shape. The foundations or 'bones' of your language must be sound if its flesh – what you want to say and how you wish to say it – is to prosper.

Of course, flesh and bone go together. A fleshless skeleton may not be much to look at, but then neither is flesh on its own: it is so much dead meat. Writers who ignore the basic structures and concentrate on disembodied style don't just fail to write well: they end up butchering the language they claim to nurture and enjoy. The sections which follow look at the bones and ligaments of language (the sentence and the clause) and its essential joints (punctuation and paragraphing).

BONE STRUCTURE **4**

4.1 WHAT IS A SENTENCE?

The sentence is the single most important linguistic structure: it is, if you like, the backbone of all writing. And it is disturbing how much **invertebrate** writing one encounters. Many otherwise quite capable writers either do not understand what a sentence is or are incapable of applying that understanding at all times.

One reason for this is that the sentence is a very difficult concept to explain and therefore to master. There are only three 'rules' which pertain, and each is of limited value.

1. **All sentences must begin with a capital letter and end with a full stop.**
2. **All sentences must express a complete thought.**
3. **All sentences must contain a subject and a finite verb.**

Comfortably straightforward, aren't they? No? You're absolutely right!

The first rule is one of the first things most of us learn at primary school. It seems elementary: using a capital letter is simple, and we all know what a full stop is. But the rule is not much use on its own:

Manchester United.   Write In Style.

Those start with capital letters, and I've [legitimately] placed a full stop after each one. They are not sentences, however; to establish why not, we need to consider rules 2 and 3.

I've often felt that rule 2 ought to be more helpful than it actually is. 'A complete thought' **seems** to be a clear and precise term: in this pair of examples it is obvious that the first is incomplete, making no sense whatsoever.

The man in a yellow.   The girl in rags.

But in what way is the second 'a complete thought'? It makes a certain amount of sense, yes, but only in terms of naming, of identification. Like 'Manchester United' and 'Write In Style', 'The girl in rags' prompts us to ask something like 'Well, so what?' or 'What **about** her?' As they stand, all three are in a kind of limbo, requiring further information to satisfy us fully.

That's where rule 3 comes in. Each of these four examples obeys rules 1 and 2; only one of them matches the requirement laid down by rule 3. Which is it?

(a) The mechanic in the oil-stained overall.
(b) The Hound of the Baskervilles.
(c) The dog bites the milkman.
(d) British Aerospace.

The answer is (c), which is an authentic **sentence**; the others are **phrases**.

In (c) an event takes place: something happens, firmly located in time. In this case that time is the present, but the sentence could equally be set in the past –

The dog bit the milkman.

or the future –

the dog will bite the milkman.

Bites, bit and **will bite** denote an action or a process – which is what all 'verbs' do. In addition, that action or process is identified in terms of time – hence 'finite', located within a definite tense/area of time. Finally, to be fully 'finite', a verb must be accompanied by a **subject** – and this tricky concept needs a little exploration.

In 'English studies' we use the term **subject** in two quite separate ways, and this can forgivably cause students a lot of confusion. In its broader, more general sense, **subject** means **topic**. In these remarks

(a) **Can you remember the subject of this chapter?**
(b) **He is bored: we should change the subject.**

subject refers to what the chapter or the conversation is about: strictly speaking, the term should be expanded to **subject matter**.

But **subject** has a narrower, technical meaning too. In grammatical terms, **subject** means that which governs the verb – the person or thing 'in charge' of the action or process described. In that earlier sentence

The dog bites the milkman

'the dog' is the 'doer' of the action (**bites**). It is the **grammatical subject**.

As a summary for the time being, let's see how the two separate meanings of **subject** apply to my three most recent examples.

(a) Can you remember the subject of this chapter?

Topic/subject matter: the question of what the chapter is about.
Grammatical subject: 'you'[+ finite verb 'can remember'].

(b) He is bored: we should change the subject.

Topic/subject matter: the speaker's desire to talk about something else.
Grammatical subjects: i) 'He' [+ finite verb 'is'].
                             ii) 'we' [+ finite verb 'should change']

(c) The dog bites the milkman.

Topic/subject matter: An incident involving a dog, a milkman and an act of biting.*
Grammatical subject: 'The dog' [+ finite verb 'bites'].

* You might find this explanation clumsy, vague or pompous. I rather hope you do: I phrased it in that way to highlight further the complete separateness of the two meanings of **subject**. For I could re-arrange the words in that sentence so that the **subject matter** definition still applied but the **grammatical subject** was radically different:

(d) The milkman bites the dog.

That still concerns 'a dog, a milkman and an act of biting'; but now it is the 'milkman' who is 'in charge' of the action: he is 'the doer', not the dog!

To qualify as a sentence, therefore, a verbal structure must possess three principal properties. It must describe an action or process that is located in a specific time-zone; the 'doer' [grammatical subject] must be identified; and the thought expressed must be complete, fully satisfying. If you are not yet comfortable with the first two, then please read through the material again; if you're then still uncertain, it might be wise to consult the Grammar Primer at the back of the book. If you're happy about those two but continue to find the concept of 'a complete thought' problematic, it is time to introduce another term: the clause.

4.2 SENTENCE AND CLAUSE: WHAT'S THE DIFFERENCE?

When uncertain about a meaning, most sensible people refer to a good dictionary. *The Shorter Oxford* defines 'sentence' as:

A series of words in connected speech or writing, forming the grammatically complete expression of a single thought.

And 'clause' as:

> **A short sentence; a distinct member of a sentence, one containing a subject and a predicate.***

The trouble is that unless you already know the difference, I suspect that this pair of definitions is not only of little help but probably increases your confusion! The most we can deduce from them is that

> **All sentences are clauses, or contain several clauses; but a single clause does not necessarily form a sentence**.

And a fat lot of help **that** seems to be, no doubt prompting the reaction, 'Thanks a whole bunch!' I hope I can clear things up by studying some examples, in the form of a little exercise.

Exercise 3
Which of these is a sentence, which a clause?

1. Although you broke the window.
2. I forgive you.
3. I have a hunch that.
4. You dislike cheese.

All four start with capitals and end with full stops; all four have a subject and a finite verb – as follows:

	Subject	Finite verb
1.	**you**	**broke**
2.	**I**	**forgive**
3.	**I**	**have**
4.	**You**	**dislike**

But do all four express a **complete** thought?

I hope you can see that 1 and 3 do not – we need more information for them to satisfy fully. Both are left hanging in the air. In 1 the use of 'although' sets up an expectation that is not fulfilled, while 3 is even more frustrating, leaving us entirely ignorant of what this 'hunch' is about. Both 2 and 4 are complete. They may be somewhat bald, even uninteresting; nevertheless, they require nothing else to make complete grammatical and intellectual sense.

However, it is relatively easy to make 1 and 3 part of an authentic sentence: we can merge them with 2 and 4.

* Don't worry about the term 'predicate'. It is defined as 'the statement made about a subject'; in effect this simply means everything in the sentence or clause apart from the subject. By definition, the predicate includes a finite verb.

5.   **Although you broke the window, I forgive you.**
6.   **I have a hunch that you dislike cheese.**

These make complete sense, and are now, perhaps, more interesting! 5 and 6 now consist of two clauses – each has two subjects and two finite verbs. And both consist of a **main clause** and a **subordinate clause**. The latter term describes a clause that cannot stand on its own –

> **Although you broke the window . . .**
> **I have a hunch that . . .**

Subordinate clauses are 'grammatical juniors', dependent on the main clause for complete sense. They are not 'subordinate' in any other way; they need not be stylistically inferior, and indeed may be more informative than the main clause they depend on, as in this example:

7.   **If you go on with a diet that consists exclusively of cottage cheese, dry toast and Brazil nuts, I shall worry.**

The main clause is **I shall worry:** it is, I think, rather feeble in view of what precedes it, a sad anticlimax to what was promising to be a fairly arresting sentence. But although that previous clause is much more interesting in every other way, it remains grammatically subordinate: it could not stand on its own.

If we return to my metaphor of grammar as a skeleton, we could say that sentences/main clauses are **bones**, and that subordinate clauses are **ligaments**. Bones may well be the basis of everything, but without ligaments they remain stiff and limited; it is often the ligaments, or the 'junior' members of a sentence that give it charm and impact. Once those bones and ligaments are in good shape, the chances are high that the flesh that covers them – the actual material and individual words chosen – will be sound and pleasing.

   If you need further guidance on clauses and how they can form various kinds of sentence, the matter is covered fully in the section on **syntax** in the Grammar Primer. My next chapter looks at how a number of professional writers create widely different shapes and effects out of the basic properties we've so far covered.

4.3. BIG BONES OR LITTLE BONES:
HOW LONG SHOULD A SENTENCE BE?

'How long is a piece of string' is often cited as the classic useless question, and to ask 'How long should my sentences be?' might seem equally idiotic. In fact it is both intelligent and important. For once you've understood how and why your sentences work, you can **fashion** them to your taste – and that partly involves a decision about how long and complex, or short and snappy, they need to be for your purposes. Effective writing comes in all shapes and sizes: the key is in judging which shape and size is most appropriate to a given task.

Please read this passage from Ernest Hemingway's *Big Two-Hearted River*.

> He took out his knife, opened it, and stuck it in the log. Then he pulled up the sack, reached into it, and brought out one of the trout. Holding him near the tail, hard to hold, alive, in his hand, he whacked him against the log. The trout quivered, rigid. Nick laid him on the log in the shade and broke the neck of the other fish in the same way. He laid them side by side on the log. They were fine trout.
>
> Nick cleaned them, slitting them from the vent to the tip of the jaw. All the insides and the gills and the tongue came out in one piece. They were both males, long grey-white strips of milt, smooth and clean. All the insides clean and compact, coming out all together. Nick tossed the offal ashore for the minks to find.
>
> He washed the trout in the stream. When he held them back in the water they looked like live fish. Their colour was not gone yet . . .

And so on. I admire this a good deal, but I've chosen it for this section because it is precariously close to being monotonous. There is some variety – but only in that some sentences are even shorter than others!

Hemingway is famous for this kind of style. In the example chosen, the profusion of full stops is designed to make the reader focus on each simple action and perception, and in its stark way it is a very physical piece.* I think it works well, but it is a most unwise model. In your own writing it is best to aim for a greater variety of sentence-length.

The next passage goes to the opposite extreme.

> When the director in the field sends the executive in there's got to be a professional set-up. We didn't have one.
>
> I suppose Loman had thought of a dozen angles of attack and obviously the one he'd chosen was the one he thought was right and he was wrong.
>
> 'I think you're showing an unreasonable bias towards –'
>
> 'Is that so?' I was really very fed up. 'We've been called in by a panic directive to clear up the wreck of an operation that went off half-cocked and killed one man and exposed another and by a

---

* The hero, Nick, is in fact still suffering from trauma, so the simple style is movingly appropriate, his stiff halting sentences analogous to the tentative steps someone might take when first walking after breaking a leg. Another example of such surface simplicity hiding deeper truth and trauma can be found in Aston's speech at the end of Act II of Harold Pinter's *The Caretaker*.

bit of luck I missed a bomb and last night they picked Fyson out
of Tunis harbour and it'd be nice to think that when they grilled
him he didn't break but the last time I saw him his nerve had gone
so they wouldn't have had any trouble. How safe's our base now,
Loman? . . .'   from *The Tango Briefing* by Adam Hall

If a homework-marker would criticize Hemingway for too many short
sentences, then Hall would be equally castigated for writing an eight-
line sentence devoid of punctuation. Yet I consider this excellent writing.
The narrator, Quiller, is very annoyed, and his outburst is the result of
cumulative frustration. It explodes in a single 'breathless' rush, which
makes the absence of punctuation entirely appropriate.

Once again, however, that is not a model I'd advise you to copy.
Creative writers can break 'rules' in this way provided they succeed as
a result. That is also true for you and me, but in most of your discursive,
non-fiction writing it is better to stick to a middle course than emulate
either of those extremes.

That middle course will be easier to negotiate if you stay constantly
alert to your readers' pleasure and comfort. There follow three more
passages which do this very well; they make their subject come alive
by **varying** the rhythms and shape of their prose. The first is from 'Iron
In The Soul', from *Selected Essays And Notebooks* by Albert Camus.

> I arrived at Prague at six in the evening. I immediately took my
> suitcases to the left-luggage office. I still had two hours in which to
> look for a hotel. And I was full of a strange feeling of liberty because
> I no longer had my two suitcases hanging on my arms. I came out
> of the station, walked by some gardens, and found myself suddenly
> thrown into the middle of the Avenue Wenceslas, swarming with
> people at that time of the evening. Around me were a million
> people who had been alive all this time and whose existence had
> never impinged upon mine. They were alive. I was thousands of
> kilometres away from a familiar country. I could not understand
> their language. They all walked quickly. And they overtook me,
> they all cut themselves off from me. I felt lost.*

This is crisp and graphic. Camus eases us into his situation with three
simple, informative sentences; then, as we get used to him and he gets
more used to his environment, his sentences lengthen. They become
more complex in other ways too: the focus on facts gives way to
something more philosophical. And as the sense of his isolation

---

* In deference to those purists who might feel that an extract from a French work
should not be used in a book on English style, I can say that the translation faithfully
reflects the original's sentences both in their structure and variety of length, which
characteristics are my concern here.

bears down upon him, the sentences get shorter again, emphasizing the anxiety and feeling of helplessness that stab at him. At all times Camus is sharply **aware**, both of his own responses and the effect they should have on us.

That extract was from the beginning of the chosen piece. The next occurs at the end of a portrait of 'Arnold' by John Wain, in his book *Dear Shadows*.

> Long before the mile was covered, Arnold was wilting. There was simply no strength left in that old body which had weathered malnutrition and disease seventy years earlier and had gone on at a cracking pace ever since. We walked more and more slowly. I was about to suggest that he sit down while I fetched the car when we heard behind us the drumming engine of a tractor. It came up, towing behind a flat wagon which had been emptied of its load. We flagged it down. The driver, a good-natured young fellow, let us scramble up on to the wagon, and sitting on its smooth boards, dusty with fragments of straw and chaff, we finished our excursion. Arnold looked round with satisfaction at the landscape, and remarked that this would be a good way of taking a holiday: touring the British Isles by tractor and trailer.
>
> That was the last of my excursions with Arnold. His bed, and then the grave, claimed him in the first height of summer, the time of year he loved so much, and his life ended among springing green leaves and clamorous birds. But I remember him jolting along behind the tractor, enjoying the fun of it, finding zest in that last outing as he had found zest in all the others.
>
> I was very proud of Arnold. He was my father.

The last sentence reveals Arnold's identity for the first time – a wonderfully touching ending.* Elsewhere there is again a variety in sentence-length pleasing in its richness and also appropriate. The shorter sentences tend to be about Arnold's weakness – his own 'shortness' of breath and stamina – while the longer ones meander gracefully, reflecting the gentle panorama of the landscape. Like Camus, Wain is always alert to why a specific length or rhythm is apposite, and how it will benefit the reader.

Lastly, an extract taken from the middle of an account of the Greek genius, Archimedes.

> There are other stories about Archimedes. One is that when asked by Hieron how great a weight could be moved by a small force, Archimedes demonstrated how he alone could pull a three-masted

---

* Incidentally, it is also a perfect example of the power of a short paragraph, a technique to be examined later.

ship which had been lugged ashore by a host of men. For this demonstration Archimedes used compound pulleys, and while it seems he did invent the compound pulley, the story has a distinct ring of fantasy about it. Not so Archimedes's supposed remark, 'Give me a place to stand on and I will move the earth,' which underlines the principle of the lever. Yet whatever the authenticity of the many stories of Archimedes, they all emphasize that his reputation as a mechanical inventor was immense. Indeed, he is even credited with designing and using vast burning mirrors to set fire to ships in the Roman fleet which later besieged Syracuse – the siege which led to Roman occupation and the death of Archimedes – though the report that he designed and built celestial globes depicting the heavens and a kind of planetarium for displaying planetary movements seems to have more of a ring of truth about it, as it was referred to by Cicero, who had seen the instruments.

from *The Cambridge History Of The World's Science*,
by Colin A. Ronan

I find that the hardest of the three to read; it is good writing nonetheless. Its rhythms are purposeful and invigorating, reflecting the author's mastery of his material. There is an attractive variety to its sentences: although they are on average longer than those in the Camus or Wain extracts, it's worth stressing that they occur in the **middle** of Ronan's account – by which time the reader has settled into the flow and 'voice' of the writing, and can thus absorb complex structures more comfortably than at the beginning.

SENTENCE LENGTH: SOME CONCLUDING GUIDELINES

It is impossible to give watertight advice on how long and how varied your sentences should be. As we've just seen, different kinds of writing require different things and express different priorities. However, there are guidelines which can be of assistance in shaping your sentences; they all hinge on the need to 'hear' what you're writing and to calculate its effect on others.

[Note: ** denotes an illustration or exercise to follow.]

1. It is usually a good idea to make your first sentence reasonably short. This is not an absolute rule, naturally, but your readers will be grateful if you ease them into your material with crisp straightforwardness.
2. Too many short sentences will quickly tire and irritate your readers.**
3. Equally, avoid too many long sentences. These tire readers in a different way, and you risk bewildering and eventually losing them.
4. Avoid constructing sentences that are too complex or needlessly intricate.**

5. It is often wise to follow a sentence containing a lot of information with a short one that, while not duplicating your material, summarizes or clarifies it.**
6. Make sure each new sentence actually *says* something. Mere repetition of already-established material is of no use, however elegant your style. Deliberate repetition for effect is another matter, but it is a difficult skill and should in any case be used sparingly.

Finally, two 'golden principles':

1. Trust the *feel* of your prose. By all means be self-critical and alert to danger, but if, all precautions admitted, you're convinced that the three successive long [or short] sentences you've written are effective and pleasing, *keep them in*. Slavishly to write one long, two short, or one long, one short, one long and so on, is just silly. To approach your prose as if it is some kind of elaborate Morse code is no way to achieve competence, let alone true 'style'.
2. Assume your readers are intelligent. Don't patronize; don't be indifferent either. You can expect them to be prepared to do some work, but try to make their working environment as comfortable and stimulating as you can.

ILLUSTRATIONS AND EXERCISES

Passage A: Exercise 4
This is potentially a vigorous piece, but it is marred by too many short sentences. Keeping as close as you can to the original, try recasting it so that it acquires proper fluency. My suggested version is on page 341.

Prohibition was known as 'The Great Experiment'. The experiment was a remarkable one. It occurred in the United States of America. It took place in the years 1920–33. The sale and consumption of alcohol was prohibited throughout those years. But the people's liking for alcohol did not disappear. Therefore alcohol was distilled illegally. It was sold in 'Speakeasies'. 'Speakeasies' were clubs owned by gangsters. Some of those gangsters became enormously powerful. Al Capone of Chicago was for a time considered to be the most powerful man in the country. He was eventually imprisoned for tax evasion. The gangsters' control nevertheless continued. The experiment came to an end in 1933. By this time the damage had been done. America has had to live with organized crime ever since.

Passage B: Exercise 5
This next sentence is much too 'fiddly' and intricate. The writer has not done enough prior planning, and tries to cram too much in, with increasingly confusing results for the reader. Try re-writing it so that it is clear; use two sentences if you wish. Again, my suggested version is on page 344.

Counsel maintained that the accused, if he had, as was alleged by some, though not the most reliable of the witnesses for the prosecution, taken the articles in question, had been subject to temporary lapses of memory as a result of shell-shock sustained during the war.

Passage C
No exercise this time – just an example of how to 'clinch' and clarify information listed in a long sentence with a snappily short one. It comes from Joseph Heller's *Catch-22*.

One day Clevinger had stumbled while marching to class; the next day he was formally charged with 'breaking ranks while in formation, felonious assault, indiscriminate behaviour, mopery, high treason, provoking, being a smart guy, listening to classical music' and so on. In short, they threw the book at him.

Passage D
Again, no exercise – simply a demonstration of what a gifted writer can build out of concentrated repetition. In this extract from *Other People* Martin Amis produces an almost mesmerizing effect that prompts both laughter and something more disturbing.

Alcoholics: you know what *they're* like, don't you? Certainly you do. Chances are, you know one or two personally, or you know someone who does. Think about it. How many do you know? There are an awful lot of drunks about these days. It wouldn't really surprise me if you turned out to be one yourself. Are you?
    Drunks are people who can't stay sober. They would rather be drunk. They can't bear being themselves. They have a point. It is harder being yourself than it is being drunk.
    Drunks aren't themselves: they're drunks. They aren't like other people, though they used to be before they started being drunks. People are various; drunks aren't.
    When drunk, drunks all think, feel and behave in exactly the same way. When sober, drunks think about drink all the time. They do.

That's what they're thinking about. If you ever wonder what they're thinking about when they're not being drunk, that's what they're thinking about: being drunk.

Most of them know some things about why they can't bear being themselves, and some of them know a lot. But they all think they know things that other drunks don't know, and they think they are special. They are wrong about that. They aren't special: they're drunks, and all drunks know the same things. It seems sadder and more interesting from their end. It is, too, in a sense. They all have their reasons, and some of their reasons are good. I don't blame anybody for being one.

It is my theory that everybody would be a drunk if they could bear to get that way. We'd all feel so much better if we were drunk all the time. But it's very hard going, getting to be a drunk. Only drunks seem to be able to manage it.

It is given to very few people to write as well as this, and I would not propose it as a model you should at once try to emulate. But its brilliance has a sound foundation that **should** be emulated. The basic idea is simple and clear, for all the mastery with which it is developed. The performance has been carefully planned; it has an enviable unity. Most of the sentences are short, gradually increasing in punch; by the end, the cumulative repetition has the force of hammer-blows. Above all, the sense of 'voice' is paramount: although *Other People* is a novel, this extract could easily be a drama script. Indeed, as a little exercise after all:

Read Amis's piece aloud.

I'll be surprised if you do not find yourself almost instinctively 'performing' it, for its immediacy and attack assume the presence of an audience – and that quality characterizes all good writing.

I have described sentences and clauses as the bones and ligaments of writing; if you construct them well, you will invariably produce a sound and durable 'skeleton'. But before we can go on to consider the 'muscle and flesh' that make the body of your writing come fully alive, a detailed study of punctuation and paragraphing is needed. For these are 'joints', essential if your prose is to be flexible and attractive.

JOINTS

5.1. PUNCTUATION: WEIGHT-TRAINING

From Amis *fils* to Amis *père*. Towards the end of Kingsley Amis's 1966 novel, *The Anti-Death League*, Jagger, a senior Government investigator, explains how he came to determine the authorship of a seditious poem that had been circulated within a top-secret Defence establishment.

> 'Whereas there are a number of illiteracies in spelling, the punctuation is correct all through. Now that's odd, you see. For every twenty people who can spell there's hardly one who can punctuate. Pretty well everyone who can punctuate can spell as a matter of course. So our man isn't really semi-literate: he's just pretending to be.'

The argument may be overstated, but I think it is substantially true.

Figure 5. *'Poor spelling is highly visible'.*

As a teacher I have come across hundreds of students – children and adults – who only rarely make errors in spelling or grammar but whose punctuation is either incompetent or dangerously limited. And I fear that nowadays this is also true of many professional communicators. In the newspapers and periodicals you read, you won't find much misspelling or many grammatical errors, but you will find a lot of wretched punctuation. Even the book-publishing trade is no longer reliable: on several occasions in the last few years I have been sent books to review awash with errors that ought to embarrass a decent GCSE student.

Something even more significant is suggested in the extract above. Jagger implies, in effect, that the skills of punctuation are harder to master than those of spelling, that they are subtler and more elusive. I think that is true too. Poor spelling is highly **visible**; so is bad grammar. Poor punctuation obtrudes less perceptibly; perhaps for that reason it matters less?

On the contrary: punctuation is the most important of all 'bread and butter' skills. Good grammar and correct spelling are not exactly incidental, naturally, and any proficient writer needs to be flawless in both. But bad punctuation is insidious, just as good punctuation is at times hardly noticeable. A spelling mistake may leap out of the page at you and interrupt the flow of your reading. That is regrettable, but unless the mistake is comically bad, it is improbable that you will fail to grasp what the intended word is. Similarly, a sudden dive into bad grammar will deflect and irritate, but it's unlikely to destroy meaning completely.

But inadequate punctuation can rapidly cause disaster. A writer who ignores essential full stops or uses the comma as the sole, carry-all signal [two common flaws in the work I encounter] will soon create a mess that is either permanently incomprehensible or requiring much arduous 're-coding' before understanding dawns. To use a building simile, punctuation is like mortar: unless you put it in correctly every time, your bricks will eventually collapse, leaving only a wrecked heap.

Before going any further, I want to list all the punctuation devices available, and to grade them according to 'weight'.* For once you understand the relative strength of each one, you'll be in a good position to decide which you should use when a punctuation point is needed.

There are ten grades of pause used when punctuating. I list them in ascending order of status; to the right is my idea of their weight as pauses, on a scale of 1 to 10.

---

* I am not at the moment concerned with the punctuation of speech and quotation. These techniques are important [they are fully covered in Chapter 22] but they have nothing to do with pause and **weight** of pause, my focus here.

1. The comma	1
2. The dash	$1^1/_2$
3. Brackets/a pair of dashes	2
4. The semi-colon	3
5. The colon	3
6. The full stop/exclamation mark/question mark	5/6
7. The paragraph	7
8. The sub-chapter	8
9. The chapter	9
10. The volume	10

I would imagine that numbers 8 to 10 are larger units/pause signals than most of you will currently be concerned with; number 7 has a section to itself later. What I most wish to make clear about the remainder is threefold:

- That the comma – the commonest and also the most wildly overused punctuation point – is very much the weakest.
- That the full stop, although it is [rightfully] used a great deal, is a very 'senior' pause, several times stronger than the comma. Indeed, for most writers there is only one larger device – the paragraph.
- That there are a number of invaluable devices in between the comma and the full stop which should be a regular part of every writer's equipment.

We shall return to those six devices shortly; first, let us see how bad punctuation can destroy potentially competent writing.

Mind the stop*

These four instances of inadequate or incorrect punctuation are in order of increasing length. The first appeared in a popular Sunday newspaper. Can you put it right?

Passage A: Exercise 6
Lady X refuses all blandishments to go on the stage or into films. Though her sister, Lady Y, is an actress. Appearing in *People Of Our Class*.

It should be written as one sentence. As it stands, it is jerky, damaging flow and meaning by separating components that belong naturally

---

* I have borrowed this neat phrase from G.V. Carey, who made it the title of his classic monograph on punctuation skills. See Further Reading.

together. You may by now see that the second and third 'sentences' do not meet the three criteria laid down in the previous chapter: strictly speaking, they are not sentences at all.

You could restore flow and grammatical accuracy in several ways: the simplest is to substitute the first two full stops with commas:

> Lady X refuses all blandishments to go on the stage or into films, though her sister Lady Y is an actress, appearing in *People Of Our Class.*

That first example suffered from absurdly overweighted pauses. What's wrong with this second one?

Passage B: Exercise 7
It should be noted that plastics can vary considerably in ruggedness they can be heavy or thin, plastic dials and knobs can have a metal sleeve to take the screw or they can be just plastic, the latter are the more likely to pull off in your hand.

Please attempt these two tasks.

1. Read Passage B aloud. Obey as if your life depended on the pauses and the punctuation signals; if **no** pause is signalled, obey that too. I'd be very surprised if it sounded 'right' as you spoke the words. The passage induces breathlessness, doesn't it? And didn't you find you were rapidly approaching a point where the meaning was so misty as to seem lost?
2. With a piece of paper to hand, read it aloud again, as slowly as you like, and write down
   (a) every word that you think requires a signalled pause after it;
   (b) the 'weight' of the pause you think is best – comma, full stop or something in between.

Then write out the piece in its complete 'improved' form. My suggested version follows in a moment.

Passage B was a piece of instructional prose. I would not say that clarity is more important in such writing than elsewhere – clarity is **always** of prime importance, whatever the task. But I'm sure you know how maddening, imprecise or confusing instructions can be, especially if you've just spent a lot of money on some new hardware [hi-fi equipment, super-de-luxe lawn mower] and find yourself at the mercy of instructions originally written in Japanese and translated by someone not fully at home with English! Instructional writing needs to be absolutely precise; it is therefore essential that the shape and rhythm of the prose match that ordered process.

So, to come to my own version of the breathless flurry above, the information must be clearly and calmly presented one step at a time. In this case, full stops are ideal, although there also needs to be a colon where the original included no punctuation whatever. My corrections are underlined.

> It should be noted that plastics vary considerably in ruggedness: they can be heavy or thin. Plastic dials and knobs can have a metal sleeve to take the screw or they can just be plastic. The latter are the more likely to pull off in your hand.

Now we have three clear, telling sentences instead of one hopelessly entangled one. All it took to effect such a decisive change was a little reflection and a moment or two of putting oneself in the reader's place.

Those first two examples are straightforward illustrations of poorly-judged pauses, at either end of the scale. The third is less obviously bad or incorrect; all the same, ways of substantially improving it may well occur to you.

Passage C: Exercise 8

There is a stretch of coast in North Norfolk that has a special place in my affections and it lies between Sheringham in the east and the delightful village of Stiffkey in the west. It is an especially beautiful coast because it has not been spoilt by
5   modern developments and it is much the same as I remember it as a small child twenty years ago and more when I regularly visited it in the school holidays. I return there most years now and stay in a small cottage in Weybourne which overlooks the sea although it may not survive as a safe habitat for very
10   long as it is close to the cliffs whose erosion continues apace year by year so that eventually it may just fall into the sea! Norfolk is famous for its wildlife and from March to October you can see a rich variety of beautiful creatures and flowers, ranging from the hundreds of baby oystercatchers that are
15   hatched every year on the Blakeney Point Nature Reserve to the bitterns that are very rare now and almost extinct apart from certain quiet areas of the Norfolk Broads whose thriving tourist trade threatens them just as it once drove out the otter and the coypu . . .

The strengths here include knowledge and charm; the weakness is that it simply smashes along, quickly becoming very hard work to read. As a result, the very enthusiasm that is the piece's greatest potential strength comes to seem irksomely gushing and distracting. In intriguing contrast to the previous two illustrations, there are no formal errors; one would still have to judge this seriously underpunctuated and indifferently designed.

As an exercise, try re-writing the piece so that it is properly enjoyable to read. No major adjustments should be necessary, although you might consider dividing it into two paragraphs; otherwise all it needs is a few judicious pauses to get rid of its rather frantic quality. My suggested version is on page 344.

The final example displays all the separate flaws of the other three. Like the last piece, its considerable potential is marred by a sense of headlong rush. And in this case that **is** due to formal error: the technical inadequacy noted in passages A and B above is also present here, and is even more damaging because the passage is so much longer.

Passage D: Exercise 9
   Cholesterol, a steroid alcohol found in certain fluids and substances, stored by the body, is a potentially deadly phenomenon, it promotes arteriosclerosis, this precipitates high blood
   pressure, which increases the chances of having a heart
5 attack, or angina, or a host of similarly dangerous conditions,
   its main carriers are foods we eat regularly, like butter, cheese,
   milk and salt, let alone things like cream and rich puddings.
       If you have too many of these, and I haven't yet mentioned
   eggs or anything fried, oil and dripping are simply loaded
10 with cholesterol, your arteries harden prematurely, this makes
   it more difficult for the blood to flow, obviously enough, they
   also get coated and, in general, unhealthy, contaminated and
   weak, you run a high risk, at the very least, of premature
   illness, or incapacity, or even death.

I have come across many hundreds of paragraphs like those over the years, and all of them suffered from what happens here. Not only does the passage become increasingly tiresome to read: the writer's control over his material and over his very thinking gets progressively weaker.

In this case, there's a wealth of detailed information: the writer evidently knows what he's talking about. But he hasn't worked out how best to deploy his material: by halfway his sense of destination is cloudy and his ability to register separate points has almost vanished. In lines 8–10, for instance, he desperately inserts something he should have included earlier, and then adds a larger point about oil and dripping. However, such poor planning would matter less if the punctuation were better.

The root of the problem is simple but very serious – most of the commas are **wrong**.

The comma is the weakest possible pause; most of the time the writer should have chosen a stronger alternative. As it is, the prose is a series of incontinent spasms in which the commas buzz across our eyes like the spots one sees after a racking cough. And this is not just a matter of taste or reader-comfort: those guidelines are underscored by the fundamental fact that

> **It is grammatically incorrect to separate two clauses with <u>only</u> a comma**.

With that essential principle in mind, re-write the piece. Read the passage aloud as it stands: you should find that your delivery will help you to decide how long each pause needs to be. Plenty of devices are at your disposal; you need not overdo the full stop, but I'll be surprised if you don't use more than the solitary instance the original provides! You may find that certain minor changes in word order are advisable, that the paragraphing would benefit from slight modification, and that a few words need to be added or substituted. But in essence you should be able to transform the piece into clarity and elegance simply by choosing correct and varied punctuation. My suggested version is on page 345.

Passage D was infested with a chronic condition sadly prevalent in much writing today: I call it 'the yob's comma'. The next section is dedicated to a full diagnosis of that condition and, I hope, its cure; this section closes with a detailed study of each punctuation device.

Weights and measures: an annotated 'hierarchy' of punctuation

1. The comma
Denotes a brief, hardly perceptible pause. If used with a conjunction [**and, but, for** etc.] it acquires the same weight as a semi-colon; otherwise it should be chosen only to separate individual words or phrases. **Never** use it on its own to divide two full clauses.

2. The dash
Equivalent to a 'strong' comma. The dash is very useful towards the end of a clause or sentence when the writer wishes to stress an additional and important point.

3. Brackets/a pair of dashes

Used to isolate a thought or piece of information that is worth including but is **secondary** to the main thrust of the material. The pair of dashes is slightly the weightier, but essentially they do the same work.*

4. The semi-colon

As might be deduced from its form [; – a full stop above a comma] its weight is almost exactly halfway between the comma and the full stop. It should be used to separate two clauses whose subject matter is closely related. Intelligent use along these lines prevents overuse of the comma and also preserves the full stop for when a significantly large pause is required.

5. The colon

Identical to 4 in both weight and sad underuse nowadays. Whereas the semi-colon denotes a pause between two related clauses, the colon separates two that directly interlock – i.e. each is to an extent dependent on the other for full sense or impact.

6. The full stop

A major pause: it should therefore be used as sparingly as possible. If you do want your reader to pause significantly, then of course use it, but be ready to take advantage of 4 and 5 as more lightweight alternatives. A profusion of full stops prohibits flow and can irritate.

7. The question and exclamation marks

These have the same weight as a full stop, but are specific **technical** devices. Any time a question is asked or implied, a question mark is obligatory. Exclamation marks are used to highlight remarks that should surprise or amuse. Beware, however, of using them too often for 'jokes'. The practice is not a bad one, but the reader might soon tire of seeing every third sentence or so advertised as a 'laugh'.

In speech punctuation, exclamation marks should be used if the tone and especially the volume of the speaker are strong (see Chapter 22).

All these devices are examined further during the remainder of this chapter, including plenty of illustrations of their correct use. It's also worth pointing out that I've been using every kind of punctuation device throughout this book. If you're unsure of how they work or

---

* The dash has a dubious status in some circles. I imagine this stems from primary-school days, when the dash is discouraged lest it become the **only** punctuation used. That is fair enough at such an early stage; adults will find the dash a most valuable 'heavy' alternative to the comma. It does roughly the same work but visually highlights the subsequent material in a very neat fashion.

are not yet clear about what I mean by 'weight of pause', you might find it helpful to re-read a couple of my paragraphs and work out how my punctuation works. It's quite possible that you'll find some mistakes or less than perfect choices; if so, write and let me know. I'll be interested and grateful (albeit somewhat ashamed) and you'll feel terrific!

5.2 'PUNK-TUATION' (I): THE YOB'S COMMA

> The notes I handle no better than many pianists. But the pauses between the notes – ah, that is where the art resides.
>
> *Artur Schnabel*

The single biggest and most common punctuational disease is the abuse of the comma. Like many diseases, however, its symptoms are not always obvious to the patient, who indeed may not even recognize them until it is too late. I've already referred several times to 'weight of pause' and the need to 'hear' how your writing will strike the reader; I'm also uncomfortably aware that unless you half-instinctively know what I mean by all that, you may as yet be not too much the wiser. A couple of analogies may help to clarify matters.

Nearly everyone listens to music at some time or another, and music depends on **rhythm**, from the simplest nursery rhyme to the most grandly-scored symphonic masterpiece. Rhythm involves the use of space, pauses and changes of emphasis; even a tone-deaf person will register such things, and can certainly respond to the use of **dynamics** [changes in volume].

Figure 5a. 'Music must intrigue and engage the listener'.

It doesn't take much imagination to realize how dull any kind of music would quickly become if there were no variety in volume or rhythm. Admittedly, there are a few works in all musical genres [rock, jazz and classical] which turn monotony into an hypnotic virtue; by and large, however, lack of variety leads to grinding tedium. So to be enjoyable, music must intrigue and engage the listener, and it achieves that partly by the use of 'rests', changes from *piano* to *forte*, and the use of a sudden increase in volume [*sforzando*]. In short, every piece of music has, in addition to the notes on the page, a host of 'secondary' but essential instructions denoting required volume, weight of touch and sound, design of phrasing and so forth.

Punctuation does the same kind of work. It **orchestrates** your words in the way that a composer orchestrates his notes; you assist and grip your reader by varying your pauses, and making that variety part of a pleasing overall structure that makes satisfying sense.

The 'yob's comma' destroys that possibility. If you provide merely a deluge of single-weight pauses, your writing will become monotonous and rapidly lose both meaning and impact. If there is no differentiation between one phrase and another, one point and another, one sentence and another, the result can only be visual anarchy and visible meaninglessness.

To use a second and briefer analogy: imagine how boring would be a football match where the only kind of pass attempted was a soft five-yard effort. [Yes, I know some of you find football boring anyway: bear with me for a moment!] The rhythm and excitement of football lie in the rich variety of its movement, the potential range of length and 'weight' of passes. A good side will employ any number of different devices: the long through pass, the deft headed pass, the 'wall' pass, the back pass, the 'one-two', the swerve pass with the outside of the foot, and so on. It is through such variation that players hope to achieve – literally – their goal.

Your aim as a punctuator is much the same. You should aim to use the most appropriate device for the task of the moment, just as do the footballer and composer. A footballer won't last long if all he uses is the delicate five-yard pass; you'll be in similar trouble if the only 'weight' of pause you use is the weakest.

Now to some illustrations and exercises.

Yob's comma: recognition, rules and remedies

Take a good look at this sentence.

(1) **It was a fine day, the sun was shining.**

It seems O.K., doesn't it? The two clauses appear so closely linked that the comma appears to be adequate as a separating device. Well, as I hope you may have realized from earlier examples, the comma is not enough. To repeat a fundamental principle:

It is always wrong to divide two clauses with only a comma, no matter how closely related in subject matter they may be.

You may remember that this rule can be also expressed in a different way:

If the subject and the verb are changed, more than a comma is needed between the relevant clauses.

In Example (1) there are two subjects [**it** and **sun**] and two finite verbs [**was** and **was shining**]. Therefore we need something stronger than a comma. Virtually any substitution would be correct, but some alternatives are stylistically better than others. Let's consider them in ascending order of aptness.

(1a) **It was a fine day. The sun was shining.**

This is grammatically correct, but it isn't very good: the sentences are too closely related for such a major pause to be appropriate. Furthermore, to continue writing in such a way for even a short time would render one's prose infuriatingly jagged.

(1b) **It was a fine day, and the sun was shining.**
or   **It was a fine day, for the sun was shining.**

This is much better: the connection is made fluently and comfortably. In fact, several other conjunctions would fit – **since, because**, even **while**. So there's no flaw or problem about this method; it's just that there are still better ways.

(1c) **It was a fine day – the sun was shining.**

Here we find an almost perfect example of the correct use and value of the dash. The root sentence consists of two such closely related clauses that the weakest correct device above the [banned] comma might be considered ideal. Not everyone approves of the dash, however, so perhaps the best version of all is . . .

(1d) **It was a fine day; the sun was shining.**

This is flawless and mud-proof. It signals the clauses' close connection while recognizing their separate grammatical integrity. It elegantly avoids both the excessive abruptness of a full stop and the inadequate comma. It is, in short, a classic model of how and why the semi-colon should be used.

Perfect though (1d) is, there remains one other way to punctuate the sentence. If you think that the two clauses are not just related but mutually dependent, you should use the colon:

(1e) **It was a fine day: the sun was shining.**

There is no real difference between (1d) and (1e): it is a matter of taste, based on your judgment of 'voice'. If you think the 'speaker' was concerned to stress the interlocking nature of the clauses, use the colon; otherwise, the semi-colon shades it. Such a subtle matter deserves a brief further section to itself.

Colon or semi-colon?

What is your opinion of the way this passage is punctuated?

> In one respect they were better off in this camp. There was a doctor in attendance. Some of the children were treated for malnutrition. The commonest complaints among the adults were exhaustion and heat-stroke.

There are four sentences. They are quite dramatic in themselves, and together they quickly paint a powerful picture. However, such clipped brevity could easily become irksome if continued for any length of time.

If we study the sentences as a sequence, we can see that they divide into two pairs: the first and second go together, as do the third and fourth. But these 'pairs' are subtly different.

The first two sentences interlock. The former is of course complete in itself as a grammatical structure, but in addition it fulfils a hint or expectation raised by **In one respect** in the latter. To put it another way, the information about the doctor answers the question raised in our minds as to why these people were **better off**. In such cases of 'fulfilment' or 'answering', the colon is the perfect separating device*:

> In one respect they were better off in this camp: there was a doctor in attendance.

The second pair does not function in quite the same way. Once again, the separating full stop is excessive in weight; but these sentences do not interlock so much as balance each other. There is no dependent or fulfilling logic operating: it is more a case of 'On the one hand . . . and on the other'. In such instances the semi-colon is the ideal device:

> Some of the children were treated for malnutrition; the

---

* The colon is also used to introduce 'lists'. This is much more straightforward than the 'interlocking' signal discussed above, and can I hope be explained via a single example:

> You will need the following things for your trip to Wales: a tent, a sleeping bag, eating utensils, a signed photograph of Tom Jones, the sheet music of 'Bread of Heaven', and a large brown paper bag.

commonest complaints among the adults were exhaustion and heat stroke.

If you have not as yet used either colon or semi-colon with any regularity or comfort, my advice would be to ignore for the time being the distinction between them: just get into the habit of using one of them on occasions when that degree of 'weight' is required. As you become more adept at this, you should soon feel confident enough to use both; when that time arrives, this summarizing formula may further assist you.

> Colon: links sentences on the basis 'Given A, then B'. Often it can replace 'because' or longer *causal* phrases.
> Semi-colon: links sentences that balance each other without being directly complementary. It is most often used as an alternative to comma + conjunction.

The exercise at the end of this section includes plenty of practice on these two subtle devices; now it is time to look at a longer and more complicated 'yob's comma' model.

What is wrong with the punctuation here?

> **(2) There are two things which really annoy me about you, firstly, you never look me in the eye, secondly, you're the untidiest slob I've ever met.**

There are four commas: only two are legitimate [those after **firstly** and **secondly**]. The other two fail to recognize that a new clause has begun, introducing a change in subject and verb. How do we put things right?

The sentence consists of a preliminary announcement

> **There are two things which really annoy me about you** . . .

followed by two clauses which identify what those things are. In other words, that announcement interlocks with the remainder – the ideal situation for a colon.

> **(2a) There are two things which really annoy me about you: firstly, you never** . . .

Moving on, the comma after **eye** is similarly wrong. Although the subject is the same (**you**), the verb changes from **look** to **are**; there are two good alternatives.

> 2b . . . **you never look me in the eye, and secondly** . . .
> Or 2c . . . **you never look me in the eye; secondly** . . .

Remember the equation: **comma + conjunction = semi-colon**. Either way is fine; if I suggest that (2c) is preferable, it is because

A. **Using the semi-colon whenever you can will soon make it an automatic and valuable part of your technical armoury.**

B. **It prevents the over-use of that very common word 'and', too many instances of which can get on a reader's nerves.**

The full amended sentence now reads:

(2d) **There are two things which really annoy me about you: firstly, you never look me in the eye; secondly, you're the untidiest slob I've ever met.**

Summary

The 'yob's comma' is a very common and also chronic ailment that disfigures the work of many otherwise proficient writers. The good news is that it can be quite easily cured; all it takes is a certain amount of careful thought, allied to the fundamental grammatical principles I've outlined several times. The bad news is that if such care is not taken, other aspects of your writing will soon begin to disintegrate. Just as a composer who has no sense of rhythm will produce music that makes little sense and has no real impact, so a writer who cannot punctuate competently will eventually be unable to transmit his thoughts properly. 'Punk-tuation' reduces both style and content to ugly inadequacy.

Please try the summarizing exercise; after that, we look at another aspect of 'Punk-tuation' – the abuse and non-use of the apostrophe.

Exercise 10
Correct the faulty punctuation in these sentences. You will find my versions in the Appendix.

1. He was fed up, the bus had left without him.
2. His promotion was not due to any particular skill or merit, he had bought his way up.
3. Stuck out here in the heart of the Yorkshire moors, in the vicinity of a bog, there is no problem parking the car, a little difficulty extricating it may be experienced, though.
4. The fridge worked, the food stayed fresh, the milk remained cold, the little light came on when you opened the door.
5. He was caught in a vicious circle, nobody would hire him as a portrait-painter until he was well known, he couldn't become well known until people hired him.
6. The recent BAFTA awards prove one thing if nothing else, when it comes to excruciating self-indulgence the TV industry has no equals.

5.3 'PUNK-TUATION' (II): THE APOSTROPHE – AN ENDANGERED SPECIES

It would be overstating the case to suggest that the correct use of the apostrophe matters as fundamentally as the things we've just been studying. It is nevertheless important. Misuse of it looks amateurish; more significantly, there are times when missed or inaccurate apostrophes damage sense and muddle the reader. Above all, incompetent use of the apostrophe is a telling symptom of a writer's failure to listen to the words, and it can easily lead to further lapses into slovenly and unhelpful writing.

It is commonly believed that the apostrophe has two main functions: to denote the omission of a letter or letters and to denote possession. This is not so: **all apostrophes denote omission**, and the latter function is both inaccurate and redundant.

Most students are aware how the former function works in straightforward instances. On motorways one finds such abbreviations as **B'ham** for **Birmingham** or **M'chester** for **Manchester**, where the apostrophe saves sign-painters the bother of providing the full name while ensuring that they neatly offer clear directional advice. I also find that practically everyone understands how and why the apostrophe is used to denote sloppy speech:

huntin', shootin', fishin'.   **It was 'orrible.**

However, the apostrophe seems to cause severe difficulty when it comes to denoting possessives and subtle contractions. Such problems can be greatly reduced once it is understood that the apostrophe always signals something which has been left out. To understand why this is so, and how the apostrophe really works, we need briefly 'to boldly go' where few students dare or want to go – back a thousand years and more to Anglo-Saxon.

Anglo-Saxon is the basis of Middle English, Shakespeare's English and modern English. By the time Shakespeare was writing, however, English was far less inflected than it had been in earlier forms. To put it simply for the present: in inflected languages many words change their form according to how they are used grammatically. This invariably involves the use of cases, as is prevalent in Latin and German, and to a lesser extent in French. Modern English remains inflected to a certain degree; one of the cases that remains is the **genitive** – which is where the use of the apostrophe comes in.

In Anglo-Saxon the genitive case was indicated by the ending **-es,** as in

Johnes book   **the Churches land**

The addition originally called for two spoken syllables. The **e** gradually eroded in speech, and in writing this omission was indicated by an apostrophe:

John's book   **the Church's land**

Believe it or not, that simple piece of linguistic history explains everything, you need to know about using the apostrophe nowadays. **All** apostrophes denote the omission of a letter, whether the word is a genitive or otherwise: that really is all there is to it.

That said and established, let us at once look at two functions the apostrophe does **not** have, both of which are nonetheless disturbingly prevalent.

1. It must *not* be used as an alternative spelling of ordinary plurals.

Thus, despite the thousands of instances you will see in shops, on menus, in newspaper headlines and on television, it is completely wrong to write such alleged plurals as:

potato's 25p a pound.
Do you like **egg's?**
Please close all **door's** after you.
West Indian **cricketer's** get pay rise.

Figure 6. 'The apostrophe – an endangered species'.

2. It is *not* automatically used in words that include the successive letters '. . . nt . . .'

It is therefore comically illiterate to write:

I **mean't** to write but forgot.
The man **lean't** over the balcony.
Are you going to the **pagean't**?
No, **Sergean't,** I have not been drinking.

One can understand why these absurdities occur: it's because of such contractions as

can't   don't   won't   hadn't

– all of which use the apostrophe correctly. Writers who insert apostrophes in **both** sets of cases are either not thinking properly or do not know that the apostrophe only signals omission: they respond in a Pavlovian way to the mere sight of the . . . **nt** . . . formation.

Does it really matter whether we write these out correctly? Well, yes. Misuse of the apostrophe looks amateurish and often ridiculous, and nothing undermines a writer so much as looking a sudden idiot! It can also confuse. It so happens, for example, that there are two nouns, **cant** and **wont**, that don't take the apostrophe:

1. can't	short for **cannot**. The apostrophe signals the omission of one **n** and the **o**.
1a. cant	hypocritical or spurious language; words used out of empty fashion/trendiness.
2. won't	short for **will not**. An admittedly odd contraction: the apostrophe signals the omission of the **o**.*
2a. wont	habit, custom.

Similarly, to prevent serious confusion one must distinguish between

3. your	belonging to you
3a. you're	a contraction of **you are**
4. their	belonging to them
4a. they're	a contraction of **they are**
4b. there're	a contraction of **there are**†

So the apostrophe is not merely an optional decoration. It is an aid to

---

* The change of the original . . . **ill** . . . to a single **o** was evidently considered too complicated to punctuate fully without tiring the reader and sacrificing clarity. Good thinking – as is **fo'csle** for **forecastle**. Strictly speaking, that contraction should be written **fo'c's'le**, but life is too short for such eye-straining fiddliness!
† Perfectly correct but very rarely used – it looks [and indeed is] too cranky to be helpful. Stick to the full **there are**.

meaning and precision: remove it, and something valuable is lost, as this exercise should demonstrate.

Exercise 11
There follow three pairs of sentences. Each pair is identical save for the presence/absence or position of the apostrophe. Explain the consequent difference in meaning in each case. My suggested explanations can be found below.

1a. The huge cliffs threatened.
1b. The huge cliff's threatened.
2a. He cares less about his children's welfare than his friends'.
2b. He cares less about his children's welfare than his friends.

3a. The village's well has been poisoned.
3b. The villages' well has been poisoned.

Commentary

1a. means that the cliffs threatened something unspecified – presumably a village, a group of people, or suchlike. Here **The cliffs** are the grammatical subject; the finite verb **threatened** is active in mood and in the past tense.

1b. means that something is threatening the huge cliff – erosion and/or the sea, perhaps. **The cliffs** remain the grammatical subject, but the finite verb has changed radically. The apostrophe signifies the omission of the **i**, making the verb **is threatened**: it is passive, not active, and in the present tense, not the past.

These are major changes in grammatical function and consequent meaning – all done by the briefest flick of the pen!

2a. means that he cares less about the welfare of his children than about the welfare of his friends. Put more simply, his friends matter to him more than his children do.

2b. means that his friends care more about the welfare of his children than he does.

The difference here is perhaps less dramatic than in the first pair, but it remains a sizable one.

3a. means that the well which serves the village has been poisoned.

3b. means that the well which serves **several** villages has been poisoned.

The difference in **scale** here is important. A poisoned well is obviously serious anyway, but sentence 3b could indicate a major disaster affecting villages and villagers for miles around.

The last of those three pairs illustrates the use of the apostrophe in plural possessives – the first 'specific problem area' I want to consider.

The apostrophe in plural possessives
What's the difference in meaning here?

1. **The boy's football shirt was filthy.**
2. **The boys' football shirt was filthy**.

The first sentence means that a football shirt belonging to a particular boy was filthy.

The second sentence means that a football shirt belonging to **several** boys was filthy. Presumably they have to take turns in wearing it, while everyone else in the team wears a T-shirt or whatever!

After such a comically unlikely example, let's return for a moment to the serious business of Anglo-Saxon. Remember that the genitive ending was originally **-es**; this applied in plurals as well. Thus:

the dog<u>ses</u> bones   the Church<u>eses</u> Bibles

In such cases the 'gradual erosion' referred to earlier led to the dropping of both the **e** and the **s**, creating the modern

the dogs' bones   the Churches' Bibles

So plural possessives are, in the main, relaxingly easy: all that is required is an apostrophe after the **s** that signifies the plural number. However, beware of **irregular** plurals. Fortunately, there aren't many of them; less fortunate is the fact that they tend to be in very frequent use.

Men's clothing   **women's** rights   **children's** games

These may be plural **in concept** but they are singular **in grammar**; they must therefore obey the singular possessive form.

Names ending in 's'

Let's introduce this tricky and nowadays quite controversial matter with a little exercise.

Exercise 12

Which of these uses of the apostrophe is wrong?

1. I admire Charles Dicken's novels very much.
2. Really? I find Dickens' work turgid and unfunny.
3. I despise Jone's taste in flashy cars.
4. What you mean is that you wish you had Jones' money.

They **all** are!

Sentences 1 and 3 are, I hope, obviously wrong – although a surprising number of otherwise literate students make this kind of idiotic mistake. I say 'idiotic' because a moment's ordinary thought can prevent it. The names at issue are **Dickens and Jones**; I suppose that somewhere there may be an author called Charles **Dicken** and a car-fancier named **Jone**, but I doubt if the above examples had such obscure figures in mind. 1 and 3 are even more absurd when one recalls that the apostrophe always denotes omission: if asked to work out what letters could possibly be missing in those names, the mind surely boggles.

Contrary to common usage – which I admit seems increasingly to be receiving 'official' sanction – sentences 2 and 4 are also wrong. They are lazy and unhelpful substitutes for the real thing:

5. **Dickens's** work   6. **Jones's** money

This is not mere pedantry; if it were, I wouldn't waste your time on it. Forms 5 and 6 are superior because they reflect how the words are **pronounced**: in conversation we would make an extra syllable out of the possessive signal –

Dickenses work   **Joneses** money

You may notice that these pronunciation models exactly match those original Anglo-Saxon genitive forms; in keeping with modern practice, we omit the **e** when writing, replacing it with an apostrophe.

However, in very long words ending in **s**, it is accepted practice to add only the apostrophe, on the basis that the extra syllable seems to create a real mouthful:

7. **Coriolanus'**   8. **Pythagoras'**

Even so, it is not wrong to write **Coriolanus's** or **Pythagoras's**: even with such multi-syllabled words we tend to add the extra one in pronunciation, 'real mouthful' or not!

As I mention above, the form taken by 7 and 8 now seems to be accepted usage for all words ending in s, and people like me should perhaps concede defeat graciously. But I would encourage you to use the form exemplified by 5 and 6: it is a genuine aid to clarity and precision, and anything that effects such qualities is to be valued and preserved.

Possessive adjectives and pronouns

The apostrophe is **never** used in possessive adjectives or pronouns. The correct forms are:

Adjectives: my; your; his/her/its; our; their; whose
Pronouns: mine; yours; his/hers/its*; ours; theirs; whose

Only one of these causes trouble – **its** – but it does so in large measure! The problem arises because there is a form **it's,** and virtually everyone confuses the two at some time or another. Here are three separate 'recipes' designed to dispel that confusion once for all.

A. By now I'd like to think that you have nailed to your memory the fact that **all apostrophes denote omission.** If you keep that thought uppermost, the distinction ought to be clear:

its = belonging to it; no omission has been performed.
it's = it is; the second **i** has been omitted.

If that isn't clear, try the next.

B. If in doubt as to whether to use **its** or **it's,** try mentally substituting **it is** in each case. If it sounds O.K., then **it's** is correct; if you end up with gibberish, you must write **its.**

Examples:

1.   The dog licked **it is** paw. Obvious drivel: you need **its:**

     The dog licked **its** paw.

2.   I must say **it is** nice to see you. No problem: write **it's:**

     I must say **it's** nice to see you.

If that doesn't work, on to the final one.

C. A four-stage 'theorem' – convoluted, maybe, but thorough!

1.   **its** is the neuter equivalent of **his** and **her.**

---

* Hardly ever used in this pronoun form, as it happens.

2. I imagine you would never be tempted to write **hi's** or **he'r.**
3. So if you remember that the possessive adjective or pronoun **its** follows the same formation as **his/her,** you should now get that one right, and then . . .
4. . . . remember to use **it's** in **non**-possessive contexts.

If **none** of those three recipes solves the problem, then I'm afraid there is nothing for it but to learn slowly by getting it wrong again and again until, somehow, it all sinks in!

The apostrophe with abbreviated verbs

In recent years a number of abbreviated verbs have become part of our language, and the apostrophe is a vital ingredient in their correct spelling.

1. **She OK'd the merger.**
2. **He was KO'd in the fifth round.**
3. **They OD'd on barbiturates.**

Unlike those illiterate plurals [**potato's, door's** e.g.] discussed earlier, the apostrophe is entirely legitimate here. Indeed, it is **essential**: not to signal the dropping of the **e** invites the reader to 'mispronounce' the verb, with potentially confusing results. For if the **e** is signalled, explicitly or implicitly, one ends up with verbs which sound like

1a. **She 'oaked' the merger.**
2a. **He was 'code' in the fifth round.**
3a. **They 'oded' on barbiturates.**

I can't pretend that such instances would cause anyone a real problem for very long. But it's worth taking the trouble to present these abbreviated verbs in a clear and accurate way – partly because doing so confirms your mastery of the apostrophe and the reasons for its use.

I hope this section has demonstrated that the apostrophe is a handy and badly neglected tool. Although it is true that your writing will be pretty proficient if the only errors you commit concern the apostrophe, using it properly will sharpen your work and add to your readers' precise understanding of it.

5.4 PARAGRAPHING: ART OR SCIENCE?

Proper words in proper places make the definition of a style.
                                                                    Jonathan Swift

While Swift's remark naturally applies to every aspect of writing, it is particularly germane to the business of paragraphing. The idea of 'proper words in proper places' seems simple enough, but all writers rapidly get to know otherwise. It is very difficult to be sure that one has chosen every word unimprovably **and** placed them all in the best possible position. And the more one writes, the harder it gets. Thousands of writers coin beautiful phrases and fashion exquisite sentences; to achieve the perfect paragraph is something else again. That goal is made all the more elusive by the fact that, unlike the rules of punctuation or even of sentence structure, the skills of paragraphing are not entirely a matter of 'scientific' logic.

For paragraphing is ultimately an art. Its good practice depends on 'feel', voice and instinct rather than on any formula or techniques that can dutifully be learnt. Conversely, its bad practice is as often due to poor instinct or inadequate 'feel' as to anything straightforwardly mechanical. Happily – and somewhat paradoxically – instinct and feel can be substantially improved by training and experience; this chapter offers a number of guidelines that should at least ensure that you never paragraph badly, even if I cannot promise that they will guarantee perfect paragraphs every time.

Perhaps more than any matter analysed so far, paragraphing skills are best understood via illustrations and exercises. As usual, I look first at how **not** to do it.

Avoiding eye-strain

Take a good look – in all senses of that noun – at the three paragraphs which follow. None of them is in my view badly written in any obvious mechanical way; yet all could have been rendered punchier, easier to read, or more aesthetically pleasing. Make a mental note of your reactions as you read, and compare them to mine.

The first example appeared in a local newspaper.

Passage A

Like many other able-bodied people, I had never thought very much about the problems of those confined to wheelchairs.

But after spending just one morning in a chair, I now realize how difficult even a simple shopping trip is for the disabled.

We borrowed a wheelchair from the Red Cross and set out along Station Road. It might be thought that I had an easy job just sitting in a chair being pushed around, but I found the ride both frightening and uncomfortable.

The pavement was very uneven – many slabs were cracked and few were actually aligned with each other. Shock absorbers should be fitted as standard on all wheelchairs.

Added to the problem of bumpy pavements was the fact that Linda, my pusher, took some time to get used to steering the wheelchair up and down the dips in the pavement. She was, of course, further hampered by my weight in the chair.

Kerbstones were another major difficulty. She almost tipped me out several times before she learnt how to negotiate them properly.

Because she had to go down the kerb backwards, I experienced a couple of moments of minor panic, when she had difficulty turning the chair round again in the middle of the road . . .

There is a certain amount to admire here. The 'voice' is clearly audible – concerned and intelligent; the sentences are nicely varied; the vocabulary is appropriately direct and physical.

On the other hand, in the space of just twenty lines there are **seven** paragraphs, which is excessive. The end of a paragraph signals a pause of some magnitude: after all, the next highest is the end of a chapter. To insist on a major pause every few lines ruins snap and flow; should the writer continue in this vein – and there's obviously a lot more to come, since pusher and passenger haven't even arrived at the shops yet – the reader will surely become fed up with the prose's stop-start jaggedness. It might be argued that such a feature brilliantly reflects the difficulties of locomotion described in the article, but I think that would be over-generous!

You will notice that none of the paragraphs contains more than two sentences. While the writing is significantly better than the *Daily Express* piece studied in Part One, there is a comparably irritating sense of being pulled away from an idea just as one was becoming gripped by it. Unlike that earlier example, though, it can be rescued.

Passage A: Exercise 13
Re-design the extract to give it proper flow and a more sensible shape. It might help you to work out first how many 'topics' or specific considerations the writer tackles: that should determine the number of paragraphs you go for. This time my version follows immediately – so try not to look at it until you've decided on your own.

Commentary

I would run together paragraphs 1 and 2, 4 and 5, and 6 and 7; with 3 left as it is, that makes four paragraphs in all. Even now they're on the short side; the subject warrants reasonably terse units, however, and each of the four addresses a distinct topic:

1.   An introductory statement about the difficulties of wheelchair-confinement and attitudes to it.

2. A sharp, disturbing summary of what being in a wheelchair actually feels like, even on mundane trips.
3. The problem of pavements.
4. The problem of kerbstones.

The next example, an extract from a letter to an 'Agony Aunt', was evidently written under great stress, and I'm afraid it shows.

Passage B: Exercise 14

From the moment I was promoted [not before time, since I'd been passed over twice for no good reason], I was not only nominally but practically the head of the firm, for I had ceased to occupy myself with details, although nothing of importance was decided without my being consulted, so that I was the pivot on which the management turned, but in the tenth year, after a long illness, my wife died, and I was very ill myself, and for months not a paper was sent to me.

There's nothing wrong with the material or the basic grammar; why, then, is this flawed writing? Again, try not to consult my remarks until you've made your own judgment.

Commentary

The overall problem is that of trying to do too much, too quickly. This is a long and involved account, yet it consists of **just one sentence**.

There are too many clauses; the whole thing has a feverish air, as if the writer is hardly in control of what he's doing. Because the connections are clear in his mind, he imagines that the reader will register them just as sharply. This is not so; his promising material is rendered confused and frustrating.

The extract concerns itself with three matters, all of which need a separate paragraph.

1. His promotion and its delay.
2. The proposition that he in effect ran the firm.
3. His wife's long illness and death, and his own subsequent illness and incapacity.

Organizing the material in this way calms it down and makes it much more accessible. Indeed, with that more generous paragraphing framework, it may be possible to include **more** information, not less: the reader is able to proceed more comfortably, and therefore can absorb further detail.

Passage C: Exercise 15
No prizes for guessing what's wrong with this – it is much too long. How would you 'sub-divide' it? And can you detect any inconsistency in the argument?

Twelfth Night is justly considered as one of the most delight-ful of Shakespeare's comedies. It is full of sweetness and pleasantry. It is perhaps too good-natured for comedy. It has little satire and no spleen. It aims at the ridiculous
5 rather than the ludicrous. It makes us laugh at the follies of mankind, not despise them, and still less bear any ill will towards them. Shakespeare's comic genius resembles the bee rather in its power of extracting sweets from weeds or poisons than in leaving a sting behind it. He gives the
10 most amusing exaggeration of the prevailing foibles of his characters, but in a way that they themselves, instead of being offended at, would almost join in the humour; he rather contrives opportunities for them to show themselves off in the happiest lights, than renders them contemptible in
15 the perverse construction of the wit or malice of others. There is a certain stage of society in which people become conscious of their peculiarities and absurdities, affect to disguise what they are, and set up pretensions to what they are not. This gives rise to a corresponding style of comedy, the object of
20 which is to detect the disguises of self love, and to make reprisals on these preposterous assumptions of vanity, by marking the contrast between the real and the affected character as severely as possible, and denying to those, who would impose on us for what they are not, even the
25 merit which they have. This is the comedy of artificial life.

Commentary

That was very hard work! As I hint above, length is not the only – or even the main – problem: the paragraph lacks **unity**. It begins by proposing *Twelfth Night's* essential 'sweetness', yet ends by suggesting that the play is distinguished for its vinegary exposure of artificiality and pretension. All the remarks stimulate, but they do not sit easily together within a single unit. One can sympathize with the reader who wonders irritably if the author could not have made up his mind before starting to write.

Engineering appropriate breaks would have prevented such annoy-ance. New paragraphs at line 7 [after **towards them**] and at line 17 [after

malice of others] would signal the distinct shift in focus and allow readers a moment or two to mull over the material in each completed paragraph.

Incidentally, the author is William Hazlitt – one of our finest essayists ever. It's comforting to think that even great writers can get things wrong sometimes!

All three passages subject the reader to needless eye-strain. One jumps around too much; another is inadequately thought out, forcing the eye to 're-code' the material into clear messages; the third offers no respite for too long. Despite containing, in varying degrees, much that is praiseworthy, each would have benefited from more astute paragraphing.

So even if paragraphing is an art and cannot be reduced to a set of prescriptions, it **is** possible to offer some pointers. I must stress that none of what follows is a 'rule': there can always be legitimate

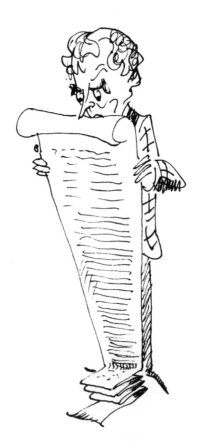

Figure 7. 'It is much too long'.

exceptions to every guideline I shall suggest. That said, those anxious to acquire an elementary grasp of how to divide their prose into efficient and agreeable units should find them useful.

Designing paragraphs

> Always design a thing by considering it in its larger context – a chair in a room, a room in a house . . .
>
> Eliel Saarinen, *Time*, July 2, 1956.

And a paragraph in a story or an argument. Your overall piece is your reader's overall environment, which he or she will enjoy and benefit from in direct proportion to how pleasingly you shape it. When designing your paragraphs, all of these suggestions are worth bearing in mind.

1. Each side of the paper [assuming A4 size] should usually contain 2 or 3 paragraphs.
2. Except for occasions when you wish to stress or highlight something, each paragraph should contain **at least three** sentences.
3. A good paragraph normally resembles a miniature chapter or essay: it should be clearly set up, properly developed, and then satisfyingly rounded off.
4. The first and last paragraphs of a piece should usually be fairly short.
5. A paragraph should have **unity**. You will probably ensure this by staying alert to 3; in addition, you should always be wary of moving in mid-paragraph from one topic to another. It can happen that the idea you're exploring sparks off another related but different one: this is a pleasing experience, but you mustn't *rush*. Your further idea must wait until you [and the reader] can give it full attention.
6. Try not to start a sentence until you're clear about how it's going to end. This is always important anyway, and I've mentioned it before; if you adopt it as a regular discipline, you will soon acquire a much better 'feel' for when one paragraph should end and another begin.
7. Within reason, try to vary your sentence-length within each paragraph.
8. Good paragraphs tend to have a **nucleus** – a sentence to which all the other material can be seen to gravitate.

The topic sentence

What I have just termed the **nucleus** of a paragraph has long had an alternative description – the 'topic sentence'. Most of the English primers of my acquaintance clearly think it valuable and illuminating;

I have never been entirely happy about the term and its taught use, and it might be helpful briefly to explain why.

The standard wisdom is that the topic sentence controls the paragraph: it either announces or encapsulates the central subject matter. Depending on how it is used and where it is placed, therefore, it operates either as an essential signpost or the paragraph's headquarters. Nothing wrong with any of that; my disquiet arises when the practice is insisted upon as a guarantee of successful paragraphing, together with the parallel assumption that a paragraph without a clearly identifiable topic sentence will be automatically inferior or even inadequate.

This is just not true. Yes, good paragraphs do, as I phrase it in 8, above, 'tend to have a nucleus' of this kind; but two further things need to be said.

1.   Many good paragraphs do not contain an obvious topic sentence. The material may be so condensed [albeit clear] that there are **several** apparent candidates. As we shall see shortly, there is no reason why such a feature need damage the writing; sometimes the reverse is true.
2.   Many paragraphs with a definite topic sentence still aren't all that good! Consider the Hazlitt extract above: the topic sentence would seem to be the first, but it does **not** operate as a nucleus for the whole piece. As we've seen, he changes his mind somewhat; his paragraphing is parsimonious – a fault which the inclusion of a topic sentence cannot rescue.

To be fair, the concept can be of considerable help to writers who are nervous about paragraphing and about organizing their material in general. In such cases, the topic sentence performs two valuable, interlocking functions.

1.   Ensuring its presence means that the **writer** makes a controlled decision about what he or she wants to say in a given paragraph.
2.   Such a sentence should guarantee the **reader's** trouble-free understanding.

If you consider yourself a real 'beginner' in paragraphing matters, you might further find it sensible to place your topic sentence at, or very near, the start of each paragraph. This will make your prose predictable in its rhythms for a while, but at least it is likely to be clear and efficient prose.

However, for more experienced and confident writers, the 'topic sentence' should be viewed as just one of many available guidelines, not a mandatory feature. If you keep in mind all eight of those guidelines above, the chances are high that you will write crisp, well-designed paragraphs. And once this has become a regular habit, it should not be long before you're ready to experiment, to vary their structure.

Types of paragraphs

There are probably as many ways of constructing an effective paragraph as there are points to explore therein or writers to write it, just as there are as many ways of writing 'well' as there are good writers. Nevertheless, I have chosen six types of paragraph, incorporating six 'patterns' of development, to demonstrate the varying ways in which material can be deployed. In my view, all are excellent pieces of writing; intriguingly, not all of them have a readily identifiable 'topic sentence'.

Type A: Illustration

> We had taken up an oil stove once, but 'never again'. It had been like living in an oil-shop that week. It oozed. I never saw such a thing as paraffin oil is to ooze. We kept it in the nose of the boat, and, from there, it oozed down to the rudder, impregnating the whole boat and everything in it on its way, and it oozed over the river, and saturated the scenery and spoilt the atmosphere. Sometimes a westerly oily wind blew, and at other times an easterly oily wind, and sometimes it blew a northerly oily wind, and maybe a southerly oily wind; but whether it came from the Arctic snows, or was raised in the waste of the desert sands, it came alike to us laden with the fragrance of paraffin oil.
>
> from *Three Men In A Boat* by Jerome K. Jerome

I would say there's a choice of topic sentences here – either the first or the fourth. The former establishes the horror and unwisdom of using oil stoves; the latter directly sets up the wittily graphic illustration that comprises the rest of the paragraph. Yet there can be no doubt that the most important word in the whole passage is **oozed**, which first appears in the second sentence – and that makes the issue even cloudier.

You might reflect that none of this seems to matter much, since the writing is compelling throughout, and you'd be quite right. That is very much the point I've been making: a clearly identifiable topic sentence is not a prerequisite for an exemplary paragraph. Jerome's account has unity, an attractive variety in sentence-length, and his sense of what he wants to say, and how he can best say it, is unimprovable. Those strengths are more important.

Type B: Catalogue

> What appealed to Bradman . . . was the range and quality of Sobers's stroke production, both in attack and defence. In this innings, which contained three sixes and 33 fours, Gary played all the recognized shots [plus a few of his own]: the delicate placement, the lofted

straight drive against a fast bowler, the square drive off the back foot to both off and leg, the controlled flick off the legs, the imperial hook, and the flowing front-foot drive were just some of the delicacies featured in a batting tour de force. From start to finish everything was correct: timing, footwork, judgment and execution. They had to be. Nothing less would so have satisfied, captivated and delighted the Don.

from *Sir Gary* by Trevor Bailey

Another fine paragraph; another one where the 'topic sentence' is hard to identify. You could legitimately cite the first, the third and the last sentences; in addition, the clause **Gary played all the recognized shots** has an equal claim. Once again, it doesn't matter. Two things guarantee the paragraph's success. First, the 'catalogue' is comprehensive, well-organized and interesting [provided you like cricket, I suppose!]. Second, the unity of structure is flawless: the last sentence returns us to Bradman's admiration, which opened the paragraph, even though the bulk of the material has naturally focused on Sobers's art.

Type C: Definition

In trying to distill the particular mesmeric quality of Miles Davis, Kenneth Tynan has referred to the Spanish word *duende*. 'It has no exact English equivalent,' he explained, 'but it denotes "the ability to transmit a profoundly felt emotion with the minimum of fuss and the maximum of restraint" . . . Miles Davis has *duende*.' Indeed, he has it not only in his music but also when he is not playing on stage – and when he is away from music entirely.

from Nat Hentoff's album essay on Davis's *My Funny Valentine*

A cogent paragraph; this time, it seems to me, there is a definite topic sentence – the brief **Miles Davis has *duende***. It may not appear until over halfway through the paragraph, but everything else flows to or from it. Even so, notice that the paragraph's over-riding strength is its unity: in this case the topic sentence is directly responsible, but we now know that there are other ways of achieving it.

Type D: Comparison and contrast

I think it unfortunate that [Sonny] Rollins felt it necessary to experiment as much as he did. When he permitted himself to play straightforward hard bop, he could be a truly magnificent improviser. During this period he made a set with Dizzy Gillespie and Sonny Stitt that contains a fourteen-minute cut called 'The Eternal Triangle'. The tune is based on 'I Got Rhythm', and it represents a peak of hard-driving ferocity in this style. The saxophonists solo separately, and then exchange fours and eights, rolling on minute after minute in a torrent of musical ideas. Rollins here demonstrates that he is capable of that extraordinary inventiveness, that tumbling outpouring of phrases which characterizes the work of both his mentors, [Coleman] Hawkins and [Charlie] Parker. Here there is none of the broken, jagged phrasing that he used in 'Blue Seven' and other pieces. But the jagged phrasing, which was seen at the time as 'sardonic' or 'humorous', foreshadowed the experimental jazz of the 1960s.

from *The Making Of Jazz* by James Lincoln Collier

This is an ambitious paragraph whose range and control impress. There is no topic sentence – inevitably, since there is no **single** topic. The centrepiece is an analysis of a particular performance, but that doubles as a contrast with Rollins's previous work and with imminent developments in jazz as a whole. You will notice that the first sentence sets this up admirably, but it does not control the material.

Paragraphs that deal in such dense patterns of comparison require very careful design: it is all too easy to get bogged down in detail at the expense of the overall thrust of the argument. Collier keeps the latter always in view: his knowledge is authoritative, and he has clearly worked out in advance exactly what he wants to cover.

Type E: Cause and effect

These examples of the growth of and belief in machinery, which we state lightly enough here, are yet of deep import, and indicate a mighty change in our whole manner of existence. For the same habit regulates not our modes of action alone, but our modes of thought and feeling. Men are grown mechanical in head and in heart, as well as in hand. They have lost faith in individual endeavour, and in natural force, of any kind. Not for internal perfection, but for external combinations and arrangements, for institutions, constitutions – for Mechanism of one sort or another, do they hope and struggle. Their whole efforts, attachments, opinions, turn on Mechanism, and are of a mechanical character.

from *Signs Of The Times* by Thomas Carlyle

Just now I commented that 'Comparison and contrast' paragraphs are by their nature unlikely to have a topic sentence. The reverse is true of Type E: an analysis of 'Cause and effect' is almost bound to centre on a particular observation. In this case it is the third sentence – **Men are grown . . . in hand** – and it is not only contextually but **geographically** central: all the causes and effects discussed depend on it. At the end we are left with a 'chicken and egg' problem: are we mechanical in our sensibility because of the growth of machinery, or is it the other way round? So far as Carlyle's paragraph is concerned, the answer matters less than his success in identifying a crucial question.

Finally, here is a paragraph that seems to have several of the characteristics examined in the first five types. In the midst of such echoes it has a pattern of its own – that of relentless logical development.

Type F: Logical development

> There was only one catch, and that was Catch-22, which specified that a concern for one's own safety in the face of dangers that were real and immediate was the process of a rational mind. Orr was crazy and could be grounded. All he had to do was ask; and as soon as he did, he would no longer be crazy and would have to fly more missions. Orr would be crazy to fly more missions and sane if he didn't, but if he was sane he had to fly them. If he flew them he was crazy and didn't have to; but if he didn't want to he was sane and had to. Yossarian was moved very deeply by the absolute simplicity of this clause of Catch-22 and let out a respectful whistle.
>
> from *Catch-22* by Joseph Heller

There is an obvious topic sentence here – the first, which is then further defined, illustrated and examined in terms of cause and effect. But the paragraph's wonderful unity is primarily due to the joyous, 'crazy' yet inexorable logic with which the opening premise is explored. And if we cannot aspire to Heller's genius, a lot of our ordinary paragraphs will follow this pattern, especially in the middle of a piece, where satisfying logical development is a key criterion.

I hope the above advice and illustration will enable you to become confidently proficient in designing your paragraphs. Once that is solidly established you should be ready to use your imagination and initiative.

Breaking the rules

Thus far I've laid down some useful 'rules of thumb'. They are not true 'rules' in any prescriptive sense, merely broad conventions designed to make writing life more comfortable. And as you develop as a writer, acquiring confidence and a sense of independence, you can safely leave some of those rules of thumb behind. For example, I know several excellent science text books which rarely contain more than two sentences to a paragraph. They are clearly and informatively written, and it doesn't matter in the slightest that they 'disobey' one of the elementary guidelines taught earlier on.

In the same way, there is no reason why an unusually long or an unusually short paragraph cannot be both pleasing and highly effective. This next example is fully thirty lines long, but it is masterly.

It's hard to make travel arrangements to visit a dream. The voyage I was planning was on a river which existed only in my head. The real Mississippi was an abstraction. I studied it with impatience, feeling that the facts were just so many
5 bits of grit in my vision of a halcyon river. I learned, without enthusiasm, about the construction of the lock and dam system. Figures began to swim in my head where the dream ought to be. In 1890, 30 million tons of freight had been carried downriver; in 1979, after a long and catastrophic decline in river trade,
10 business was up again to 40 million tons. The Civil War and the coming of the railroads had almost smashed the river as a commercial highway, but the oil crisis of the 1970s had brought the Mississippi back to life. A river barge, I read, 'can move 400 tons of grain a mile on a gallon of fuel, compared with only 200
15 tons for a locomotive'; and a lot of people were now wanting to move a lot of tons of grain because the United States had raised its quota of grain exports to Russia. So the port of New Orleans was busy with ships casting Midwestern wheat and corn and soybeans off to Murmask and Archangel. To someone
20 somewhere, I suppose, this kind of information has the ring of industrial poetry; it didn't to me. It was reassuring to find that the river was important again, a central artery linking north and south in a drifting procession of towboats and barge fleets, but I found the details of its renaissance grindingly dull. They
25 threatened to contaminate that great, wide, open stretch of level water which was far more actual for me than those tawdry scraps of intelligence from the real world.

from *Old Glory* by Jonathan Raban

This isn't easy: it outdistances the Hazlitt extract which I criticized for excessive length. (See pages 54–6). But I wouldn't make the same criticism here: the paragraph has a unity which the Hazlitt lacked. Moreover, I find the length appropriate to the subject – a 4000+-mile river that has dominated the author's imagination for years.

It opens with a memorable observation, moving elegantly into the controlling topic – the 'real' Mississippi versus Raban's 'dreamed' one. Perhaps you then find the catalogue of facts and figures hard to take in, even annoyingly opaque. Such a reaction supports rather than undermines the writing, for it is Raban's own response. He is 'impatient' at such things, finding them 'grindingly dull' and so many 'bits of grit in my vision of a halcyon river'. But having identified those disappointing realities, he stays with them and puts us as fully in the picture as he can, before returning gracefully to the image of the river with which he began. In effect, he has it both ways. If we find those statistics and commercial phenomena interesting [as I must say that I do], well and good; if not, we share his own instincts, which protects the writing against reader-alienation.

Raban wisely keeps his sentences relatively short. If you're going to tax the reader's stamina with a very long paragraph, it is sensible to ensure that no individual sentence within it gives any trouble. Most readers will contentedly follow you down a long, even arduous road, provided that the way is reasonably clear; if however it's also tangled with weeds, shrouded in mist or pitted with sudden holes and traps, they're going to get fed up.

From unusual length to unusual brevity. The **one-line paragraph** can be a shrewd and dramatic tactic, as these next two passages show. The first I composed myself.

> G. V. Carey published *Mind The Stop* in 1939. Drawing on his experience as a schoolmaster and in publishing, Carey compiled a no-nonsense guide to clear and accurate punctuation that quickly became a standard work of reference, a 'Bible' to teachers and writers alike. It was not only sensible and readable: it was the most authoritative and comprehensive book yet published on the subject.
>
> Over fifty years on, that is still the case.

The single-line paragraph serves to highlight Carey's achievement, and it does so by **visually isolating** the point. As a result it acquires immediate extra impact.

This second passage is from 'Death', an essay on boxing by Norman Mailer in *The Presidential Papers*.

> Their bodies made a contrast. Liston, only an inch taller than Patterson, weighed 214 pounds to Patterson's 189. But the difference was not just in weight. Liston had a sleek body, fully muscled, but round. It was the body of a strong man, but the muscles looked to have been shaped by pleasure as much as by work. He was obviously a man who had had some very good times.
>
> Whereas Patterson still had poverty in his muscles. He was certainly not weak, there was whipcord in the way he was put together, but it was still the dry, dedicated body of an athlete, a track man, a disciplinarian: it spoke little of pleasure and much of the gym. There was a lack eating at it, some misery.
>
> The bell rang.
>
> Liston looked scared.
>
> Patterson looked grim.

Not one but **three** single-liners: this not only 'breaks the rules' but seems to glory in flouting them! Yet it is a legitimate visual orchestration of a hugely dramatic moment. Set out in this way, the prose causes us to concentrate fiercely on three stark occurrences and to absorb their highly-charged simplicity one at a time. A good sports journalist should try to make readers feel 'they were there'; Mailer brings this off superbly, and a key factor in that success is his daring triple use of the one-line paragraph.

Such audacity must always be accompanied by sober thought. The one-line paragraph should be used sparingly, and you must be convinced it is the right device for your needs. If it is employed as anything other than an occasional powerful 'weapon', your writing can soon degenerate into the kind of thing analysed on pages 4 and 5, where virtually every sentence is made into a separate paragraph. But if you are sensible and alert about it, such variation can valuably broaden your style and give it added muscular force.

Afterword

Even the most stunning architecture – physical or verbal – relies on sound foundations, just as the supremely-tuned body of a crack athlete is based on the known properties of bones and muscles. If you are serene about the material covered in Part Two's pages, you should find that your foundations or 'skeleton' are in good shape, and that you will write accurately and clearly. Accordingly, that concludes for the time being our detailed study of the mechanics and structures of English. It has not been exhaustive: there are further sections on these matters elsewhere, mainly in the Grammar Primer. Nevertheless we are now ready to consider more sophisticated skills.

Later we'll be considering the various tasks your writing may encompass – the letter, the essay, the report and so on. First it is time to reflect in depth on how to achieve a truly individual and supple style – the comely flesh that clothes and gives life to your healthy body.

STYLE

INTRODUCTION: 6
STYLE VERSUS FASHION

Style is the dress of thoughts; and let them be ever
so just, if your style is homely, coarse, and vulgar,
they will appear to as much disadvantage.
Lord Chesterfield

When we see a natural style, we are astonished
and delighted: for we expected to see an author,
and we find a man.
Pascal

Fashion condemns us to many follies; the
greatest is to make oneself its slave.
Napoleon

Style is not unlike genius: we reckon to know it when we see it, but find it hard to define. And because we confidently recognize style in others, we often assume that to acquire it ourselves we need only copy the original model. That may be the basis of **fashion**; it is not the basis of good **style**.

Fashion is fun; it can also be tyrannical. As I write, just about the quickest way to induce fits of mirth in the street is to appear there wearing flared trousers. Yet twenty years ago they were the height of fashion, and – who knows? – may be again by the time this book is published. That example is trivial; yet isn't it rather sad that someone who feels idiotic wearing Chinos, rejuvenated 'Oxford Bags' or trousers cut straight and narrow*, should be mocked if he chooses a style that suits him better or in which he feels more comfortable?

A similar constraint can affect one's speech and writing. People often use language in a way that is unnatural – a way they've adopted for reasons which have little to do with how they feel or what they want to say. As with fashion, the process can be insidious. When you buy a certain garment, you may privately feel ridiculous in it, but seeing others wearing similar things will at once make you feel better. As with much else in life, once you get used to it, it soon strikes you as comfortable and 'right':

* In Jasper Carrott's phrase, 'looking like a two-pin plug'.

familiarity breeds serenity. In the same way, the adoption of a linguistic style may at first seem alien, but quickly comes to seem natural.

The trouble about this – and here the analogy with high-street fashion breaks down – is that language is a more complex expression of what you want to 'say' than appearance can ever be. It is also – unlike matters of dress, hair-style and so forth – fundamental. Fashion may create a startling first impression, but language – written or spoken – expresses the 'real you', as this brief excursion into a recent trend might illustrate.

Picture someone with multi-coloured and/or shaved hair, whose face is an alarming amalgam of scrap iron and Druidic war-paint and whose garments suggest a cross between a sadistic jailer and a hob-nailed Geronimo. In short, a Punk stereotype. Now consider how many such blood-curdling figures turn out to be charming, gentle, public-spirited people! Such a 'surprise' is both pleasing and salutary: it teaches us not to judge by appearances, not to (forgive the cliché) 'judge a book by its cover' but to appraise the true man/woman under such essentially superficial 'masks'.

However, the way you talk and write **does** define you in a direct and persistent manner. It is therefore important that your style is not only clear to others but an unsullied reflection of yourself and what you wish to communicate. For true 'style' has nothing to do with fashion or others' usage. Of course there are – as we've seen – certain basic

Figure 8. 'Fits of mirth in the street'.

rules you need to obey. It would be crazy to attempt to wear trousers as if they were a shirt, or vice versa; similarly, you need to respect the intrinsic grammatical properties of words and structures. Indeed, just as everyone needs clothes, so must all writers clothe their thoughts in clear and decent forms. Once that is secure, you are free to develop your best method of expressing yourself: it will be all the more effective for being yours and nobody else's.

There are plenty of people in the public eye who are not in the least 'slaves to fashion' but who are indisputably 'stylish': Ian Botham, Judi Dench, Simon Rattle, Meryl Streep and Nick Faldo come quickly to my mind. They are household names and supreme in their field precisely because they have each obeyed Polonius's advice: 'To thine own self be true'.

In sum: a good style is not imposed from without but emerges from within. It should combine naturalness, flow and pleasure for all; as Somerset Maugham deftly observed,

> A good style should show no sign of effort. What is written should seem a happy accident.

The achievement of such apparent ease is far from easy. In the words of a friend and colleague of mine, 'the art which conceals art is bloody hard work.' I hope to make your progress towards Maugham's ideal less hard and certainly less bloody! And I start by looking at all the things you **don't** need or shouldn't use, which will greatly lighten your way and your burden.

FIGHT THE FLAB **7**

All our life is crushed by the weight of words: the
weight of the dead.

Luigi Pirandello

When in doubt, strike it out.

Mark Twain

Why begin in such a negative way? Why focus on what **not** to do instead
of addressing what is desirable?

Well, bad style and bad writing usually stem from things which should
have been jettisoned rather than the absence of things which should
have been included. This does not just apply to those times when your
writing will improve by being edited and honed down; it also takes in
a catalogue of practices which should be avoided on principle and as
a matter of course. One of the soundest ways of arriving at your own
'voice' – your individual style – is first to be aware of all the accumulated
junk that disfigures our language.

Hamlet speaks of 'the thousand natural shocks / That flesh is heir to.'
The afflictions that can impair the 'flesh' of your style may be fewer
in number, but they are still considerable. Firstly, a group of ailments
characterized by obesity.

7.1 WAFFLE AND PADDING

Waffle: to talk or speak ignorantly or aimlessly. (OED)

We all waffle sometimes – in speech at least. We have all known occasions when we drivel vacuously on, through ignorance, embarrassment
or love of the sound of our own voice. It is not something to encourage,
naturally; but it will inevitably happen from time to time, especially
when we're 'put on the spot' or caught unprepared.

Written waffle is another thing altogether and must always be
avoided. The diagnosis is simple and the remedy brutal. Writers
waffle when they have nothing to say and/or no control over their
material: this is the result of pure ignorance, and the only cure is to
stop writing, go back to one's books and do some more preparatory
work. If you waffle in an exam, I'm afraid the condition is likely to be
terminal. All you can hope for is an indulgent marker!

Padding is a different matter – less obviously ruinous but a major threat to the writer's command. Padding is any word, phrase or structure which does no real work or damages impact and tempo. It can seriously weaken prose which is essentially sound, where the writer does not know what he/she is doing; if the writing is not kept taut, it can reach a stage where muscle and sinew disappear.

There are two kinds of padding to avoid: 'surplus fat' and 'deliberate fleshiness'. The first is the more innocent, arising from clumsiness or ignorance rather than the more sinister desire to hide one's meaning on purpose.

Surplus fat

All bodies need some fat; so does a good style. Lean sentences fashioned like whipcord can be both beautiful and riveting, but few can get away with a style consisting solely of such an approach. **Surplus** fat refers either to words and structures that are superfluous by definition or to once-muscular expressions that have lost sheen and power.

Figure 8a. 'All bodies need some fat'.

1. Tautology

A tautology is an expression where at least one of the words is redundant. Two obvious comic examples would be

a dead corpse   **a round circle**

Most tautologies are more subtle, and therefore more dangerous. I've heard or read all these recently, often from highly-educated people:

1. this new innovation
2. at this moment in time
3. whys and wherefores
4. unnecessary fripperies
5. quite unique
6. quite dead

All are illiterate.

1. **Innovation** already includes the idea of newness, so **new** is useless.
2. You cannot have a **moment** in any other dimension but that of **time**. Use **now** instead!
3. **Why** means **wherefore**; it therefore makes as much sense to use the absurd expression **whys and whys**.
4. **Fripperies** are *by definition* **unnecessary**.
5. **Unique** means 'one of a kind'. Something is either unique or it's not: you cannot have grades of uniqueness. **Quite** is therefore foolishly redundant.
6. Even more obviously, you cannot have **degrees** of death!*

You can avoid the trap such examples illuminate by sharp attentiveness, and that applies to larger-scale tautologies too. Look at this ludicrously conditional sentence:

If we had some bacon, we could have bacon and eggs, if we had some eggs.

I find that a charming joke; if one were to be more solemnly analytical about it, one would see that its intrinsic idiocy derives from the speaker having no idea where the sentence was going to end up. Such floundering characterizes many inadequate sentences, and poor sentences often start with flabbily thought-out phrases. Here are six in a little exercise.

---

* It can be (legitimately) comic to refer to someone as 'very dead' or 'seriously dead': the masterly Raymond Chandler does this several times, as do other good thriller writers. The key is humour or irony: if that's not your intention, stick to strict accuracy.

Exercise 16
Each one of these opening remarks contains at least one redundant word. Can you tighten them up? Answers in the Appendix.

1. Throughout the whole chapter . . .
2. The final incident with which the chapter ends . . .
3. These factors combined together to produce . . .
4. It was no more than a mere passing thought . . .
5. But after a while, however, he realized . . .
6. He can do no more than just follow blindly . . .

At all times, watch and listen to what you write: as Kingsley Amis observes, 'The price of a good style is eternal vigilance.' Once you train yourself to spot these little bits of flab, you will avoid their minor idiocies and also tune up your writing in a healthily alert way.

2. Useless or unwise qualifiers

There are a number of words, in common and forgivable use in speech, which should be deleted from all developing writers' vocabulary. They are at best useless and at worst actively damaging.

1. **incredible**   Arguably the single most stupidly used word of all. Its true meaning is **unable to be believed**; its colloquial meanings range from 'mildly surprising' to 'excellent'. Find another word – there are plenty to choose from. Otherwise you risk the kind of inanity perpetrated by Lord Asa Briggs, distinguished historian and Chancellor of Sussex University: we've seen the line before in Part One, but it's worth repeating.

   We thought this story incredible – very convincing.

One or the other, please: it cannot be both!

2. **fantastic**   Nowadays used as a vague synonym for 'excellent' or 'supreme'. Avoid that usage in all formal writing. The word means **pertaining to fantasy**; however, the colloquial use of **fantastic** has taken such a hold that you risk being misunderstood even if you use it correctly, so try to use the noun rather than the adjective.

3. **pathetic**   Again, try to stick to the noun – **pathos** – if what you wish to signify is the idea of **evoking pity or sadness**. If you intend the idea of 'ridiculous' or 'contemptible', then use those words, not **pathetic**, which will confuse readers and possibly rebound damagingly on you.

4. **brilliant**   Used far too loosely as a synonym for 'very good'. If you wish to draw attention to qualities that **shine**, well and good; thus it is fine to refer to a hot sunny day or an innings by Viv Richards as **brilliant,** because in each case you capture a central quality. But it is not an appropriate word to describe something impressive which does not also **scintillate**.

5. **definitely**   A curious word: its use often undermines an argument rather than endorses it. If you come out with something like

> **Macbeth is definitely a tragic hero . . .**
> **Time is definitely relative . . .**
> **Nuclear reactors are definitely controllable . . .**

one somehow gets the impression that the matter is in doubt – that Macbeth is neither heroic nor tragic; that time is absolute; that nuclear reactors are frighteningly dangerous. The emphatic tone causes a twinge of suspicion: the reader detects rhetoric, not evidence. Alternatively, it can carry an element of childish triumph – 'Wow! I've made up my mind about that, so there!' In any event, the word is hardly ever used beneficially; leave it alone.*

6. **situation**   This has become an all-purpose suffix that is usually both ugly and redundant. In all five examples below, **situation** is useless:

> **Practice is different from a game situation.**
> **We're in a riot situation here.**
> **Tomorrow you're likely to encounter a rain situation.**
> **And Manchester City have a free kick situation.**
> **Hamlet has an eyeball-to-eyeball confrontation-situation with his mother.**

Above all, avoid the horrible construction based on the words **ongoing . . . situation**. My 'favourite' was this attempt to say that two people were having a love affair:

> **They are in an ongoing carnal knowledge situation.**

7. **no way/in no way**   A recent arrival in yob's English that has infected far too many. It is ugly and dubiously emphatic, like **definitely**, and it often involves needless and unsightly double negatives, as in these charmless structures:

> **No way is Macbeth not a tragic hero.**
> **There is no way you can move an object without expending energy.**

After the World Cup of 1974, Billy Bremner, the Scottish captain, defiantly answered criticisms of his team's performance with, 'There

---

* If you **must** use it, at least spell it right! It's **definitely**.

is no way I'm not proud of what we did do.' Why didn't he just say, **I'm proud of what we did,** which is simpler, more dignified and clearer? After all, if what you are claiming is that certain, why make such a syntactical big and complex deal of it?

8. **over the top**   A slang expression meaning **excessive, extreme, over-done.** It should be banished from formal writing at all times. Nothing destroys snap and dignity faster than such remarks as

> **Shakespeare goes way over the top here . . .**
> **The Green Party's diagnosis of pollution is over the top.**

The phrase is casual and complacent, and invariably removes the focus from what's being said, putting it firmly and damagingly on who's saying it.

9. **human**   Not much help if what you mean is 'caring', 'sensitive' or 'sympathetic'. Human beings are capable of the noblest responses; they are also capable of cruelty and any number of things that place them below any animal. **Human** is too big, too basic a concept to be a good choice for subtler ideas. Use **kind** or any of the three alternatives mentioned above.

10. **literally**   Almost invariably used wrongly. It means **without mysticism, allegory or metaphor;** if incorrectly and emptily used for emphasis, the opposite sense is produced, as in these comical remarks from, respectively, Trevor Bailey and Ted Lowe.

> **Boycott has literally dropped anchor.**
> **Higgins has literally come back from the dead.**

Those are the ten 'useless qualifiers' which I come across most often or which most annoy me.* There are many others – words that are empty, ugly, unclear, or all three. A little fierce thought should protect you from their harmful use.

---

* For literature students only: I'm tempted to add the word **sincere** to those ten when it is used in aesthetic criticism. If you say a poem or song is 'sincere', you claim a privileged insight into the private motivation and feelings of the composer. That can look conceited; worse, it rarely persuades – unless you document it at length and in dense biographical detail. Even then, your labours may be fruitless or simply inappropriate, as this remark by the poet Liz Lochhead warns: 'poets don't bare their souls: they bare their *skills.'*
   Do not confuse the artist's private [even unconscious] spurs and ideas with their effect on you. The latter is your business and what you wish to communicate: use the word **convincing** instead. If ever tempted to use 'sincere', remember that your prime job as a critic is to say whether and how the writing works, not to pass moral judgments on the writer. Besides, 'sincerity' is not an unambiguously praiseworthy quality anyway: Hitler was sincere, as were Savanorola and Nero. Find a safer compliment!

Leaden lead-ins

Boastful or arrogant writing is as repellent as a boastful or arrogant person. On the other hand, false modesty or lack of nerve can be just as unattractive. You should always assume that your reader is interested enough in what you're saying to give you a fair hearing, so there's no need to apologize for what you're about to write or to 'wind yourself up' into it. Accordingly, avoid all these:

It is interesting to note that . . .	Kills all interest at once.
It may perhaps be said that . . .	Well, why shouldn't it be?
It is worthy of note that . . .	Ugly, pompous and wasteful.
We can safely say that . . .	If so, why not just **say** it?
From certain points of view . . .	**Whose** points of view? Looks vague and timid.

These five constructions slow everything down to no purpose. They create a flabby and timorous impression; the attempt to 'cover oneself' either wastes time or is annoyingly unspecific.

Such effects are unfortunate anyway, and can lead to worse problems. Consider this sentence, which appears in the first paragraph of a well-known critical work.

> We should like to make it impossible for any academic authority . . . to tell us with the familiar easy assurance that Dickens of course was a genius, but that his line was entertainment.

What do you make of the **tone** here?

I find it suspect in its hectoring vagueness. I want to know just who these critics are who insist with 'easy assurance' that Dickens is mere 'entertainment', and I start to wonder if such a mixture of aggression and imprecision indicates a lack of conviction or serenity. In this case, the answer is 'Yes'. The writers are F. R. and Q. D. Leavis, in their *Dickens The Novelist*, published in 1970 and rightly acknowledged as a cogent account. But, as many reviewers pointed out at the time, the only critic who had ever sought to dismiss Dickens as 'a mere entertainer' was one F. R. Leavis himself!*

I have no wish to pillory a brave and valuable critic; the fact is that such imprecise militancy is as bad a strategy as needless apology. And the two things are curiously related. If you get into the uncorrected habit of writing dully vague 'lead-ins', you may soon find yourself coming on strong in an unspecified and suspect way. That is poor tactics: you must document your argument **at once**. Otherwise, your problem will be graver than flabbiness: it will seem that you've got something to hide.

---

* In *The Great Tradition*, 1948.

Unnecessary complexity

Please read these six examples.

1. The poet succeeds in creating an arresting picture . . .
2. Mozart manages to convince us . . .
3. Einstein is trying to put over the point that . . .
4. . . . embodies a representation of . . .
5. . . . the way this is brought to realization is . . .
6. . . . promotes a general level of satisfaction . . .

All are in the first place clumsy, in the second flabby, and in the third disagreeable.

In the first three, the slim-line verbs **creates, convinces** and **puts over** are doubly superior. They are clearer, and they avoid the originals' **tonal kick-back**:

1. **succeeds in creating**   suggests that the poor old poet had a hell of a time getting his work up to scratch.
2. **manages to convince**   is patronizing, as if giving a Brownie point – 'Well done, Wolfgang, old chap!'
3. **Einstein is trying to**   Inaccurate, and in a most unfortunate way. It's not Einstein who's making the effort but **you**. You're struggling to articulate your ideas – something he managed rather well.

At best such structures sound naive; at worst they are condescending. You will benefit in every way if you **keep it simple**.

Similar advice applies to the remaining three examples, which all suffer from pompous timidity.

4. embodies a representation of   = is
5. the way this is brought to realization is   = this happens by
6. promotes a general level of satisfaction   = satisfies everyone

Of course, you want to avoid using the same simple verb time after time, just as you should avoid the Chinese water-torture repetition of **and, but** and **then**. But by and large the virtues of simplicity far outweigh its problems; besides, your writing should never be ugly, which 4–6 are. As the American philologist Wilson Follett remarks:

> The writer who fills his pages with ugly dissonances and tells himself that they are not worth the trouble of rectifying, because not one reader in fifty will ever test him **by voice**, is deluding himself. His bad readers may not mind, but his better readers will follow him with pain and inward protest if they are sufficiently interested in his contents, and otherwise not at all.
>
> from *Modern American Usage* (Longman, 1968); my emphasis

Finally in this section, do not clutter up your formal writing with over-use of the first person. **I** itself is not so bad, although it should be watched carefully; but **to me, in my view, in my opinion, it seems to me**, and **I think** should be occasional at most.* You're doing the writing; you know you're doing it; the reader knows you're doing it. Regularly to remind everyone of the obvious is tiresome; moreover, there are times when you need to stress that what follows is **your** opinion as opposed to another specified one. In speech, the structure **I think** is very common, but it is only really noticeable when the pronoun is emphasized, as in, **Well, I think . . .** – i.e. in contrast to anyone else. When writing, if your projected use of **I think** has that force, keep it in; if not, strike it out.

In speech, all of us lapse at times into other 'verbal tics' – **you know, I mean, sort of**, and of course **um** and **er**. I need hardly say that such things must be ruthlessly banned when writing. Even more obviously than over-use of first person phrases, they are forms of 'stuttering': they do no work, and either embarrass or irritate.

5. Clichés

Clichés are expressions which have lost all charm, power or currency. I know of no better definition than that offered by Clive James:

> On *Nationwide* (BBC1) there was a lady whose cat had recently survived a complete cycle in the washing machine. 'What sort of condition was he in?' asked Frank Bough. The lady answered without smiling: 'My husband said he looked like a drowned rat.'
>
> The essence of a cliché is that words are not misused, but have gone dead. To describe a wet cat as a drowned rat is to use language from which all life has departed, leaving mechanical lips and a vacant stare.
>
> from *Glued To The Box: TV Criticism From The Observer 1979–82*

In a language as rich and globally used as English, there are bound to be plenty of clichés, and the number increases all the time. It is almost impossible to avoid using them altogether; but one should at least try, for two reasons:

1.   Clichés are **dull**; no reader enjoys being bored.
2.   As Clive James suggests, clichés reflect a mind that is not **thinking**. No reader will follow for long a writer who trafficks in stale, inappropriate and empty-headed expressions.

The stress on thinking is crucial, which is why this defence of the use of clichés is unconvincing:

* I shall assume you to be incapable of using the appalling **I myself personally**!

> **Phrases become clichés because so many people have found them attractive and useful. Furthermore, they're *clear*: everyone knows what you mean by them.**

There is something in the first sentence; the second is decidedly suspect. Many clichés are widely misunderstood and misused, and their effect is anything but clear. Consider these four sadly well-known examples:

nose to the grindstone	**grist to the mill**
hoist with his own petard	**nigger in the woodpile**

These employ metaphors that are obscure and out-of-date, if not positively alien.

Nose to the grindstone is used to express the need for single-minded hard work. It is not much of an image for late twentieth-century life, is it? People who use it invariably have no idea what a grindstone looks like, let alone how it's used. In addition, the phrase strongly suggests discomfort and danger, which are not appropriate to most forms of intellectual work!

Grist to the mill is even more obscure. Hands up all those who are fully aware what **grist** is or visualize the milling process when using the phrase? Not a lot, I'd guess; avoid it.

Hoist with his own petard is fascinating in its useless way. It has a distinguished pedigree for a start [*Hamlet*, III:iv:208], and it has nothing to do with strangulation, which virtually everyone I've heard use it seems to imagine. It means **blown up by his own bomb**, and while therefore appropriate to a gruesome incident in Belfast or Beirut, isn't over-apposite in normal circumstances. The term **own goal** is more in tune with our own society, and it is immeasurably clearer too – though be careful, since it has already become a cliché itself!

Nigger in the woodpile means, I believe, **troublemaker** or *agent provocateur*, but nobody has been able to explain to me why it should mean that. In addition, it is highly offensive: indeed, as a mixture of unpleasantness and imprecision, the phrase takes some beating.

Clichés are not just stale: they are usually woolly. For all their reputed clarity-through-familiarity, they often confuse through laziness and sloppy thinking, characteristics notably evident in the use of proverbs and lifeless similes.

Proverbs

There are two words to say to a young writer on the subject of using proverbs and they are, **forget it**. Proverbs are handy things to **know**: some people still insist on using them, and it helps to have some idea of what they're talking about. But to encounter a proverb in the midst of a vigorous piece of writing is a dreary experience.

There are three things about proverbs that render them a disease. First, nearly all of them seem to go in contradictory pairs:

> Too many cooks spoil the broth / Many hands make light work

> Everything comes to him who waits / The early bird catches the worm

> Honesty is the best policy / Nice guys come last

> Out of sight, out of mind / Absence makes the heart grow fonder*

Second, they are rigid and surprisingly abstract. Like other clichés, they had an appropriate and telling power – once. They grew out of a particular situation, and as such had a particular instructiveness. What happens nowadays is the reverse: they are imposed upon a situation as an allegedly perfect summary of it. In fact, most human predicaments are subtle, special, even unique: they require more than some hackneyed formula to do justice to them. And like those pre-industrialization phrases we looked at in the last section, most proverbs are absurdly out of date: when, for example, did you last hear of anyone, anywhere, **crying over spilt milk**? Someone prepared to shed tears over a few drops of UHT dairy produce is a leading candidate for the funny farm, wouldn't you say?

Third, more than a few proverbs are either incomprehensible or simply illiterate. Consider these four:

1. **Fair words butter no parsnips.**
2. **Still waters run deep.**
3. **Don't let the grass grow under your feet.**
4. **You can't teach an old dog new tricks.**

The first proverb manages to be ludicrously self-evident and totally baffling at the same time. Just who, in the entire course of human history, has ever suggested that words ['fair' or otherwise] **can** butter parsnips? But what does it mean anyway? That 'actions speak louder than words'? That 'all this talk won't buy Auntie a new frock'? Those are clichés themselves, of course, but at least they make some kind of sense.

Both 2 and 3 are absurd and/or illiterate. The point about **still waters** is that they don't run at all: that is, funnily enough, why they're still. The broad idea behind this expression is sound enough – that surface appearance can belie a deeper reality. But on the principle that you risk

---

* I rather like the 'renegade' version: **Absence makes the heart go wander**. At least it matches its 'twin'!

losing your readers if you include incongruous expressions, this is one to avoid and pour gleeful scorn upon.

Proverb 3 is even sillier. How can grass grow if it's blocked off from sun, rain and organic chemicals by around ten stone of human flesh culminating in two shod [and probably smelly] feet? The governing idea, implying ambition, is satisfactory; but it is undermined by the inadequacy of the **literal** image – a definition that encompasses all bad metaphors.

Proverb 4 is, quite simply, incorrect. You **can** teach an old dog new tricks, as I and many other dog-owners will testify. Since this inane proverb is often employed as an excuse for laziness or the refusal to consider another point of view, it's highly satisfying to point out that it serves only to expose the speaker: a 'natural truth' it ain't!

I hope this destructive detour has proved amusing. I stick to the terse point with which I began it: never use proverbs in your writing – unless for humorous or ironic purposes. They are dull, rusty and rarely more than vaguely apt. The same goes for lifeless similes, which I deal with next.

Lifeless similes

When we're very young, learning about not only language but such basic physical things as heat, colour and so on, similes like **as white as a sheet** and **as hard as nails** are vibrant and valuable. But it really ought not to be beyond the wit of sophisticated students with a five-figure vocabulary to come up with something better than those standard structures, especially as many of them are so much linguistic junk. Here are ten leading candidates for the scrapyard.

1. **As green as grass**. Yawn, yawn. Also astonishingly vague: botanists estimate that the various grasses between them account for over 100 colour shades.
2. **As plain as the nose on your face**. An absurd remark if you're attempting to point something out to someone: it is extremely hard to focus on one's own nose without severe ocular pain.
3. **As thick as two short planks**. Exceptionally boring; and mystifying too: what has the **length** of the planks got to do with it?
4. **As sober as a judge**. Ha ha.
5. **As happy as Larry / As happy as a sandboy**. Meaningless unless you happen to know a cretin named Larry who's always laughing his head off, or number several blissful sandboys – whatever **they** are – among your acquaintances.
6. **As bold as brass**. What does this mean?
7. **As plain as a pikestaff**. What **is** a pikestaff? Is it plain?
8. **As fit as a fiddle**. How many violins do you know that go jogging, or work out regularly in the gym?

9. **As brown as a berry**. Why not 'as red/black/green as a berry'? The berries we eat – and therefore notice most – are those colours.
10. **As right as rain**. Again, what does this mean?

You may have noticed that 6–10 are alliterative – that is, the adjective and noun start with the same letter. Alliteration, though a neat device, should always be used as an **enhancement** of meaning and impact; in these cases the wish to alliterate is for its own sake, and meaning is buried. They may have had a degree of giddy charm when freshly coined; now they are drab as well as nonsensical.

Those ten are a tiny sample: our language abounds with fossilized and opaque similes. Unless you can find a witty variant with which to refresh them, they should be left alone. Make up your own similes: it's more fun, both for the reader and yourself.

Summary

As I remarked earlier, it is almost impossible to avoid **all** clichés: I'm sure you will find at least a few in this book! Clichés are numbered in millions, and each generation produces its own. Recent additions include

> **at the end of the day; acid test; grass roots; stable relationship; nitty-gritty; U-turn; high profile; toy boy; in this day and age; quantum leap; motorway madness; personal organizer; viable alternative**

– all the more insidious because we hear them so often. There may be occasions when you deliberately use a cliché because it really is the best way of getting your meaning across. For all my scorn of proverbs, there is one – **the proof of the pudding is in the eating** – that I do sometimes use, because I haven't come across or invented another expression that so clearly registers what I want to say when I use it. But such moments should be rare. As always, stay alert. Vibrantly idiomatic English is always pleasing; just watch for those idioms that have become stale or obscure and keep them out of your writing.

6. Redundant qualifiers

An earlier section looked at **useless or unwise qualifiers** – words you should banish from your writing or select only after careful thought. There are other qualifiers that are not suspect in the same way but should nevertheless be used sparingly.

There will be times when you wish to modify your statements with an adverb. But don't do it too often: you must trust your material enough to state it plainly. So be ruthless about the following: **very; quite;**

extremely; absolutely; utterly; rather; really; somewhat; completely; totally.

Save them for times when they're essential or make a genuine difference; certain words cannot be qualified, and others need it less often than you might think. For example, all the following phrases are flabby and weak:

1. **quite evil**
2. **rather tragic**
3. **somewhat wicked**
4. **very true**
5. **completely and utterly defeated**
6. **extremely empty**

In 1–3 the adjectives **quite, rather** and **somewhat** modify are so powerful that it seems timid, or indeed plain silly, to 'reduce' them in such a way. The remaining three are further instances of **tautology**, looked at earlier. In 5, **completely** and **utterly** duplicate each other; in 4 and 6 **very** and **extremely** are redundant because the word each one modifies is already an absolute – just like those absurd phrases cited before: **a dead corpse** and **a round circle**.

These are comic because you cannot qualify **corpse** or **circle** in any way that thereby touches on their intrinsically-defined properties. You can however safely say **a rotting corpse** or **a white circle** because these qualifiers **add** information, not duplicate it.

So if your root word is already forceful, make sure that any qualifier does some real work. Thus **a wicked villain** is useless, but **a smiling villain** is additionally powerful. Similarly **a sudden shock** is padding, but **a valuable shock** is intriguing, moving the reader forward rather than wasting his/her time.

Redundant qualifiers can take the form of whole clauses and phrases, not just individual words. In each of these cases, the second clause is valueless, repeating an idea already covered in full:

> **The tale never becomes monotonous: it is always varied and interesting.**
> **She had a dependable husband – someone she could rely on.**
> **The speaker kept to the point and never wandered off into irrelevancies.**
> **We consider the enterprise to be unacceptably risky and think it too much of a gamble.**

Sometimes what may seem to be mere repetition can be defended as subtle distinction. For example:

> **The accident was sad and tragic.**

Is this a tautology or a legitimate nuance? Something can be sad without being tragic; but can anything be tragic that is not also sad?

Such questions are interesting, and there will be times when you need to 'worry at' a phrase in this delicate way. A simple test you can apply if in doubt is mentally to put **both . . . and also** in front of the words you're proposing to use.

1. **Both scared and also frightened** is clearly repetitive.
2. **Both sad and also tragic** is at least possible, even if you still decide to omit **sad**.
3. **Both famous and also revered** is certainly all right; someone could be either without being both, so the combination is a telling one.

Finally, a rather curious qualifier that should be used with care. What, precisely, do these constructions mean?

not unworthy   not unkind   not unfashionable

No doubt you've been taught in mathematics that 'two minuses equal a plus'; hence you might think that those three structures operate on an identical principle. They don't! Their 'weight' is substantially less than the three single-word alternatives (**worthy, kind, fashionable**) and thus take on a more cautious, even grudging air.

The **not un-** construction has its uses, but many writers employ it too often, which amounts to its abuse. Besides, it carries echoes of George Orwell's Newspeak. That reduced the treasure-house of English to minimalist poverty, with for example the structure **double-plus good** replacing **superb, excellent** and indeed all such adjectives; conversely, **ghastly, dreadful, abject** and the like were all replaced by the single term **double-plus *ungood***. Such chillingly deliberate destruction of man's greatest asset – language – is doubtless alien to your own aims; even so, keep your use of **not un-** to a minimum. The simpler and more positive alternative is nearly always superior.

In many cases, decisions about **redundant qualifiers** will arise during the editing stage of your work, not in the first flush of composition. It is nevertheless a good idea to be alert to such things as early as possible: if you start your project fully switched-on to how your language sounds and to exactly what you're saying, you will do a more efficient job and your eventual editing will be less arduous. And I must end by confessing that over-use of qualifiers is a fault of mine when I write, which I and others have to edit ruthlessly. You may find some such redundancies even after the thorough going-over this text has had!

Summary

This kind of flab is 'innocent', in two separate ways. First, it is akin to puppy-fat in that it characterizes the young, learning writer. Lapses into

Figure 9. '"Innocent" flab'.

tautology, cliché and redundancy, the tendency to be awkward, or taking a long time to get to the point are all symptoms of a writer struggling to acquire mastery. They are not minor: unchecked, they can become a serious threat to healthy style. On the other hand, they can be put right given alert and judicious thought.

Second, the irritation and confusion they cause is not deliberate. Often writers are not aware of their 'surplus fat' and imagine their style to be in fine shape – just as many overweight people think they're 'in the pink'. Pointing out the need to lose that weight may be hurtful; but most such writers are, I find, impressively humble and anxious to improve once the faults have been identified. Most are successful in doing so, too.

But there's another kind of flab – one that the writer is not only aware of but seems positively to revel in. That is my next target.

Deliberate fleshiness

This involves the calculated, even cynical use of complex structures and highly sophisticated vocabulary. Sometimes such a style is employed to impress; at others it is used to intimidate; and on occasion it is designed to conceal, which is worst of all.

It would be incautious to suggest that such intentional flabbiness abounds more than ever before. But there's certainly a lot of it about, and that makes life tough for the learning writer: a good number of

Figure 10. 'A style employed to impress or intimidate'.

the 'models' he/she encounters will be of this sort. So both as an encouragement and as a warning, I offer this observation:

An 'adult' style is not necessarily one to emulate. A great deal of adult language is ugly, dull or inept, and it often obscures more than it reveals.

A cautionary example is provided by George Orwell in his essay 'Politics And The English Language':

I am going to translate a passage of good English into modern English of the worst sort. Here is a well-known verse from *Ecclesiastes*:

'I returned and saw under the sun, that the race is not to the swift, nor the battle to the strong, neither yet bread to the wise, nor yet riches to men of understanding, nor yet favour to men of skill; but time and chance happeneth to them all.'

Here it is in modern English:

'Objective considerations of contemporary phenomena compels the conclusion that success or failure in competitive activities exhibits no tendency to be commensurate with innate capacity, but that a considerable element of the unpredictable must invariably be taken into account.'

That is a parody, but not a very gross one. . . . The whole tendency of modern prose is away from concreteness.

Orwell's parody highlights three centrally damaging things that can characterize such allegedly sophisticated prose. First, as he says, it veers away from the concrete, almost as if terrified by it. Second, it not only destroys the poetry and music of the original, but virtually obliterates its meaning as well. The simple power of the original's images and the lilt of its rhythms grip the imagination and the intellect, whereas even a highly-educated person will find the process of 'decoding' the translation joylessly laborious. Third, the translation is much longer than the original – even though quite a lot of the latter has been by-passed, as Orwell recognized.* And although he wrote the essay nearly fifty years ago, let there be no doubt that his remarks are just as relevant today, if not more so.

In short, a certain kind of 'adult' writing seems to pride itself on three major vices: excessive abstraction; indifference to clarity and the reader's comfort; self-indulgent verbosity.

1. The desire to hide

The word **simple** is, paradoxically, a very complex one. For a start it has a host of meanings: *The Shorter Oxford* lists no fewer than twenty-four. The six most relevant to my discussion here are:

1.	**straightforward, unelaborate**	a simple sentence; simple diet
2.	**absolute**	the simple truth
3.	**feeble-minded**	simple Simon; hence simpleton
4.	**insignificant, trifling**	simple people
5.	**easily done or understood**	give a simple explanation
6.	**natural**	a simple heart; simple joys

You will quickly see that these meanings are not only separate: they can be opposites. One of the most famous questions ever asked was Pontius Pilate's: **What is truth?**

That strikes me as 'simple' in senses 1, 2 and 6. It is emphatically not so under the other definitions, especially 5: it is as difficult as anything in human history, and indeed nobody has yet answered it satisfactorily.

When I recommend simplicity, therefore, I do not have meaning 3 in mind, which would be silly; or 2, which is usually impossible. Nor am I suggesting that your efforts will reduce to 4. But you **should** strive for 1 and 6; and if you find the **easily done** part of 5 involves a lot of (hidden) work, you must always try to ensure the **easily understood** part for your readers' sakes.

As your vocabulary and technical skill increase, you will want to make as much use of them as you can. This shows admirable enterprise, but

---

* He goes on to say:

> The concrete illustrations – race, battle, bread – dissolve into the vague phrase 'success or failure in competitive activities'. This had to be so, because no modern writer of the kind I am discussing – no one capable of using phrases like 'objective considerations of contemporary phenomena' – would ever tabulate his thoughts in that precise and detailed way.

The original passage is from *Ecclesiastes*, 9: 11; 1611 version.

don't let it lead you to ignore the virtues of simplicity and harmfully inflate your writing. This next exercise features a very clever man with plenty to say who has forgotten how to write naturally.

Exercise 17
The following passage is some 120 words long. Can you paraphrase it in 40?

In the affluent society, capitalism comes into its own. The two mainsprings of its dynamic – the escalation of commodity production and productive exploitation – join and permeate all dimensions of private and public existence. The available material and intellectual resources [the potential of liberation] have so much outgrown the established institutions that only the systematic increase in waste, destruction and management keeps the system going. The opposition which escapes suppression by the police, the courts, the representatives of the people, and the people themselves, finds expression in the diffused rebellion among the youth and the intelligentsia, and in the daily struggle of the persecuted minorities. The armed class struggle is waged outside: by the wretched of the earth who fight the affluent monster.

Commentary

That is the first paragraph [**first**, mark you!] of *An Essay On Liberation* (1969) by Herbert Marcuse. He was a political philosopher of the first rank, so we should not perhaps expect his work to be easy. But is it efficient or natural writing?

No, surely not. The language is top-heavy, abstract, turgid; above all the passage is **verbose**. As noted, it is 120 words long; have a look at this 33-word paraphrase of mine and compare it to your own.

> Capitalism dominates the affluent society at all levels. By enlarging the range and intensity of its influence, it sucks in and emasculates most potential rebels, leaving only the abjectly poor to fight it.

That is just over one-quarter of the original's length. It may sacrifice the odd nuance, but it captures the essentials of the argument without distortion or omission. And unlike the original it is, I hope, almost immediately comprehensible.

Why do people write like that? Why did Marcuse, an internationally-renowned figure, feel it necessary to use four words where one would do and in general write as if he were almost afraid of making himself clear?

Fear may be the key. Marcuse's subject [the state of the earth and its oppressed poor] may be a large one; his treatment of it is common-place – orthodox post-Marxist attitudinizing. Since he's addressing a presumably educated and well-informed audience, he seeks to dress up his unremarkable ideas in the most imposing fashion he can find. So he reaches for the grandest 'power terms', hoping they will cow the reader into dutifully accepting that his argument is both important and fresh. In short, the passage tries to bully the reader; bullies are notorious for their underlying insecurity.

All that may strike you as unfair. You might instead feel that Marcuse is an innocent victim of the drift away from the concrete that Orwell identified half a century ago. Whatever one's view, the fact remains that Marcuse attacks the reader with a string of Latinate words and complex constructions that resist quick understanding. Those 'power terms' – **suppression, escalation of commodity production, potential of liberation** and **persecuted minorities** – fail to prompt any clear physical image. And they surely should: the passage centres on basic physical truths – violence, torture, poverty, mass production and, indeed, how life is lived. Only the phrase **the wretched of the earth** resonates appropriately; and by the time it appears, the damage has already been decisive.

Such writing is dishonest. Once any writer allows a gap to develop between the concrete reality addressed and the language used to express it, muddle and deception result. Intriguingly, that dishonesty does not have to be malicious or sinister: a lot of misleading language can be considerate in intention – which brings me to the topic of **euphemism**.

2. Euphemism

Euphemism: the substitution of a mild or vague or roundabout expression for a harsh or blunt or direct one.

The three commonest causes of euphemism are death, sex and going to the lavatory. If a friend of yours has recently suffered a death in the family, it is sensible and considerate to seek the least painful way of referring to it – 'passed away', 'moved on' or whatever. Similarly, if you're at a formal dinner-party and become aware of the urgent need to relieve yourself, it is just crass to rise abruptly and favour the table with, 'Gotta piss, folks.' Judge your audience!

On such occasions, the roundabout expression is commendably tactful. In most instances, however, euphemisms are cowardly and deceptive rather than courteous. Their dressed-up, inexact nature betrays fearful dislike of unpalatable fact; as such they are enemies of clarity and truth. Furthermore, they are insidious. Shying away from direct linguistic contact with certain ideas and facts can quickly spread to your handling of other ideas and facts; before you know it your language has become woolly and coy. So I believe one should, within reason, call a spade a spade.

For euphemism, whether decorous or deceitful, is everywhere. It permeates all matters of everyday life – not just death, sex and urination but money; serious illness; any kind of mental disturbance; political and business practice; warfare; housing; advertising; education; travel; food and catering; and so on. The more you kow-tow to it, the more your style and its ability to communicate will suffer.

Now to some examples.

The first is from an A level essay on *Othello*, a play centrally concerned with sexual infatuation and obsession. A good many students get into difficulties when writing on this theme – not because they are adolescently giggly about it, but because it takes a lot of courage to 'go public' in a direct manner about the subject. As a result, they write things like this:

Othello and Desdemona have a huge crush on each other which interferes with their judgment.

The basic idea is sound, but the language diminishes it to a near-comic extent. It is not true that the characters' passion 'interferes with their judgment': it **obliterates** their judgment. And I suspect that such a cripplingly diluted phrase was the inevitable consequence of starting with the feebly coy 'huge crush', which relegates the relationship to a Mills and Boon level.

Appropriateness and 'weight' of vocabulary are all-important. Here the student felt diffident about registering the instinctive ferocity of the lovers' passion, seeking refuge in a phrase that would not embarrass him. But in another way, of course, it **did** embarrass him: the expression is factually inappropriate, and suggests that he has not grasped a point of fundamental significance.

How far you go in a corrective direction is tricky! Perhaps the following is a good compromise between genteel inadequacy and excessive raunchiness:

The sexual delight Othello and Desdemona share in each other bypasses and eventually annihilates their judgment.

That is also an extract from an A Level essay. Both students make essentially the same point; the second, which records the intensity of the pair's sexuality in an accurate and dignified way, has an authority that the first's blushful reticence does not approach.

That first example of euphemism may be gauche, but it is hardly a sinister abuse of language. The next illustration **is** morally disreputable. It is a famous example of the language of war, taken from the *pro forma* letters sent to bereaved relatives of servicemen killed in the Great War (1914–18). The central clauses invariably read:

He died instantly and felt no pain.

In many cases this was simply not true. Most soldiers did not die instantly: a considerable number died in slow agony spread over days often hanging inaccessibly alive in 'No Man's Land' until they became too weak or infected to survive.

It could be argued that the formula was designed from the best of motives – to cheer the bereaved, to offer them comfort and even some pride in their loss. But it could equally be said that it amounted to flagrant lying, that it cynically blinded the recipients [and thus others] to the lunatic waste and cruelty of a war that political bosses were determined to see carried on. That determination may not have been dishonourable or wrong in itself; it is, however, harder to believe that when such devious methods were used to safeguard its continuation.*

'War is hell' may have become the stalest of clichés†, but the official language of war has shown an increasing fondness for a bland abstraction void of any hint of infernal torment.

Ever since **casualty** was coined for a soldier killed in combat, war-mongers have worked at ways of making the horrific seem tolerable, and the Vietnam war was distinguished, if that's the word, for the way language itself was 'conscripted' as if it were part of the war effort. One of the terms the Pentagon used in their press releases was **defoliation** (literally 'the stripping of foliage from trees and shrubs'). This comfortable Latinism was mobilized to anaesthetize the public to what was really involved – the blanket-bombing with napalm and dioxin of whole areas of the jungle, including of course the Vietnamese peasants within them. The truth was indeed hellish, as this account by Adam Sweeting shows:

> By the end of the Vietnam war, these sinister bat-like machines (B-52 bombers) had created most of the 26 million craters which perforated the landscape. More bombs were dropped on Vietnam than were used in the Second World War. While these were being delivered, something called Operation Ranch Hand was systematically carpeting South Vietnam with 72 million litres of Agent Orange defoliant, ossifying two million hectares of forest and mangrove swamp in a well-organized pattern which suggested a form of intensive farming run by the devil. 'Help prevent a forest,' went the slogan among the Ranch Hand crews . . . [*The Guardian*, 4/11/88]

* Such tawdry phoneyness is wonderfully satirized in *Catch-22*, where the manically self-seeking Colonel Cathcart sends his own *pro forma* letter to all bereaved relatives without even deleting the unapplicable terms. Thus a Mrs Daneeka's letter of condolence reads:

> Dear Mrs, Mr, Miss, or Mr and Mrs Daneeka: Words cannot express the deep personal grief I experienced when your husband, son, father or brother was killed, wounded or reported missing in action.

† The remark is attributed to General Sherman of the Union forces in the American Civil War; I imagine a similar idea may have crossed the minds of Julius Caesar, Marlborough, Napoleon and all those involved in the Charge of the Light Brigade.

It's a pity that there wasn't more reporting of this kind while the war was going on, when the American people were fed mendacious abstractions as 'information'.

I'm not of course suggesting that you will be capable of such callous manipulation of language. But I do want to stress that language can be a malignant smokescreen as well as an illuminating beam. The more we fail to call a spade a spade or allow others to hold forth blandly about things that are unambiguously horrible or starkly distressing, the more we risk surrendering the independence that language affords us. That is why Harold Pinter is to be applauded rather than prudishly censured for his sudden dive into obscenity during an otherwise temperate literary interview:

> I'll tell you what I really think of politicians. The other night I watched some politicians on television talking about Vietnam. I wanted very much to burst through the screen with a flame-thrower and burn their eyes out and their balls off and then enquire from them how they would assess this action from a political point of view.*

The journal *Private Eye* has always been good at 'de-coding' the kind of humbug that so angered Pinter. Here is its 'corrective' explanation of the US Air Force's botched 1986 raid on Libya.

THAT LIBYAN RAID
Glossary of Terms

What they said	*What they meant*
The mission was 100% successful	We really screwed it up
Surgical precision	All our bombs hit Libya
We only hit selected military targets	Tough luck on all those embassies, schools, kids, hospitals, etc.
We had no intention of assassinating Gadaffi	We missed
We deeply regret any casualties	They're only Arabs
This will teach them once and for all that terrorism doesn't pay	Gadaffi More Popular Than Ever Shock
We have made a major contribution to effectively reducing terrorist capability in the world	Cancel your holiday plans
As a result of what we did Americans can walk a little taller in the world	We're still cancelling our holidays
We've shown that they can't push us around	Did you see Rambo?
We're not contemplating a second strike	Bombs away!

* From *Writers at Work: The* Paris Review *Interviews; Third Series* (1977) ed. G. Plimpton, Penguin, p. 361.

The piece is overstated, naturally, and you may think that measured accuracy would have been more effective than its irreverent anger. You might also think that to attack politicians is itself a cliché: they've been pilloried by satirists for centuries.

I find such debunking scorn healthy and important. When writers aim their vitriol at politicians, it is not things like the shaping of policy, the difficult business of government or even electioneering that prompt their rage: it is bogus conduct. It is the politician as liar that *Private Eye* and Pinter are attacking – and 'politician' in that derogatory sense means anyone in public life whose task it is to provide the people with information and who fail to tell (or face) a known truth or wraps it up in misleading language.

I stressed earlier that you'll find euphemism everywhere. Here are ten of my 'pet hates' over the years; you might then like to try the similar exercise that follows them.

1. **industrial action**: On strike/doing no work.
2. **strategic labour reserve**: The unemployed.
3. **I've got a cash-flow problem**: I'm broke.
4. **I'm going to South Africa to help break down apartheid in cricket**: They've offered me £100k for two winters' work.
5. **He is suffering from a chemical imbalance in the right hemisphere of the brain**: He's potty.
6. **The site has been rationalized**: All the buildings have been demolished.
7. **The property is in easy reach of good communications**: The house is 100 metres from the M25.
8. **He underachieves on paper and is anonymous in class**: He's a lazy sod and I can't remember what he looks like.
9. **The conditions are not propitious:** We haven't a chance in hell of surviving.
10. **Inexpensive dresses for mature women with the fuller figure:** Nasty cheap frocks for fat old women.

Exercise 18
Now 'decode' these expressions; my versions appear afterwards.
'Nukespeak'*

1. strike potential.
2. 'soft'†targets.

---

* i.e. the language of nuclear weaponry.

† 'Hard' targets are military bases and missile sites. Both 1 and 2 are standard expressions in the language of strategic defence [i.e. war] planning.

The world of work and business

3. My members' material aspirations have been grossly betrayed.
4. I'm not running a charity, you know.

Medicine

5. The patient is in a stable condition.
6. He is a disturbed personality with schizophrenic and paranoid tendencies.

Housing

7. This property would benefit from a degree of renovation.
8. This attractively idiosyncratic flat is distinguished for the communal friendliness of its adjoining residents.

Catering

9. A pleasant full-bodied red wine that is always in demand.
10. Gratuities at the discretion of the customer.

General

11. I'm sorry about your birthday – I forgot.

12. Eh, lad, you must take us as you find us.

These are my alternatives to the euphemisms of Exercise 18.

1. The ability to kill hundreds of millions of people in a few minutes.
2. Concentrated areas of population.
3. We haven't got the pay rise we asked for.
4. I'm interested only in making as much money as possible.
5. The patient is in very bad shape and will probably die.
6. He is a dangerous lunatic.
7. The place is falling apart and is currently uninhabitable.
8. This flat is decorated in appalling taste and you have to share a bathroom and lavatory with twenty other people.
9. The house plonk.
10. If you don't tip us, you're just a mean sod.
11. I couldn't be bothered to remember your birthday.
12. We're very unpleasant to all strangers and we don't give a toss what you think.

Figure 11. 'The patient is in a stable condition'.

Summary

Not all the euphemisms in my illustrations and that exercise are sinister or devious; one or two even have a certain charm. Nonetheless, use of euphemism should be kept to a minimum. The choice of a roundabout expression nearly always sacrifices clarity, appropriateness or necessary concreteness; sometimes all three. As a concluding guiding principle, therefore:

> **When you've nothing to say, don't say it. And when you *have* got something to say, do so in as unadorned and direct way as is feasible and apposite.**

That will suit best your own purposes of communication, and it will also help preserve the integrity of your style. If you feel that last phrase is pompous, just look back over some of the examples of 'fleshy' writing in this chapter, and note again how ugly they are and how they abuse words as a medium of enlightenment. The more writers there are who do that, the more we risk the shrinking of our language, our judgment and our independent awareness.

That ends our detailed look at **waffle and padding**. There remain two more areas of flab to be fought – self-indulgent 'fine writing', and fake formalism. Both overlap with more than a few of the things we've considered already, but they deserve a separate look.

7.2 PUBLISHING FOR VANITY'S SAKE

This is a shorter section, designed to amuse as much as instruct. In it my concern is with the kind of florid style whose most obvious characteristic is the writer's self-love.

I have stressed from the start that all good writing embodies a delight in words. But there is a big difference between a delight that is meant to be shared with the reader and one which is, as it were, directed at a looking-glass. 'Fine writing' is **vain**: it is designed for the writer's self gratification, and clear communication to others doesn't come into it.

Here is a recent [October 1990] letter to *The Times*.

> Sir,
> Last Saturday I was bathing my visiting grandson amongst a flotilla of paper boats made from that day's *Times*. We were both so absorbed in our separate aims, I to launch and float the boats, Tobias (aged two) to sabotage and scuttle them, that we failed to notice that both boy and bath had meanwhile been marbled in a delicate tracery of black.
> This form of marbling is very like the Japanese art of *suminagashi*. However, since this new method involves only warm water, liquid baby soap, *Times* newsprint and a small boy, it is a very much simpler process, and equally pretty.

This is not badly written in any mechanical way; nor, to be fair, is it flabby in its phraseology or sentence structure. Yet it is very vulnerable to a simple question: **Why on earth was it written as a public letter?**

There can be only one reason – unless the writer meant it as a subversive joke: she did it purely to show off. A charming (and private) domestic incident is vainly transformed into a public lecture on an esoteric subject. The effect is disastrous.

My use of 'vainly' just now was doubly deliberate. For **vain** does not just mean **conceited**: it also means **useless** or **unavailing**, as in such expressions as 'in the vain hope that he would succeed' or, of course, the simple 'in vain'. Our letter writer was so pleased with her artistic discovery that she evidently did not stop to consider whether others would find it of value or even interest – and surely very few would. As I remarked before, one suspects a joke; but one waits in vain for the 'tonal kick-back' that would confirm humour as the intention. The last sentence is crowningly ludicrous, asking us to take note of a cheap* way

---

* If one wanted to be really solemn about this admitted trifle, one could add that it's 'cheap' in another sense – that of regarding a bathing infant primarily as a sub-artist's tool.

of effecting *suminagashi*: who'd want to anyway? No wonder the letter found its way into *Private Eye*'s splendid column 'Pseud's Corner'.

Now for something much more difficult, albeit just as awful.

> Non-Euclidean space, and the dissolution of our entire fabric of perception, results from electric modes of moving information. This revolution involves us willynilly in the study of modes and media as forms which shape and re-shape our perceptions. That is what I have meant all along by saying 'the medium is the message', for the medium determines the modes of perception and the matrix of assumptions within which objectives are set.
>
> from 'Explorations In The New World' by Marshall McLuhan*

This is irredeemably opaque: however many times one reads it, it still doesn't make any real sense.

Further research into McLuhan's ideas would establish that he saw the advent of television as comparable to the invention of printing in its effect on human knowledge and perception. He also maintained that all electronic forms of communication required an understanding radically different from those associated with the 'ancient' culture dominated by printing.

Even knowing all that is no help here, however: the argument neither pleases nor persuades. Groping around in a dense fog [verbal or otherwise] comes low down on any list of life's delights; and how can any of us be persuaded of anything if we don't understand what is being talked about? The language is remorselessly abstract; it is also – and this is where **vanity** comes into it – bewilderingly self-referential, indeed absurdly so. The 'revolution' he so grandly posits amounts to nothing other than going round in circles.

My third example is also an exercise. Please read this passage that I have adapted from a magazine article.

> Once my mother said: 'What I am proudest of is that I have made two beautiful gardens in my lifetime, both from virgin soil.'
>
> 5   What a splendid statement, was my own instant reaction. Is it yours too? Gardens can continue to give increasing pleasure to everyone who looks over the fence. It is with some trepidation that I plead that, if even one sentence that I have written should have eternal life, it should be this one, in that it surely epitomizes the innate longing for fulfilment, for passing on the
> 10 torch that is buried in the heart of all the human race:
> *Every mother at birth sets three crowns upon her child's head. A crown for courage, a crown for faith, a crown for happiness.*

* Collected in *McLuhan Hot & Cool* (Penguin, 1968), p. 182.

Exercise 19: Revision

I don't know what effect the content and **tone** have on you – we'll discuss that shortly. First, there are at least ten things wrong with the piece technically, and in roughly chronological order they are:

1. Factual inaccuracy
2. Faulty logic
3. Poor paragraphing
4. Mixed metaphor*
5. Bad grammar
6. Yob's commas
7. Bad sentence structure
8. Innumeracy
9. No unity of material
10. A non-sentence

Can you identify them? My commentary follows immediately, so try not to look at it until you've made your own judgments.

Commentary

1. **Factual inaccuracy.** I just don't believe that the author's mother made two gardens out of virgin soil. She may have paid for or overseen such work, done by a gang of sub-contractors and jobbing gardeners; but the idea of a (presumably) quite elderly woman

---

* A **mixed metaphor** is a construction where two separate images collide, with confusing and/or ludicrous results. For example:

> **We're skating on thin ice and will soon be out of the frying pan and into the fire.**

Both the images are clichés, of course, which doesn't help; but the biggest problem is the marriage of ice/water and heat. If one visualizes the overall scenario, absurdity ensues – a picture of a skater in danger suddenly repositioned in boiling fat and additionally threatened by a large blaze. The latter would surely cause the **thin ice** to melt at once anyway, wouldn't you say?

Another example comes from a Radio 4 news bulletin: I nearly included it in my very first section, 'Disasters':

> **The policy of non-intervention is a hot potato which has left the Government with egg on its face.**

A **hot potato** means an urgent problem; to be left with **egg on one's face** means to be embarrassed or to look foolish. The trouble is, of course, that potatoes aren't famous for being made out of eggs; a potentially vigorous statement is again ruined by the visual absurdity the images evoke.

Mixed metaphors are invariably a symptom of the failure to 'engage brain before writing' or to both 'hear' and 'see' the words chosen. As noted, they are often an additionally unfortunate consequence of relying on hackneyed phrases.

creating two horticultural masterpieces with her bare hands and a few homely tools is preposterous.

2. **Faulty logic.** The fourth sentence [lines 5–6] may seem all right; but what is its logical connection with the opening remark? Are we to believe that she 'made two gardens' with the prime objective of giving pleasure to itinerant nosey-parkers rubbernecking over her private fence?

3. **Poor paragraphing.** It is unnecessary to start a new paragraph at line 4; it is essential to do so at line 6, after 'fence', because the next sentence addresses an entirely different topic.
   [This flaw goes hand-in hand with 7 and 9.]

4. **Mixed metaphor.** I would not greatly care to have a 'torch . . . buried in the heart', and I'd guess that most members of 'the human race' would feel the same. It would be bad enough if it were a battery-operated torch; since the author is (I think) using the older idea of a burning brand, the prospect is excruciating.

5. **Bad grammar.** 'This one' in line 8 is faulty: it has no **antecedent**. That is, there is no noun or concept to which it refers back,

Figure 12. 'Itinerant nosey-parkers'.

which pronouns must always do. 'This one' refers **forward** to the pseudo-epigram that ends the piece.*

6. **Yob's commas**

7. **Sentence-structure**. These points can be taken in tandem. The sentence concerned is the lengthy 'It is with some . . . human race' [lines 7–11], and it's a right mess. It wanders all over the place; by the time one gaspingly makes it to the end, one has almost certainly lost track of how it started and what it's supposed to be about.

   There is no easy way of putting it right. The prose is so badly thought-out that it's almost impossible to improve it through mere tinkering: the whole thing needs to be dismantled and redesigned, using far fewer commas. But it might be thought that such a task is just not worth the effort!

8. **Innumeracy.** The author cannot add up. He pleads for 'one sentence' to be given 'eternal life' and then writes down two. [See also 10.]

9. **No unity of material.** In fourteen lines we move from gardens to a desire for literary immortality to a sub-biblical pronouncement about courage, faith and happiness. There is, I suppose, a potentially unifying concept: motherhood. But it is loosely set up [we're into gardens almost at once] and ignored altogether in the middle.

   The small and medium-sized errors already analysed all contribute to this absence of unity. The passage is characterized by poor thinking and indifference to the reader; it is unsurprising that its structure is blancmange-like and vapid.

10. **A non-sentence.** The last sentence isn't a sentence at all: it has no verb. Admittedly, this doesn't matter much in terms of sense; but it isn't all that wise to claim immortality for a sentence which then fails to qualify grammatically as one. Nothing punctures a writer's vanity faster than illiteracy.

To have spent several pages demolishing such a slight piece might strike you as equivalent to taking an elephant gun to a sparrow. But apart from its value as a 'revision test' on some of the things covered earlier, there are important lessons here which hinge on the writing's **tone** and implicit attitudes. What did you make of these?

As is doubtless already evident, I'm not all that impressed! The piece is a frenzy of self-advertisement; worse, it operates in a universe of one.

---

* There **is** a legitimate way to use 'this' to refer forward: put a colon after the 'this' and then go on **at once** to specify what the 'this' is. The colon is a clear signal that an explanation is imminent, and therefore the reader will not be confused. In the above instance, 'this one' would be all right provided a colon were placed after it and the very next words were the 'Every mother . . .' proclamation.

The author is so pleased with himself and all his 'lovely thoughts' that he cannot be bothered to link them in a fashion that might enlighten. That may account for why he is slip-shod at every turn – though ignorance is also a factor, I suspect: his grammar and punctuation are fragile; his grasp of structure primitive; his sense of how his words will sound or read is minimal. He's having a wonderful time and nobody else matters.

Saddest of all, perhaps, is the way the writing causes us to cringe at things which should strike us as admirable. Few would in principle want to sneer at motherhood, courage, faith or happiness. But the way they are presented is disastrously vain – it is the writer who is being held up to admiration, not the concepts. All in all, the piece inspires in me the same reaction that American wit Dorothy Parker once expressed in a review. 'This is not a book to be laid lightly aside: it should be hurled with much force out of the window.'

The three examples I've looked at are extreme cases of vanity. But we all need to keep a watchful eye on our work, and to be wary of anything that strikes us as notably pleasing. Each of us then needs to ask a few tough questions:

1. Is it really that good anyway?
2. Does it communicate properly and enlighten?
3. Why have I included it? Does it do any real work, or am I just showing off, disagreeably 'marking time'?
4. What's the lasting effect on the reader going to be?

Figure 13. 'Strike it out'.

If any of the answers has a negative tinge, it may be time to follow Dr Johnson's stern command:

Read over your compositions and whenever you meet with a passage which you consider particularly fine, *strike it out.*

'Murder your darlings', in fact. That advice is Noel Coward's, and all writers will benefit from at least considering it: for example, my original demolition of the last passage was seven pages long!

From vanity to something more innocent but no less injurious.

7.3 PHONEY RULES AND FAKE FORMALISM

English has surprisingly few hard-and-fast rules. There are certain basic laws of grammar, of course; rules of punctuation are also precise and reliable: the ones outlined in Part Two are watertight. But English spelling cannot claim a single rule to which there are no exceptions; in addition, things like sentence structure, word order and word positioning are largely left up to the individual writer. That is one of the charms, and great strengths, of English; it can also perhaps be a source of uncertainty to the student.

The position isn't helped by the wide currency of counterfeit 'rules' which shackle rather than empower the developing writer. I want to focus on four of these; then I shall look at several flabby and boring structures which many pupils are erroneously taught they must employ.

Phoney rules

1. **It is wrong to begin a sentence with 'and' or indeed any other conjunction.**

Absolute nonsense. Moreover, to believe this prevents you from stressing conjunctions, which we all sometimes wish to do.

In the normal run of things, words like **and, but** and **for**, being both very common and very small, are hardly noticed by the reader: they merely advertise a link or contrast that the brain notes automatically. Supposing, though, you want to stress such a word – just as we often do in speech by placing a heavy emphasis via our voice? The only way to do this is to draw attention to it **visually**, and the only way to do that is to give it a capital letter, advertising its unusual importance. What better method than to start a sentence with it, whereby the capitalization is automatic?

Phoney Rule 1 is believed by an enormous number of people. As with certain other things I've looked at along the way, this is probably because it derives from one's primary school lessons. At that age, we have only a small vocabulary, and we tend to use the same words again and again; it makes a lot of sense, therefore, to find a way to discourage that. By the time we reach our teens, however, our vocabulary has increased a thousandfold: there is no longer any need to follow primary-school advice just for the sake of it. And to repeat, **there is no such rule in English grammar.**

As with any stylistic device, you should not use this technique too often; but if sensibly used for maximum impact, it is not only legitimate but valuable, since it allows your voice to grace your writing.

2. **It is wrong to use a preposition at the end of a sentence**.

Again, quite untrue.

For a start, there are some constructions where the preposition cannot comfortably go anywhere but the end:

1. **What is the world coming to?**
2. **This bed has not been slept in.**

If you rewrite these to comply with **Phoney Rule 2**, you end up with:

1a. **To what is the world coming?**

Figure 14. 'It is wrong to use a preposition at the end of a sentence'.

2a. **In this bed no sleep has taken place.**

1a is just about okay, though stiff and pompous compared to 1; 2a is wholly unsatisfactory. It is not only clumsy: it makes the remark nudgingly ambiguous, suggesting that other things may have 'taken place' even if 'sleep' did not!

Besides, the 'rule' is daft anyway. As with so much else, you should not make a habit of ending sentences with a preposition; on the other hand, to worry unduly about avoiding the practice can sacrifice voice and flow. Winston Churchill once encountered a civil servant who was pedantically 'accurate' about the matter, rendering his prose ugly and tiresome to read; eventually Churchill drew a line through the man's entire memorandum and wrote at the bottom: **'This is the kind of English up with which I shall not put.'**

His sardonic good sense should be a model to us all. Always remember:

Language does not serve grammar: it is the other way round.

Clarity and easiness on the ear and eye matter most; anyone or any 'rule' that in effect rejects that principle should be regarded with considerable suspicion.

3. **In formal writing it is wrong to use contractions**.

In other words, you must never use, **it's, they're, doesn't** and so on, but must dutifully write **it is, they are, does not** and the like.

Pure phantom pedantry: no 'rule' is at issue, just formalistic prejudice. It may well be a sensible practice when very young; it even remains sensible a few years later, when pupils begin to be aware of the difference between formal writing and casual conversation. Thereafter it is just silly. The full structure isn't superior to the contraction. It adds nothing in clarity, and its extra 'dignity' is often spurious, as obsessive avoidance of informality can lead to stilted and flabby prose. There may well be times when you feel that the full construction is more appropriate: style is often a matter of 'horses for courses', and indeed Part Four is devoted to that theme. But to argue that contractions in formal writing are intrinsically wrong is just dumb.*

4. **It is wrong to say 'It's me': it must always be 'It is I.'**

Once more, quite untrue.

One reason behind this wrong-headed advice is the dislike of contractions, which we've just been into. The other stems from a technical

---

* It occurs to me that the determined avoidance of contractions may be one reason why so few people know how to use the apostrophe. (See Part Two, pages 43–51.) If you're discouraged from using it in such a way, it's not surprising if you lose all sense of its value and what it's for!

point of grammar – that it is wrong to use the accusative form with the verb 'to be'. An explanation might go something like this:

> **It is obviously illiterate to say 'Me am teacher' or 'Him am dead'; in the same way, we should not use the object pronoun (me, him) after 'is' or any other form of the verb.**

This is correct so far as it goes. However, the point is that it does not go far enough. For **me** is not only the **accusative** (object) form of **I**: it is also the **demonstrative** [= emphatic] pronoun. One uses the expression **It's me** to emphasize that it is oneself as opposed to anyone else that one is talking about. Because of that fact, it could be argued that the expression is not only an acceptable alternative to **It is I** but actually a better one.

Besides, a lot of people who pride themselves on not using **It's me** commit real illiteracies such as **between you and I** and **It's a matter for your mother and I**. The I is wrong in both cases: the accusative form must always follow a preposition [**between** and **for**].*

Somehow the idea has grown up that it's socially superior to use **I** rather than the 'proletarian' **me**. If words are an army, then **I** is officer class while **me** belongs to the ranks; and all four 'phoney rules' I've discussed contain an element of such disagreeable pretension. The feeling seems to exist that if one avoids contractions, never places a preposition at the end of a sentence or a conjunction at the beginning, and flaunts the 'correct' use of **I** as much as possible, one is more pukka both as a writer and as a person. Mere snobbish drivel, needless to say: all it actually achieves is to cramp your writing and make life needlessly difficult for your readers. If that's 'pukka', you're better off being a pleb!

There are other 'phoney rules' dealt with in Part Five. For now, I just want to repeat that, while they have a valuable function during the early stages of one's education, they quickly become obsolete, shackles rather than sails. They rob writing of its natural voice, turning it into something more impersonal and, frankly, boring. That penalty also characterizes certain formal structures that are mistakenly thought to be necessary and good.

Fake formalism

I have elsewhere† commented on the leaden phrases with which many writers open or close their essays – structures like:

---

* If you are uncomfortable or uncertain about such terms as **accusative, demonstrative** and **preposition**, they are explained and illustrated in the Grammar Primer, Part Five.
† In *Brain Train* [E & FN Spon, 1984], pp. 93–96. See also Part Three above, page 76.

> **In order to answer this question, we must first consider . . .**
> **The question is asking us whether . . .**
> **Thus in conclusion we may safely say that . . .**
> **In this essay I have attempted to bear out the title's contention that . . .**

The sad thing about such tedious and useless expressions is that nobody would ever write them down instinctively: they've all been laboriously taught, with a depressing twin emphasis on caution and lack of imagination.

Those examples were taken from sixth-form or undergraduate essays; the trouble starts a lot earlier. There follows a standard type of comprehension question – the kind of thing we regularly encounter from about the age of nine:

> **What three things do you notice about the man's behaviour as described in lines 15–20 of the passage?**

And we are taught to answer in a sentence – which invariably means that we are instructed to begin our answer with the question's wording. Thus:

> **The three things I notice about the man's behaviour as described in lines 15–20 of the passage are . . .**

after which we go on – accurately, let's hope! – to list them.

Now why on earth do we do this? It is irksome, for writer and reader alike; it wastes a lot of time; it has a zombie-esque quality that dulls any possible pleasure.

There is one answer, sensible enough but hardly clinching. That bloated format is encouraged in early years because it ensures that pupils focus on the question and thus increase their chances of answering it accurately. To be sure, this works sometimes – although it should be said that laboriously copying something out does not guarantee an incisive intellect. But the formula becomes almost impossible to defend later on. For every student that really needs it as a 'prop', there will be ten who find such preliminary ritual a valueless drag: they may even make more of a mess of the answer as a result. So what objection can there be to an answer that identifies those three things in this way:

1. **He is nervous.**
2. **He is ashamed of his shabby coat.**
3. **He seems to be drunk.**

Assuming those answers to be correct, I cannot see anything wrong with that way of presenting them. Indeed, I strongly suspect that the examiner/reader will be delighted to find the information set out in such a crisp unfussy fashion.

If you are an A level student, an undergraduate or in a profession where you're required to write regularly, you will not, of course, have to do comprehension exercises very often! But their principles – and traps – remain relevant: you too should steer clear of any structure that is no more than an empty block of words. In the first place, these are invariably nondescript clichés; in the second, they cause you to adopt a 'voice' that is not your own. And the practice is contagious: once you feel obliged to observe such 'set-piece' formalisms as

> **Thus it can be seen that . . .**
> **In this essay I shall first consider what the title says and then go on to discuss whether it is a correct statement, and finally attempt some form of summary . . .**

you risk cluttering up your style with further, regular flab. You might even become capable of this kind of thing:

1. **That is not a prerogative we have available to us.**
2. **That information is not to hand at this juncture.**
3. **Post-nutritive substance disposal.**

Figure 15. 'He is nervous, he is ashamed of his shabby coat and seems to be drunk'.

Those bulbous structures translate into normal English as:

1. **We can't do it.**
2. **I don't know.**
3. **Shit.**

And if you think that these examples have a lot in common with the euphemisms analysed earlier, you're quite right. In every case there is a flabby veering away from directness, from ensuring that one's words do a precise and illuminating job of work.

Now on to positive ways of guaranteeing that you do that.

VOICE

8

He who wants to persuade should put his trust not
in the right argument, but in the right word. The
power of sound has always been greater than the
power of sense.

Joseph Conrad

The art of conversation is the art of hearing
as well as of being heard.

William Hazlitt

Good prose should resemble the conversation
of a well-bred man.

Somerset Maugham

There follow three longish pieces of writing that I admire very much.
Their origins are various: a novel, a newspaper article, a film transcript.
But aside from my enjoyment of them – which I hope you will share –
they have something in common. Can you identify it?

Passage A

(Then) the goddam picture started. It was so putrid I couldn't take
my eyes off it. It was about this English guy, Alec something, that
was in the war and loses his memory in the hospital and all. He
comes out of the hospital carrying a cane and limping all over the
place, all over London, not knowing who the hell he is. He's really
a duke, but he doesn't know it. Then he meets this nice, homey,
sincere girl getting on a bus. Her goddam hat blows off and he
catches it, and they go upstairs and sit down and start talking
about Charles Dickens. He's both their favourite author and all.
He's carrying this copy of *Oliver Twist* and so's she. I could've
puked. Anyway, they fall in love right away, on account of they're
both so nuts about Charles Dickens and all, and he helps her run
her publishing business. She's a publisher, the girl. Only, she's not
doing so hot, because her brother's a drunkard and spends all their
dough. He's a very bitter guy, the brother, because he was a doctor
in the war and now he can't operate any more because his nerves
are shot, so he boozes all the time, but he's pretty witty and all.
Anyway, old Alec writes a book, and this girl publishes it, and
they both make a hatful of dough on it. They're all set to get
married when this other girl, old Marcia, shows up. Marcia was

Alec's fiancée before he lost his memory, and she recognizes him when he's in this store autographing books. She tells old Alec he's really a duke and all, but he doesn't believe her and he doesn't want to go with her to visit his mother and all. His mother's blind as a bat. But the other girl, the homey one, makes him go. She's very noble and all. So he goes. But he still doesn't get his memory back, even when his Great Dane jumps all over him and his mother sticks her fingers all over his face and brings him this teddy bear he used to slobber around with when he was a kid. But then, one day, some kids are playing cricket on the lawn and he gets smacked in the head with a cricket ball. Then right away he gets his goddam memory back and he goes in and kisses his mother on the forehead and all. Then he starts being a regular duke again, and he forgets all about the homey babe that has the publishing business. I'd tell you the rest of the story, but I might puke if I did. It isn't that I'd **spoil** it for you or anything. There isn't anything to **spoil**, for Chrissake. Anyway, it ends up with Alec and the homey babe getting married, and the brother that's a drunkard gets his nerves back and operates on Alec's mother so she can see again, and then the drunken brother and old Marcia go for each other. It ends up with everybody at this long dinner-table laughing their asses off because the Great Dane comes in with a bunch of puppies. Everybody thought it was a male, I suppose, or some goddam thing. All I can say is, don't see it if you don't want to puke all over yourself . . .

from *The Catcher In The Rye* by J. D. Salinger

Passage B

And now the bloody young man is lifting a young girl from the wreckage and laying her on the verge among the roadworks. She is even bloodier than he is. You've still got one headlamp working, and that is the only light on the scene. You can see the blood quite clearly by the light of that lamp. She is writhing a bit on the verge, in an attitude of complete abandonment and indecency. Then she lies quite still and he covers her. You know she is dead. You wonder about the other car, but the young man is walking over there, and you leave it to him again. Anyway, it's dark over there, and you're such a coward you don't want to go and look. You excuse yourself by thinking that as you know no first aid you could serve no useful purpose. So you stand beside what is left of your car, and you wait, and you don't really think about anything at all. You are not even in very great pain any more, but you know you've got to look at your right leg, because that's where the pain was and you use the headlamp to look, and it's all bloody and unreal-looking. That's **your** leg. It's always been all right in the past. Best not look any more. That blood will just go away if you leave it. Anyway, why stay here? What to do now? If you go away, you'll be in trouble for failing to report an accident. If you stay, you'll just see more horrible things when they uncover whatever is in that other car. You can report the accident tomorrow. Yes, that's right. Walk home now, and report the accident tomorrow. Forget about the car. Don't want that any more. Home is 15 miles away, but it doesn't matter. Just go home, and maybe tomorrow it won't have happened. That's right, down the hill, quite easy going. Leg doesn't really mind being walked on at all. But the thrillers are wrong when they talk of **warm** blood trickling down. It isn't warm; it's cold. Everything is cold. There isn't a footpath to walk on, but it doesn't matter. Just walk in the middle of the road. Walk home. Police car pulling up? Failing to report an accident? It's an offence. You know it is. But they seem to know all about it. They want to know what car you were in, but you can't remember the number. They put you in their own car. Riding in a police car indeed. Proper Z car, with radio. They are using the radio. Hold the ambulance. Fifth casualty found. Leg injuries and shock. Funny, they don't seem to mind that you didn't report the accident. They don't even seem to want a driving licence. Just as well. Left it at home. Then you're in the ambulance. And now you resist. Now you really resist. You're not going anywhere with that lot . . .

from 'Statistic', *The Guardian*, 1963

Passage C

It's impossible through words to describe what is necessary to those who do not know what 'horror' means: 'horror'. Horror has a face; and you must make a friend of horror – horror and moral terror are your friends. And if they are not, then they are enemies to be feared: they are truly enemies.

I remember when I was with Special Forces – it seems a thousand years ago – we went into a camp to inoculate some children. We'd left the camp after we'd inoculated the children for polio; and this old man came running after us and he was crying – he couldn't say why. And they* had come and hacked off every inoculated arm. There they were in a pile: in a pile of little arms.

And I remember, I cried: I wept like . . . like some grandmother. I wanted to tear my teeth out – I didn't know what I wanted to do. And I want to remember; I never want to forget it: I never want to forget. And then I realized – like I was shot, like I was shot with a diamond . . . a diamond bullet right through my forehead – and I

---

* 'They' are the Vietcong, North Vietnamese commandos in the Vietnam war of the 1960s and 70s.

thought, 'My God! The **genius** of that! The genius; the will to do that. Perfect; genuine; complete; crystalline; pure.'

Then I realized that they were stronger than we, because they could stand it. These were not monsters – these were **men**, trained cadres. These men, who fought with their hearts, who have families, who have children, who are filled with love; but they have the *strength*, the strength to do that. If I had ten divisions of such men, then our troubles here would be over very quickly. You have to have men who are moral, and at the same time are able to utilize their primordial instincts to kill – to kill without feeling, without passion, without judgment. Without judgment; because it's judgment that defeats us.'

A speech by Colonel Kurtz (played by Marlon Brando), transcribed from Francis Ford Coppola's *Apocalypse Now*

What unites the three passages?

Several things may occur to you. For a start, they are of course all long extracts – comfortably the longest I've included so far. All are dramatic, too: the Salinger is primarily humorous in intent and effect, but the film the narrator [Holden Caulfield] watches contains a fair amount of incident, and his withering account is certainly fast moving. And you may also have noticed that despite the passages' length, nearly all the sentences within them are punchily short, making focus and concentration relatively easy.

However, the quality I have most in mind is that each passage is distinguished for its sense of **voice**. All three have a 'power of sound', in Conrad's phrase, that doubles the impact of their already-powerful material.

Intriguingly, that clarity of voice enhances our visual awareness and response. I find I can not only 'see' with photographic definition every detail mentioned: I also form a very distinct picture of the person behind the voice. Add to all that the tactile crispness of the writing, and in each case one becomes immersed in it, gripped by its appeal to the senses and intellect alike.

Early on in this book I laid down a fundamental principle:

> **All good writing sounds equally good when read aloud; and all good talking will read well when transcribed**.

The sense of voice is paramount: get that right, and all else should flow from it.

Now to three examples where the voice is deliberately and revealingly disagreeable. I want to stress that the writing is in no sense bad. Each passage spotlights a character whom the author wishes us to criticize or find seriously wanting; we are led in this direction mainly by our sense of the character's voice, which tells us – faster than decoding the actual words – that something is amiss. All three form, in part, an exercise: in each case:

1. Read through the passage silently and carefully.
2. Then read it through again – **aloud**.
3. Make a detailed note of your reactions, especially what effect the 'voice' has on you.

Exercise 20

This first passage is taken from early in *Mansfield Park* by Jane Austen. It chiefly features the odious Mrs Norris, a bitter and spiteful woman who rarely misses an opportunity to bitch about Fanny, the gentle heroine of the novel. The discussion concerns an errand that Fanny has been obliged to do even though she is in frail health.

Edmund got up and walked around the room, saying, 'And could nobody be employed on such an errand but Fanny? – Upon my word, ma'am, it has been a very ill-managed business.' 'I am sure I do not know how it was to have
5 been done better!' cried Mrs Norris, unable to be longer deaf; 'unless I had gone myself indeed; but I cannot be in two places at once; and I was talking to Mr Green at that very time about your mother's dairy-maid, by **her** desire, and had promised John Groom to write to Mrs Jefferies about his son, and the
10 poor fellow was waiting for me half an hour. I think nobody can justly accuse me of sparing myself upon any occasion, but really I cannot do everything at once. And as for Fanny's just stepping down to my house for me, it is not much above a quarter of a mile, I cannot think it was unreasonable to ask
15 it. How often do I pace it three times a day, early and late, ay and in all weathers too, and say nothing about it?' 'I wish Fanny had half your strength, ma'am.'
    'If Fanny would be more regular in her exercise, she would not be knocked up* so soon. She has not been out on horseback
20 now this long while, and I am persuaded, that when she does not ride, she ought to walk. If she had been riding before, I should not have asked it of her. But I thought it would rather do her good after stooping among the roses; for there is nothing so refreshing as a walk after a fatigue of that kind; and though
25 the sun was strong, it was not so very hot. Between ourselves, Edmund . . . it was cutting the roses, and dawdling about in the flower-garden, that did the mischief.'

---

* This phrase means 'made exhausted' and must not be confused with the modern American usage, signifying 'made pregnant'. English is a fluid language, and certain expressions dramatically change in meaning over the years!

Commentary

I very much hope you dislike Mrs Norris intensely! Austen 'leads' us with an authorial comment just once – the phrase **unable to be longer deaf** (lines 6–7), which suggests eavesdropping and meddling. Otherwise, Mrs Norris is condemned out of her own mouth: her 'voice' is definitively nasty.

Her aggressive prattle is amusing, but it is also most unpleasant. She at once dives into a torrent of self-justification that is as trivial as it is unattractive; then she launches a scarcely-disguised attack on what she sees as Fanny's laziness and own self-indulgence. The suggestion that she believed that **it would do her good*** (lines 26–7) is a transparent lie, and her obvious indifference to Fanny's welfare is underlined by the inane **though the sun was strong, it was not so very hot** (lines 29–30). And at the end she behaves like a classroom 'sneak', looking to make Fanny seem a contemptible skiver with only herself to blame for her illness.

When you read it aloud, I'd be surprised if you didn't find yourself adopting a feverish and ugly tone; however you read it, though, I'd be amazed if you liked what you heard. Nor of course were you supposed to: by expert manipulation of voice, Austen has in a few sentences nailed a character who will prompt dislike and contempt throughout the novel.

Exercise 21

The second passage is from Chapter V of *Middlemarch* by George Eliot. It is a letter proposing marriage written to Dorothea Brooke – an ardent but naive young woman – by Mr Casaubon, a middle-aged clergyman who is also a supposedly distinguished scholar. Please follow the same three-part procedure as before.

> My dear Miss Brooke,
> I have your guardian's permission to address you on a sub-ject than which I have none more at heart. I am not, I trust, mis-taken in the deeper recognition of some deeper correspondence
> 5 than that of date in the fact that a consciousness of need in my own life has arisen contemporaneously with the possibility of my becoming, acquainted with you. For in the first hour of meeting you, I had an impression of your eminent and perhaps exclusive fitness to supply that need (connected, I may say,
> 10 with such activity of the affections as even the preoccupations

---

* You may have noticed that this phrase nearly always refers to things that are unpleasant and/or highly tedious, and also that it's invariably used by people who have no interest in you other than getting you to do what they want!

of a work too special to be abdicated could not uninterruptedly dissimulate); and each succeeding opportunity for observation has given the impression an added depth by convincing me more emphatically of that fitness which I had preconceived,
5   and thus evoking more decisively those affections to which I have but now referred. Our conversations have, I think, made sufficiently clear to you the tenor of my life and purposes: a tenor unsuited, I am aware, to the commoner order of minds. But I have discerned in you an elevation of thought and a
10 capability of devotedness, which I had hitherto not conceived to be compatible either with the early bloom of youth or with those graces of sex that may be said at once to win and confer distinction when combined, as they notably are in you, with the mental qualities above indicated. It was, I
15 confess, beyond my hope to meet with this rare combination of elements both solid and attractive, adapted to supply aid in graver labours and cast a charm over vacant hours; and but for the event of my introduction to you (which, let me again say, I trust not to be superficially coincident with foreshadowing
20 needs, but providentially related thereto as stages towards the completion of a life's plan), I should presumably have gone on to the last without any attempt to lighten my solitariness by a matrimonial union . . .

There's a further paragraph before he signs off, but I imagine you've got the point!

Commentary

If you've never come across the piece before, I would almost guarantee that you found the first reading not just very difficult but enragingly boring and obscure. I know I did – and the second reading too. But as with Mrs Norris, the point is that we're **supposed** to respond in this way. George Eliot's aims are, however, more complex and ambitious than Jane Austen's, in that she wants our rage and contempt to be only the beginning.

For how would you feel if you received a 'love letter' like that? Various responses occur to me: hysterical laughter, vomiting, a feverish lunge for the wastepaper basket. Or perhaps we might feel great pity for someone who expresses himself in such a way, together with alarm at the prospect of getting mixed up with him in any way. And that, I think, is what we go on to experience after that initial head-aching annoyance has worn off a bit. The prospect of Dorothea marrying a man who writes and 'sounds' like that fills us with horror. The letter 'places' Casaubon unimprovably: we really don't need to be told any more about him.

To illustrate just how decisive is the matter of his voice, try this little 'sub-exercise':

1.   Read aloud once more the first 14 lines, to 'uninterruptedly dissimulate'.
2.   Try and work out what the sentence in brackets means. You will need pen and paper, I assure you!

Tough, is it not? I ended up with two 'translations': first, an attempt to make some sense out of it while staying reasonably close to his style and tone:

I may say that my affections were so stimulated that not even the preoccupations of my important scholarly work could muffle them.

Second, a translation into direct, suitably emotional language:

I love you so much that I can't work properly.

However, that second version is of course alien to everything that Casaubon has shown himself to be. He is incapable of the warmth and naked affection those simple words communicate: his voice is hopelessly dry, and the impenetrable maze of his style is a basic index of his nature. In addition to the ghastly Latin-soaked flatulence of his phrasing, there are clear indications of smug self-absorption, sexism and delusion: it is no great shock when we later discover that he is not a real scholar at all, just a tired old hack way behind in his field. In short, Casaubon's 'voice' here is the key to everything significant about him.

Exercise 22
The third passage comes from Act III of Shakespeare's *Julius Caesar*. Brutus is the leader of the conspiracy that has assassinated Caesar, and he comes to the market place to defend and explain this deed to the Roman people. As before, please follow the three-part procedure outlined.

Romans, countrymen, and lovers, hear me for my cause, and be silent, that you may hear. Believe me for mine honour, and have respect for mine honour, that you may believe. Censure me in your wisdom, and awake your senses, that you may be
5   the better judge. If there be any in this assembly, any dear friend of Caesar's, to him I say that Brutus's love to Caesar was

no less than his. If then that friend demand why Brutus rose
against Caesar, this is my answer: Not that I loved Caesar less,
but that I loved Rome more. Had you rather Caesar were
10   living, and die all slaves, than that Caesar were dead, to live
all free men? As Caesar loved me, I weep for him; as he was
fortunate, I rejoice in it; as he was valiant, I honour him; but,
as he was ambitious, I slew him. There is tears, for his love;
joy, for his fortune; honour, for his valour; and death, for his
15   ambition. Who is here so base, that he would be a bondsman?
Who is here so rude, that would not be a Roman? If any, speak;
for him I have offended. Who is here so vile, that he will not
love his country? If any, speak; for him I have offended. I pause
for a reply.

Commentary

This is not obviously disagreeable, as were the first two examples. It is
a measured performance that commands respect, and we can see why
the crowd answers that he has offended 'none' of them.

Yet there's also something rather disquieting about it, isn't there? For
all his virtues, I have always found Brutus mildly repellent: I think this
speech shows why. He has just killed a man – his friend as well as his
leader; is he not rather too comfortably at peace with himself and the
world he has just shattered? He certainly seems very fond of his own
honour – it's the first thing he mentions and he does so twice. His aloof
control is emphasized by an old rhetorical trick – the suggestion that
anyone not accepting his argument is vile or slave-like. Finally, one notes
with dismay how **abstract** it all is. Even his beloved **Rome** is evoked as an
idea or ideal, not as a living city of people, buildings, flesh and blood.

So this is a voice one listens to with respect but not with warmth.
Its sincerity and dignity are not in doubt, but its lack of emotion is
chilling. In addition, it is fatally complacent. Antony – Caesar's devoted
friend and thus Brutus's vengeful enemy – almost immediately 'replies'
to Brutus's case, and within a few minutes has so turned the crowd
that Brutus has to fly for his life. We shall be looking at his speech
and how it contrasts with Brutus's later; for now it is enough to note
that Brutus's voice is in several key ways inadequate or inappropriate,
and that Shakespeare designs this pivotal scene with that vocal matter
centrally in mind.

Now that we've seen how six writers harness voice as a major force
in their prose, it's time to look at how the same policy can work for
you. I begin by considering the period in which the concept of voice
becomes a problem – adolescence.

Voice: the virtues of primitivism

Small children are necessarily limited writers, but their style is appealing and often very funny. Consider this short piece, written by a 7-year-old girl.

Me And My Sickness
First I got a few tummy aches. Not very bad ones, but then in the evening I got a very bad tummy ache. I then started to roll about with my hands on my tummy. Then I did some sick. I kept waking up and doing sick. I did a dreadful thing while I was asleep: I did sick everywhere. Mummy and Daddy took all the bedclothes off and took me out of my bed. Then Mummy took me and put me in the bathroom, where I did sick all over the floor. In the morning I felt much better. Today I have not done any sick so far. I can now have drinks (not food) without getting sick.

This is clear, sharp and – despite the subject matter! – quite delightful. Her natural, vibrant voice is a pleasure to experience, as is her own fresh pleasure in using language. She may not know many words yet, but those she does know have for her a huge charm – almost a touch of magic. In addition, the piece is impressively balanced: there is a strong structure and narrative thrust, but it is also fluent and great fun to read. Our 7-year-old exemplifies a principle I introduced in my first chapter – that the spirit of children's writing offers enduring lessons to writers of every age and every kind.*

The fact remains that when I was an adolescent, I wouldn't have been caught dead writing in such a way. It's not just that its obvious limitations would have affronted my 13-year-old's dignity; by then I would have been frightened of its nakedness and spontaneity. And I was **wrong** – and so would be any developing writer who took the same view.

Adolescence: voice change and changing voices

Young children have a **single** voice. They write in the same way as they speak, and they tend to speak in the same way to everyone – parents, friends, other adults, strangers. They have not yet learnt to discriminate; another way of putting it might be that they have not yet learnt to dissimulate or to select the role they think most fitting. Then comes the dawn of self-consciousness, and with it the disappearance of that singleness of voice: adolescence, in short.

* This composition – one of the girl's first homeworks – later appeared in her school magazine under the by-line 'Anon: Prep 1', and in a way one can see why the writer didn't want to be named! But one would like her identified – in order to congratulate her.

Consciousness of self is only part of the rapid expansion of consciousness and knowledge that occurs during these years. This may be a bewildering process, but it is also an exciting and entirely healthy one. Your brain is at its most active and arguably its most efficient. You learn literally tens of millions of things in a wide variety of fields; your grasp and use of linguistic structures accelerate; your vocabulary grows enormously; you start to acquire judgment and intellectual independence. And you begin to be aware of your own nature, its strengths and weaknesses, and what I will call its 'plurality of self'. You come to realize that you have **several** selves – pupil, son/daughter, friend, young citizen and so on.

All those developments are invigorating and positive. But self-consciousness is a two-edged sword: it can be weakening and negative as well. All at once you are acutely aware of how others see you, which can lead to awkwardness, a lack of confidence and a host of 'masks' designed above all to prevent you from looking foolish. These protective layers, or what the German psychologist Wilhelm Reich called 'character armour', are often most evident in your use of language. Where the child is unthinking and spontaneous in giving tongue, the adolescent is more wary. Frequently silence is preferred; otherwise, something non-comittal or even obstructive. And in writing – my chief concern – original freshness can give way to the defensive aping of 'safe' adult models and the gradual denial of all that is most natural and individual. In short, that 'plurality of self' can create a damaging plurality of voice.

Now there is nothing wrong with plurality of voice in itself. For a start it is both unavoidable and often literal in the case of male adolescents, who move from treble or alto to tenor or bass: for many, all four can come into play – sometimes within a single sentence! In addition, to have at your disposal a variety of register, tone and style when speaking or writing adds further to your increased linguistic resources and awareness, and properly harnessed is an unambiguous strength.

The trouble arises if you choose the wrong voice, or [worse] you become so confused that you speak or write in a mish-mash of voices that neither expresses with any clarity what you want to say, nor gives anyone a sense of your true self. As an initial step in preventing such confusion, try the exercise that follows.

Exercise 23
Here I have listed eight kinds of speech encounter which you may experience on any given day. Jot down what you imagine would be each one's most obvious features in terms of tone, the sort of vocabulary you might use, your general demeanour and so on; my commentary follows beneath.

1.   Conversations with your family.
2.   An exchange with a bus conductor/booking clerk/etc.
3.   Conversations with friends, or colleagues whom you like.
4.   Conversations with peers/colleagues whom you **don't** like, or with whom you are neutrally professional.
5.   Conversations with your superiors/people in authority over you.
6.   A conversation with a complete stranger – e.g. someone requesting directions.
7.   A conversation with someone you fancy.
8.   Conversations with visitors to your home.

Commentary

1.   Likely to be 'informal' most of the time: affectionate, amusing, usually unselfconscious. Such exchanges also feature a good deal of 'code' – the kind of private, intimate language that all families develop.
2.   Civil; functional; formal. Your use of language will be business-like and brief – provided you both listen properly.
3.   Very similar to 1, although the 'codes' will probably be different. The same kind of ease and informality will be present, however, as will a lack of self-consciousness.
4.   Style and behaviour will be markedly different from 3. You will almost certainly be cautious, polite, very self-aware and using a considerable amount of control. Such conversations are as a result very tiring!
5.   You will probably display a degree of deference and be anxious for approval, or at least not to offend. If you happen to like and get on well with the superior concerned, your language and manner may be quite relaxed; it would be unusual even so if they matched 1 or 3.
6.   Very like 2, except that it may lead to a more involved and complex exchange. In addition, such conversations often occur 'out of the blue', whereas 2 exchanges tend to be planned or expected. Your tone and language may differ as a result.
7.   Always different from 3, no matter how much you may like him/her

as well! The biggest difference is an extreme – and unique – self-awareness, which can radically alter both what you say and how you say it.

8. The style and register of these conversations will depend on who the visitors are. Atmosphere and behaviour may well be close to 1, and certainly 3, if the visitors are welcome and everyone's relaxed; 2, 6 or even 4 may be nearer the mark if you're less lucky!*

Those eight are just a sample of the many encounters you could have on an average day. However many I might list, you would find that ultimately they fall into three groups: those where your language and manner are **informal**, those where they are **formal**, and those where **either** possibility exists, according to circumstance. To identify our eight in this manner is simple enough, but it's worth doing, because some important insights and principles can be established as a result.

Informal: 1, 3
Formal: 2, 4, 6
Either: 5, 7, 8

Conclusions

1. We are at our most natural during **informal** exchanges, whether they involve lively banter, the sharing of confidences or just ordinary chatting. The personality is at ease, the voice relaxed; the conversation is a source of pleasure.†

2. **Formal** encounters are not so much fun but can be very satisfying: using a different kind of tone and language capably and courteously [which 2, 6 and especially 4 require] carries its own quiet pleasure.

3. The **Either** category is intriguing and instructive. In all three cases cited, the more you are confidently able to be yourself, the more informal [and therefore pleasant] the conversation will be; conversely, the more you feel obliged to be dutiful, cautious and linguistically on your guard, the more the exchanges will become a strain. That kind of formal conversation is wholly unpleasurable: you feel unnatural, under pressure and decidedly uncomfortable.

---

* It is a sad truism that relatives – especially in-laws – often make you feel false or awkward, in both speech and general behaviour. You're supposed to feel intimate and relaxed with them, but I know of few families where the kind of language associated with 1 extends to broader family get-togethers. Perhaps that's why Christmas is a strain for so many!

† Note that this is usually true even when you are unhappy or discontented. Talking informally when 'down' may not solve anything, but it's good therapy, not least because you're being listened to by someone who cares. And sometimes hearing yourself voice your thoughts can lead to a new understanding and perhaps a new mood, which is as pleasing as it is valuable.

4. The final and most crucial point concerns your writing. You cannot avoid the occasional conversation that is unpleasant or a matter of joyless effort, where your voice is constrained, dull or even artificial. **But never allow your writing to be similarly corrupted**. If the demands of formal writing reduce the pleasure you take in using words, something is badly wrong: you're using the wrong words, using them in the wrong way, or abandoning your voice. I now move on to further ways of ensuring that your formal writing is no more – and no less – than a pleasurable extension of your natural style.

Words as a window, not a wall

I've been stressing clarity from the first page of the book. If I do so yet again now, it's because a good deal of adult language disguises or hides meaning – sometimes deliberately, more often out of incompetence or a misguided belief that certain phrases sound good. In addition, the onset of self-consciousness can lead to a timidity about saying what you really think. In writing – especially in a task that requires some kind of judgment or decision – don't hide behind others' views. Consult and read them, yes: that is a key constituent of learning. But remember that it's your writing and views that matter. Say what you think and don't 'fudge': you will please and impress your readers far more by doing so than by sheltering behind a wall of received ideas, imprecise opinion and often stodgy prose.

Keep it simple, keep it clear

In a previous section, 'Fight the flab', we looked at the damage deliberate avoidance of simplicity can do. Conversely, a determination to keep things as simple as possible can bring considerable benefits. Appropriately, the guidelines are all easy to understand and should also not be difficult to put into practice.

1. **Never use a long word where a short one will do.**

This was one of George Orwell's six elementary rules of good writing in 1946, and it is just as important now.

2. **Avoid Latinate words and constructions if a simpler alternative is available.**

English is predominantly Latinate, so there will be times when you cannot find a simpler alternative, and others when you (quite rightly) may not wish to do so. But one of English's greatest strengths is that it has a host of simple, basic words to express the simple, basic facts of existence. In all these instances, the simpler word is the clearer and the stronger:

death	rather than	**demise** or **decease**
sex drive	rather than	**libido**
fast	rather than	**exponential**
road	rather than	**thoroughfare**
worsen	rather than	**exacerbate**
show	rather than	**manifest**
yes	rather than	**affirmative**
no	rather than	**negative**

The last two are comical – the kind of Americanism we could all (Americans included) do without. But **all** the right-hand alternatives are faintly absurd: few of us would ever choose them naturally. Nevertheless, there is often a temptation to forgo naturalness and choose expressions which impress. They rarely do: 'Think Simple' wherever possible. Use

meeting	not	**interface**
use	not	**utilize**
illness	not	**malady** or **condition**

That last is particularly stupid in the phrase **heart condition:** everyone has a heart condition because everyone has a heart.

3. **Avoid foreign, scientific or technical words unless they are essential.**

There will be occasions when such words are essential. But they should never be used without good reason: always be sure you fully understand them before committing them to paper.

Inappropriate use of these words looks either pretentious or evasive. Restaurant menus are notorious for both. It is ludicrous to call roast beef 'le boeuf roti' in England, even if the restaurant is devoted to French culinary methods; and virtually every wine-list I've ever read is in urgent need of a ruthless literary editor. If this is admittedly an exaggeration on my part –

This pleasingly rich-bodied Bordeaux has a notably full nose and a sensuous texture that owe their quality to the peculiar eloquence of the grapes of the region, warm-thighed and resonant as they traditionally are.

– you'll probably have encountered something similar if you dine out with any regularity. As with many of the euphemisms we examined previously, the atmosphere of the prose is all wrong. One suspects that the intimidating jargon and forced imagery hide a 'real truth' translation that might go:

A cringingly average bottle of Gallic red ink that will soon annihilate whatever palate you've got left after eating our over-spiced food, and make your mind too hazy to notice that we're charging the earth for liquid junk.

The only time jargon or imported phrases are justified is when there is no good equivalent in English. Thus it is all right to use **cliché** or **impasse:** they are valuable additions to our language because they pinpoint a concept more exactly than any available English word can. But it is not all right to use **chef d'oeuvre** when the exact alternative **masterpiece** is available. Nor is **modus vivendi** instead of **way of life** anything other than mere posturing.

Scientific and technical words carry the additional danger of inaccuracy as well as pretentiousness. It is now common to see **neurotic** used to mean 'mildly nervous' or **schizophrenic** for 'somewhat inconsistent'. Originally – and properly – both words denote a precise, and very serious, psychic illness: to hijack them for inappropriate everyday use both harms their force as clinical terms and renders one's language vague and unconvincing.

Figure 16. 'Intimidating jargon'.

4. **Take great care when using slang.**

A fair amount of nonsense is talked about the use of slang in formal writing. I believe it is absurd to disapprove of it on principle, which is what more than a few English teachers of my acquaintance do. Good slang – that is, lively and inventive contemporary idiom – is vigorous and concrete; moreover, it is a central index of the healthy fluidity and growth of English (or indeed any language). Those who argue that it has no place in formal writing at any time both overemphasize the resources of 'standard English' and underestimate the fresh precision, wit and energy that slang can achieve, and I am glad to find that no less a figure than George Eliot agrees with me:

> Correct English is the slang of prigs who write history and essays. And the strongest slang of all is the slang of poets.
>
> (*Middlemarch*, Book 2)

I would never suggest, therefore, that you should avoid slang at all times. There will be occasions when it enlivens your writing in a wholly appropriate way, and your readers may well be very grateful for a racy respite from more sedate and sophisticated structures. But the use of slang is dangerous nonetheless, on at least three counts:

- Most slang has a very short life, and nothing seems more dated than yesterday's 'in' phrase.
- Conversely, genuinely current slang is problematic in a different way: your reader may not have heard the phrase yet, and therefore be completely fogged. This is especially likely if you're a young person writing for an older generation!
- Even if a slang phrase is comprehensible and verbally precise, it may be inappropriate in tone.

When writing formally, therefore, and the possibility of using slang arises, ask yourself the following questions about each word or phrase:

1. **Will it be understood?**
2. **Will I be laughed at for using stale slang?**
3. **What is the alternative 'standard English' phrase, and does the slang equivalent do a better job? (N.B. *not* equally good, but *better*.)**
4. **Does it strike the right note, in terms of tone and reader-comfort? Is the 'voice' apt and pleasing?**

And even if all the answers to the above seem to give you the green light, add:

5. **Since the use of slang always carries a slight risk, given certain readers' views, am I really sure that I still want to use it?**

If the answer is 'yes', then go ahead.

Before moving on, I should perhaps stress something I've already made passing reference to: a lot of other teachers, writers and professional guides would offer sharply different advice – and not necessarily because they belong to the 'Slang Is Always Wrong' school of thought. They would probably argue that the potential snags and pitfalls of using slang invariably outweigh its benefits, and that it is wise to avoid it – always.

My own view, while recognizing the soundness of that advice in many respects, is that good and appropriate slang can breathe much-needed freshness into your writing, that it will often sharpen up both your sense of what you're saying and therefore the reader's, and that at its most successful it promotes an immediate sense of voice and individuality. Every major literary artist in history has used – often coined – slang words and phrases to great and memorable advantage; and although the criteria and ethos of 'creative writing' and formal writing are obviously different, I see no reason why they should be entirely cut off from each other. Writers who think only in terms of 'correct English' are not only likely to be priggish, as George Eliot observed: it's highly probable that such inner pedantry leads to their work being impersonal and dull as well.

5. **Choose concrete rather than abstract wherever possible.**

Human beings are very complex creatures; they are also simple ones. We find nice things nicer than nasty ones, we prefer pleasure to pain, and we have a fondness for clarity over obscurity.

Such fundamental characteristics are relevant to good writing. People think in pictures, not concepts, and unless you regularly stimulate their visual sense you risk losing them. No matter how elegant your sentences or interesting your material, if you fill your prose with abstractions you will not grip. The next exercise starkly demonstrates the contrast.

Exercise 24
The two pieces that follow both address sexual corruption. Which is better?

Passage A

How We Know Sex
The whole movement of 'philosophical anthropology' is opposed to the reductionism implicit in the Galilean-Newtonian-Cartesian approach to knowledge, not least, to knowledge of man, which, in its tendency to objectify, has the effect of reducing life in nature, and man especially, to the status of

'dead' objects. The difference which is being emphasized now is that between what Polyani calls 'attending to' – looking at the outside of things – and 'attending from' – entering into the experience of the creature observed, by throwing oneself, by imagination and intuition, into the 'inner experience' of the manifestation being studied. It should be obvious that much of the attention to sex in our culture is 'attending to' rather than 'attending from' – and so, lacking imagination, it lacks understanding of the meaning and inwardness of sex. The effect has been a disastrous separation of 'sex' from the personal.

from David Holbrook's contribution to Pornography:
The Longford Report, 1972

Passage B

The Sick Rose

O Rose, thou art sick!
The invisible worm
That flies in the night,
In the howling storm

Has found out thy bed
Of crimson joy
And his dark secret love
Does thy life destroy.

William Blake, c. 1792

Commentary

I hope you chose passage B!

I will admit at once that the contrast is hardly fair – on three counts. First, Holbrook's argument is just a paragraph from a lengthy exposition; Blake's poem is complete in itself. Second, to compare discursive prose with the highly concentrated language of a lyric poem is always precarious: the two genres work in different ways and by different criteria. And third, the world is full of writing that would come off second best to *The Sick Rose*, which is arguably one of the greatest short poems ever written.

Nevertheless, some important points and principles emerge. The Holbrook is very difficult to read: it took me three goes before I fully understood its first sentence. It is obviously the work of an intelligent and committed man, but the profusion of commas is distracting and the grandiose references are a further obstacle. Above all, Latinate and abstract language predominates: the potentially valuable distinction between 'attending to' and 'attending from' is, I find, blurred by such accompanying structures as **of the manifestation being studied** and even

the meaning and inwardness of sex. What do such phrases mean? They conjure up no picture for me, no physical sense of what is being addressed – and that, given that the topic is human sexuality, is surely a serious flaw. Only the last sentence – significantly, also the shortest – achieves immediate impact and clarity; by then, some might think, it's too late.

Blake's language is deceptively simple: there isn't a word in the poem that a bright 8-year-old would not have encountered. [I'm not suggesting that such a person would therefore understand the poem as a whole!] Furthermore, it paints dramatic pictures. Even if one reads the poem on a merely literal level, the evocation of a fragile plant under double attack [the worm and the elements] is gripping; when one adds the symbolic level(s), the effect is overwhelming. Potentially abstract concepts such as **joy** and **love** are made intensely concrete by the addition of **crimson** and **dark secret**, adjectives which 'nail down' guilt, passion, corruption and destruction in a precise, almost tactile way. Intriguingly, Blake demonstrates here exactly the qualities Holbrook associates with 'attending from' – the poem is indeed an immersion in 'inner experience' through 'imagination and intuition', and it achieves this by ensuring that its words have instant physical bite.

Of course, in any substantial and sophisticated writing, it is impossible to avoid the abstract altogether. Nor is it always desirable to even try: a great deal of scientific, philosophical and even literary thinking depends on abstract concepts. The secret is to make sure that they are regularly mixed with, or illustrated by, something more physically immediate. The next piece is a superb example of how to use concrete images to render clear something otherwise unimaginable.

Exercise 25

Please read this passage, which is an edited extract from *The Daily Telegraph*'s lead story on Tuesday, August 7, 1945. I find it a splendid piece of reporting, and I hope you concur. Why does it work so well? Which phrases/sentences have the greatest impact on you, and which are the **least** effective? And what, despite its many strengths, is **missing** from the account that perhaps ought to have been included?

ALLIES INVENT ATOMIC BOMB: FIRST DROPPED ON JAPAN

2000 TIMES THE BLAST POWER OF RAF 11-TONNER

ENEMY THREATENED WITH 'RAIN OF RUIN' FROM THE AIR

The Allies have made the greatest discovery in history: the way to use atomic energy. The first atomic bomb has been dropped on Japan. It had:

Over 2000 times the blast power of the largest bomb ever before

used, which was the British 'Grand Slam' weighing about 11 tons; and
More power than 20,000 tons of TNT.

Yet the explosive charge is officially described as 'exceedingly small'. A spokesman at the Ministry of Aircraft Production said last night that the bomb was one-tenth the size of a 'block buster', yet its effect would be 'like that of a severe earthquake.'

The first atomic bomb, a single one, was dropped on Hiroshima, a town of 12 square miles, on the Japanese main island of Honshu. Tokyo radio said that the raid was at 8.20 a.m. yesterday, Japanese time, and that the extent of the damage was being investigated.

The official announcement yesterday of the existence of the bomb was made 16 hours after its first use. Late last night no report had been made on the damage done because it had been impossible to see the result through impenetrable clouds of dust and smoke.

EFFECT ON WAR AND PEACE

In a Downing Street statement Mr. Churchill was quoted as saying: 'By God's mercy British and American science outpaced all German efforts. The possession of these powers by the Germans at any time might have altered the result of the war and profound anxiety was felt by those who were informed.'

Mr. Stimson, the United States Secretary of War, said the bomb would prove a tremendous aid in shortening the war against Japan. It had an explosive power that 'staggered the imagination.'

President Truman described the results as the greatest achievement of organised science in history. The Allies had spent the sum of £500,000,000 on the 'greatest scientific gamble in history' and had won.

If the Japanese did not now accept the Allies terms, he said, they might expect a 'rain of ruin from the air the like of which had never been seen on this earth.'

The method of production would be kept secret, while processes were being worked out to protect the world from the danger of sudden destruction. Congress would be asked to investigate how atomic power might be used to maintain the future peace.

Commentary

The most obvious reason for the passage's riveting power is the event itself: nearly fifty years on it still haunts our imagination. If one was in a grudging mood, it might be said that the piece almost wrote itself, so awesome is the topic: you'd have to be a singularly bad writer to render it dull! But that would hardly be just: the reporting is a first-class performance, and its key strength is the shrewd explanation of what an atomic bomb can do.

Even today, a large number of highly educated people [myself included] do not fully understand atomic fission. At the time of Hiroshima, the whole thing must have struck all but a handful of readers as science fiction. So the writer at once establishes a frame of reference that can be readily grasped: the bomb's power is explained by comparisons with known, 'ordinary' bombs, starkly and punchily expressed. Particularly effective is the emphasis on the bomb's strange, scary smallness and the instant revelation that its effect resembles that of 'a severe earthquake': these are images that people can at once visualize.

You may have noticed that the report carries no mention of damage to buildings or to human life – one of the 'missing' things I asked you to identify. The reasons for this may be various – security, genuine lack of information [as implied in the mention of 'impenetrable clouds of dust and smoke'], shame or just a shocked unwillingness to spell out the suffering involved. That's a large and separate issue; what strikes me is that the information which is given is presented in such a way as to release our imaginative powers, enabling us to speculate on what the people of Hiroshima would have undergone. That happens of course to be a horrible set of pictures, one which many of us would quickly wish to blot out; the fact remains that no such resonance would occur if the writing was not so vibrantly concrete.

To my mind the least effective moments occur in the various politicians' remarks. With one exception these are generalized and wrapped up in careful phrases designed to reassure rather than resonate. The exception is President Truman's 'rain of ruin' sentence: this has enormous impact, identifying a force that is almost Biblical in its potential anger. Once again, it is the simple concreteness of the phrase that guarantees its power.

Finally, also missing is any attempt to explain the mechanics of the fission process. As the last paragraph reveals, a major reason for this must have been security; but I would also guess that (a) the journalist concerned didn't know how to explain such things, and (b) even if he did, his readers wouldn't have been able to follow him. Even so, the piece gives one a formidably clear sense of what this new weapon can do and of some of the disturbing possibilities its invention opens up, and it does so by recourse to simple, known phenomena and images. Rooted in the concrete, it brings the inexplicable and the unimaginable within reach.

A third and final exercise follows in a moment. It is a lengthy one, returning us to the scene from *Julius Caesar* examined earlier in this section. It is perhaps best suited to readers with a central interest in literature, although the points it reveals about the power of the concrete over the abstract are I think of value to any writer. You may however prefer to skip to the section's last topic, 6, which you will find on page 135.

Exercise 26
As a preliminary, please re-read the speech by Brutus printed on pages 116–7.

To recapitulate briefly, his oratory is drenched in abstractions – **ambition, love, wisdom, valour, fortune** and most crucially of all, **honour**. Even the concrete words he uses are curiously devoid of physical impact. **Tears** is coupled to a love that was; the seemingly dramatic and blunt **death** is rendered abstract by being intimately linked with **ambition**; and even Brutus's **Rome** emerges as more a philosophical idea than a teeming city. And all this abstraction is, in the circumstances, very dangerous. Brutus knows Antony is to follow him in reply, yet his low-key approach suggests a lack of concern amounting to complacency. Events rebuke him with terrifying swiftness.

A slightly abbreviated version of Antony's answer appears below.

Please read it carefully, noting as you do as many contrasts with Brutus's speech as you can identify.

Part A

Antony. Friends, Romans, countrymen, lend me your ears;
I come to bury Caesar, not to praise him.
The evil that men do lives after them,
The good is oft interred with their bones;
So let it be with Caesar. The noble Brutus
Hath told you Caesar was ambitious.
If it were so, it was a grievous fault,
And grievously hath Caesar answered it.
Here, under leave of Brutus and the rest
(For Brutus is an honorable man,
So are they all, all honorable men),
Come I to speak in Caesar's funeral.
He was my friend, faithful and just to me;
But Brutus says he was ambitious,
And Brutus is an honorable man.
He hath brought many captives home to Rome,
Whose ransoms did the general coffers fill;

Did this in Caesar seem ambitious?
When that the poor have cried, Caesar hath wept;
Ambition should be made of sterner stuff.
Yet Brutus says he was ambitious;
And Brutus is an honorable man.
You all did see that on the Lupercal
I thrice presented him a kingly crown,
Which he did thrice refuse. Was this ambition?
Yet Brutus says he was ambitious;
And sure he is an honorable man.
I speak not to disprove what Brutus spoke,
But here I am to speak what I do know.
You all did love him once, not without cause;
What cause withholds you then to mourn for him?
O judgment, thou art fled to brutish beasts,
And men have lost their reason! Bear with me;
My heart is in the coffin there with Caesar,
And I must pause till it come back to me.

Part B

   Antony. But yesterday the word of Caesar might
Have stood against the world; now lies he there,
And none so poor to do him reverence.
O masters! If I were disposed to stir
Your hearts and minds to mutiny and rage,
I should do Brutus wrong and Cassius wrong,
Who, you all know, are honorable men.
I will not do them wrong; I rather choose
To wrong the dead, to wrong myself and you,
Than I will wrong such honorable men.
But here's a parchment with the seal of Caesar;
I found it in his closet 'tis his will.
Let but the commons hear this testament,
Which, pardon me, I do not mean to read,
And they would go and kiss dead Caesar's wounds,
And dip their napkins in his sacred blood;
Yea, beg a hair of him for memory,
And dying, mention it within their wills,
Bequeathing it as a rich legacy
Unto their issue.

Fourth Plebeian. We'll hear the will; read it, Mark Antony.

All. The will, the will! We will hear Caesar's will!

Antony. Have patience, gentle friends, I must not read it.
   It is not meet you know how Caesar loved you.
   You are not wood, you are not stones, but men;
   And being men, hearing the will of Caesar,
   It will inflame you, it will make you mad.
   'Tis good you know not that you are his heirs;
   For if you should, O, what would come of it?

Fourth Plebeian. Read the will! We'll hear it, Antony!
   You shall read us the will, Caesar's will!

Part C

Antony. If you have tears, prepare to shed them now.
   You all do know this mantle; I remember
   The first time ever Caesar put it on:
   'Twas on a summer's evening, in his tent,
   That day he overcame the Nervii.
   Look, in this place ran Cassius' dagger through;
   See what a rent the envious Casca made;
   Through this the well-beloved Brutus stabbed,
   And as he plucked his cursed steel away,
   Mark how the blood of Caesar followed it,
   As rushing out of doors, to be resolved
   If Brutus so unkindly knocked, or no;
   For Brutus, as you know, was Caesar's angel
   Judge, O you gods, how dearly Caesar loved him!
   This was the most unkindest cut of all;
   For when the noble Caesar saw him stab,
   Ingratitude, more strong than traitors' arms,
   Quite vanquished him. Then burst his mighty heart;
   And, in his mantle muffling up his face,
   Even at the base of Pompey's statue
   (Which all the while ran blood) great Caesar fell.
   O, what a fall was there, my countrymen!
   Then I, and you, and all of us fell down,
   Whilst bloody treason flourished over us.
   O, now you weep, and I perceive you feel
   The dint of pity; these are gracious drops.
   Kind souls, what weep you when you but behold
   Our Caesar's vesture wounded? Look you here,
   Here is himself, marred as you see with traitors.

                    from Antony's speeches in Act III, Scene ii of
                            Shakespeare's *Julius Caesar* (c.1599)

Commentary

For a start, it is much longer. Brutus's entire presentation takes less than fifty lines, whereas Antony's covers over two hundred. Second, it seeks to rouse the crowd rather than soothe them.* Third, Antony revels in the concrete where Brutus took refuge in the abstract – and that is why Antony 'wins'.

The opening lines are almost cornily famous: their subtlety and menacing power can therefore be missed. Antony speaks in blank verse as opposed to Brutus's prose.† Yet observe how quickly Antony gets down to earthly, physical facts – the things that the apparently more 'down to earth' Brutus ignored. The second line gives us **bury**, the fourth **bones**; from then on a concrete thrust is dominant. Antony craftily introduces early on the theme of money, that most concrete of matters, reminding the people how well off they were under Caesar's rule. Moreover, his grief seems [and to be fair, almost certainly is] genuine – and it is grief for a dead **friend**, not for some lost abstract ideal. The last two lines of Part A are a masterstroke in a speech already abounding in tactical brilliance: the crowd witnesses a man made speechless by grief. This contrasts mightily with Brutus's articulate coolness, and very much to the latter's disadvantage.

Antony also introduces the **honorable men** refrain which has a hypnotic, corrosive effect: the more he repeats it, the less the crowd believe it [which of course is his intention]. Later in Part B he develops the theme of money, playing upon the crowd's emotions as he deliberately tantalizes them over Caesar's will. The language is rich in concrete simplicity: they are **men**, not **stones**; Caesar has **wounds** and had living **blood**; he talks of their children, their **legacy**, Caesar's **heirs**. All are basic truths that hit hard, affecting the crowd more than any abstraction could possibly do. And in Part C Antony climaxes his performance by making use of that most valuable 'prop': Caesar's corpse. This is a devastating 'visual aid', its fresh raw gashes and blood cruelly obvious to everyone. The increasing repetition of **blood, traitor** and savage references to weaponry, and the clinching impact of **Then burst his mighty heart** complete the

---

* For reasons of space I have edited out most of the by-play with the crowd, since this doesn't directly advance or illustrate Antony's case. But those lines are not insignificant: the fact that the crowd gets vocally involved demonstrates the immediacy of Antony's performance, contrasting with the dutiful, slightly removed silence that attended Brutus's.

† In general Shakespeare uses blank verse as the vehicle for deep emotion, nobility of thought or any expression of intensity, whereas prose suggests reasonableness, distance or objectivity, and down-to-earth observation. In these circumstances, it is almost as if Brutus's prose is misplaced, and he allows Antony to provide the all-important physical appeal and directness, the high-flown verse notwithstanding.

utter demolition of all Brutus's sober abstractions, and the scene ends with what in effect is the start of civil war, with Brutus on the run.

In sum: Brutus is listened to because he is highly respected and his grave use of words evokes a similarly measured response. But when Antony's turn comes he at once emphasizes the physical facts that lie behind Brutus's judicious report. He wields like tomahawks words such as **bones, friend, blood, wounds, coffin, tears, testament, stabbed** and **will**: it is not hard to see why he triumphs.

None of us can write as well as that; few of us will ever be in a remotely comparable situation. Nevertheless, this scene teaches all writers – and perhaps all politicians! – a crucial lesson. For in nearly every case **you will make your points more clearly and more persuasively if you make your style as simple and concrete as you can**.

6. Within reason, call a spade a spade

I have already cited this principle (see page 91), and I've also stressed that you have to be careful about it. There are people to whom you should probably not in answer to an enquiry after your health, reply, 'God, I'm knackered!' But provided you pay proper attention to courtesy and appropriateness, you should be as direct as possible, and that means being as simple and concrete as possible.

This short extract from P. G. Wodehouse's story *Jeeves And The Song Of Songs* illustrates the point beautifully, along with most of the other 'guidelines' I've offered in this section. The speakers are Bertie Wooster [the narrator], his Aunt Dahlia and, first, his incomparable manservant Jeeves. In addition to everything else, notice how masterly is Wodehouse's capturing of the three distinct voices.

> 'In affairs of this description, madam, the first essential is to study the psychology of the individual.'
> 'The what of the individual?'
> 'The psychology, madam.'
> 'He means the psychology,' I said. 'And by psychology, Jeeves, you imply – ?'
> 'The natures and dispositions of the individuals in the matter, sir.'
> 'You mean, what they're like?'
> 'Precisely, sir.'
> 'Does he always talk like this to you when you're alone, Bertie?' asked Aunt Dahlia.

This is comic writing of a high order, and the humour resides in the radical difference between the register and vocabulary of Bertie and his aunt and those used by Jeeves. In the context, therefore, both registers are essential and appropriate. But if we take Jeeves's language **out** of context, it seems needlessly elaborate in normal circumstances. Bertie's simple **You mean, what they're like** is **precisely** what Jeeves has taken many words to say. One could further argue that Jeeves's remarks are not only lengthy: they are difficult, semi-scientific, Latinate and abstract – a combination that makes him hard to follow. No wonder Aunt Dahlia asks about their private conversations!

Punch once observed that to criticize Wodehouse was 'like taking a spade to a soufflé', and to subject that passage to my kind of analysis is doubtless equally clumsy. Nevertheless, I think the extract shows – through its wit, not despite it – that neither meaning nor impact need be lost by choosing the simple concrete approach. Indeed, both will often thereby be strengthened.

Conclusion: voice – friend or foe?

My stress on the primacy of voice may seem to contradict the kind of advice most 11- or 12-year-olds [and sometimes their seniors] receive from their teachers:

It's time you stopped writing in the way you speak.

In that extract from *Apocalypse Now*, Kurtz spoke of making 'horror' and 'moral terror' one's friends, lest they become 'truly enemies'. Less dramatically, we can say that there seem to be conflicting views about whether speech and writing are 'friends' or 'enemies'. Which should it be?

The answer is **both**. As adolescence takes hold, a difference should be emerging, yes, between the spontaneity of speech and the more considered use of words necessary for effective writing. But if that division becomes absolute, leading the student to regard speech and writing as mutually exclusive, great damage to both can result. It is essential not to regard your conversational rhythms and your written style as enemies or as separate activities that have little to do with each other. Keep your 'voice' present all the time. You need also to make your language appropriate – for example, a thank-you letter to a great-aunt will require a different vocabulary and tone from the 'friendly-rude' style you adopt with friends and peers. But that great-aunt should still be aware of you – your personality, your individual voice. Indeed, if she cares about you, a stiffly impersonal letter will hurt and disappoint her. As a final principle, keep in mind that

Adult, formal writing does not require self-obliteration, nor is 'politeness' the same as 'impersonality'.

Good adult writing is properly aware of circumstance, and respects self and audience equally. As William Hazlitt implies in one of the epigraphs to this section, the art of conversation involves good listening as well as good speaking. The same is true of the art of writing: once you stop listening to your voice – the essential 'you' defined in childhood – you're in trouble.

TAILOR-MADE

PART FOUR

INTRODUCTION

The previous sections on style have, I hope, shown you how to maintain a clear sense of voice in all that you write. I have stressed the twin needs: listen to what you write and keep your reader in mind at all times.

If you take care of those tasks, you will quickly find that your judgment becomes sound – judgment of tone, of circumstance, of what the most appropriate register might be.

You will also come quickly to realize that different kinds of writing require different approaches. This section looks at a variety of specific tasks, all of which have their own conventions and criteria. We start with the letter.

What is a letter? Well, obviously enough, it is a written communication – a means of giving information or exchanging ideas. Even in a visual age that is additionally dominated by the telephone, people still write many letters, and many kinds of letter.

The trouble is that it is easy to write a poor letter: fashioning a good one takes a lot more care and effort. But such conscientiousness is essential, because if you write a poor letter the point of sending it is lost. This is bad enough if you're writing to friends, even though they'll forgive you and give you a further chance to make yourself clear. No such tolerance should be expected from a company or any kind of officialdom: if your first letter is inadequate, you may not get an opportunity to redress things.

Regardless of type, function or length, a good letter exhibits these qualities:

- it is clearly set out and comfortable to read
- the writer's 'voice' is properly audible
- the tone and register are appropriate to
  (i) the relationship with the recipient
  (ii) the nature of the subject matter
  (iii) the letter's overall circumstances
- it gives a sense of enjoyment or satisfaction
- the points are made with impact and 'rightness'
- it makes the reader want to write back

It may occur to you that these qualities should attend any and all good writing, and of course you are right. But letters are an especially direct form of writing. As the last point implies, a good letter presupposes a kind of conversation with the reader, or sets out an agenda to be discussed. Letters are usually addressed to just one person (or to a family or committee as a unit, which amounts to the same thing), and they are written and sent for a precise, 'one-off' reason. It is therefore very important that the writer gets as many things 'right' as possible.

The first thing to get right is the basic layout. The following three considerations apply to **all** letters:

1. In hand-written letters the address should ideally be placed in the top right-hand corner. With headed paper, as used by businesses or many private individuals, it is now accepted practice to **centre** the address at the top.
2. The date should be clearly stated.
3. Careful attention should be paid to **spacing**. Many letter writers seem terrified of space and cramp their design. You should work out in advance all that you want to say in your letter (q.v.), and use the space accordingly.

   If in doubt about what I mean here, take a look at the three specimens on pages 146, 148 and 150 and my comments on them.

Other matters of layout depend on the **kind** of letter being written; there are, essentially, three such broad 'types':

A. The formal business letter to someone you don't know.
B. The less formal business letter, to someone you **do** know and may indeed know very well.
C. Informal letters to friends and intimates. These range from chatty notes to family and close friends to long passionate love letters!

Let us look at how these differ.

1. All business letters (types A and B) should print the recipient's address on the left-hand side, above the greeting ['Dear so and so . . .'].
2. The greeting and closure should obey the following conventions, in tune with the types A, B and C outlined above:

A. If you do not know the person, you begin 'Dear Sir' or 'Dear Madam' and conclude 'Yours faithfully'.
B. It may be that you do know the person's name ['Dear Mr Jones' or 'Dear Ms Bates']; in which case you should close 'Yours sincerely'. This remains the case even if you now use each other's forename.

   In fact, 'Yours sincerely' is much the most frequent closing device, for it covers every kind of letter between the first formal approach and the 'code' one adopts with friends and loved ones.
C. For intimate letters there are no such conventions or rules, although they too should be set out clearly. You can begin any way you like – 'Dear Rat-bag/Darling Squidgy-Thighs/Hello, you old bastards . . .' – and you may also close in a style of your choice: 'Yours ever/Luv 'n' stuff/ Lots of love/Bumperoodles of great smacking soggy kisses . . .'

Indeed, such letters are **so** personal and so much a matter of 'private' language and intimate code that a book like this can offer only limited advice on how to write them – although we shall look at an example shortly. It is Types A and B that exercise people most, and it is those I've had chiefly in mind when constructing the above guidelines.

To augment and make more specific those guidelines, here is a set of 'rules' that should be borne in mind when writing any kind of business letter.

1. Know what you want to say

You can't expect your correspondent to read your mind, only your letter. Therefore be clear about what you want to say and ensure that you cover all the points you need to. For all 'business' letters, it is wise to look over all previous correspondence before you start.

2. Put your material into sequence

Once you've decided on all the points you wish to cover, you must now organize them into a logical sequence – logical from the **reader's** point of view.

3. Make each step a separate paragraph

Your letter will be much easier to digest if each significant idea has a separate paragraph devoted to it. If one topic needs a lot of coverage, break it down into sub-paragraphs and number them if necessary. This will ensure greater clarity and comfort for the reader.

4. Have an introduction and a conclusion

Make these brief but definite. You should ease the reader into your letter, and lead him/her graciously into your 'goodbye'.

5. Identify the subject with a heading

In truth, this practice may not always be necessary or appropriate – you will have to be the judge of that. But if your letter is to cover a specific project or a particular financial matter (a tax claim, an insurance policy enquiry), 'titling' your material in this way will at once concentrate the reader's attention on your concerns. This is also the place to quote any policy, account or reference numbers.

6. Make sure your correspondent knows what to do next

You can undo all your good work so far if your reader is left wondering, 'Where do I go from here?' Make sure that your conclusion is positive and indicates what, if any, response you want. Even if the matter is now dealt with and requires no response, say so.

7. Write your letter out

Once you're clear about your material and its organization, write the letter out in full. Read it through, checking that you've obeyed rules 1 to 6 or all those that apply, that it makes sense and that it reads well.

As with all writing, the more experienced you become, the easier all this gets. You will soon automatically follow the rules; you won't need to jot everything down. If you're dictating, you'll probably be able to handle short letters without notes, although for longer letters it's always wise to list your main points, so as not to forget any.

8. Always check the finished letter

Once you (or someone else) has typed the letter, check it thoroughly. [The same goes for any letter written in longhand.] Make sure it says what you intended, that there are no spelling or typing errors, and that any figures or information given are accurate. Ensure that anything you've promised to enclose is enclosed, and that 'enc.' has been typed at the bottom of the letter to let the recipient know. If the letter is particularly important to you, it is a good idea to ask someone else to proof-read it, or even read it backwards!

Finally, send the letter out as soon as possible: don't leave it lying around until it's out of date.

It's time to look at some examples – both good and bad.

First, look at Example 1 overleaf, which outlines a skeletal model for a business letter, and then read my comments on it.

Example 1 The letter: standard design and format

24, Faber Street,*
London,
EC1E 4PP

Joseph Gardiner Esq.,*
288, Biddenham Road,
Liverpool,
L23 6SX

May 5, 1991

Dear Mr Gardiner,

T

E

X

T

Yours faithfully,

E. S. Jennings (Dr)

---

* It is now common practice to use 'open' punctuation in business letters, i.e. the omission of commas and full stops in both the recipient's and the sender's address.

1. The writer's address is placed in the top-right-hand corner. It is however not **cramped** in there but sensibly spaced.

2. The recipent's address is placed above the greeting; notice that it starts a little further down the page than the sender's address. This further attention to spacing gives the letter an attractive sense of shape.

3. The date is clearly stated and occupies a space of its own. It could be placed on the left above the recipient's address, but where I've placed it is still standard practice. Such a minor point is however now a matter of taste rather than a 'rule'.

4. In this instance the writer closes 'Yours faithfully', suggesting that this is a first contact. Any subsequent correspondence should use 'Yours sincerely'.

5. The writer prints his name, but leaves plenty of room for his signature. He also records his title: in this case it is **Dr**, but a woman writer might find it even more important to register her title – **Mrs, Miss** or **Ms**. In either case the title may be inserted after the writer's name, as shown in the example. All three features are essential: the recipient needs to know who has sent the letter – name, gender and title – and a signature on its own will not be enough: many are quite indecipherable! On the other hand, even an illegible scrawl introduces a needed 'personal touch'.

6. I have of course left the 'text' blank. All I'd say here is to repeat the need to work out in advance what you want to say, and **how much** you want to say. If the letter will extend to two pages or more, design it sensibly. Try not to leave yourself with a last page of just two lines or so: space out the previous one more generously so that the final sheet has at least one substantial paragraph.

Now we turn to some 'real' letters. The first, printed alongside, is an example of the 'intimate' letter; it was written by the novelist Scott Fitzgerald to his daughter. Please read it, and then consider my comments that follow on page 149.

Example 2

521 Amestoy Avenue,
Encino,
California.

March 27, 1940

Dear Scottie,

I am going to work on 'Babylon' at a lousy salary – a week from Monday. Anyhow it's something.

A letter from Baltimore disturbed me this morning – what have you done to your hair? Three different people have seen fit to correspond with me about it. Can't you tone down the effect a little? You heightened it so gradually that I don't think you realize yourself now just what it looks like. Nobody minds if a woman of thirty wants to touch hers up but why imitate a type that is passé even in pictures? It was a cute trick when you had one blond strand that looked as if the sun might have hit it, but going completely overboard defeats any aesthetic purpose.

Best luck for the spring term. I know it's always the hardest and I have that almost uncanny fear for you at the moment that comes sometimes. Perhaps it's the touch of overconfidence and self-justification in your letters (i.e. the Daisy Chain) that I haven't seen for over a year. Please give yourself a margin for hard luck.

Love,

Daddy.

P.S. I can <u>understand</u> the overconfidence – God haven't I had it? But it's hard as hell to recognize it in oneself – especially when time's so short and there's so <u>much</u> we want to do.*

* Andrew Turnbull (ed), *The Letters Of Scott Fitzgerald* (Penguin, 1968), pp. 82–3.

There are one or two things here we can't understand – for instance, the reference to 'the Daisy Chain'. But that is as it should be. It is an intimate letter from father to daughter, and like most intimate letters, a kind of shorthand or code operates from time to time. In all other respects, this letter's strengths are warmingly obvious:

1. The voice is clear and appropriate – worried, loving and sympathetic.
2. He says what he wants to say with no fuss and a lot of impact; it is fluent and direct.
3. Despite his concern, it is evident that Fitzgerald **enjoyed** writing it – mainly because it brought him into contact with someone he loves dearly and also likes very much.
4. It is distinguished by its complete **naturalness**: he writes nakedly, with no pretence and no reservations.

The next example is a formal business letter, from the Eastern Gas Board to the author. As before, please read it and then consider my comments on it.

Figure 3

Tower Point,
Sydney Road,
Enfield,
Dr R. H. Palmer,   Middlesex
64, Levinson Road,   EN2 6TT
Bedford,
MK40 2LU   JY/JHK/LR
                                                    45 1267 0400 20

27 June, 1989

Dear Dr Palmer,

I thank you for your letter dated 15 June 1989, and I very much regret that your previous letter received on 3 June did not receive the courtesy of a reply.

I have examined our records and find that the two accounts rendered to you previously were to estimated readings. I am of the opinion that one or both of these was understated, resulting in the larger than expected account that you have now received.

I would in the first instance suggest that you again check the meter reading to ensure that the index previously supplied by yourself was correct. If this is so, I am prepared to accept payment by instalments, as you suggested. I suggest an immediate remittance of £186–94, followed by two further payments of £150 each at monthly intervals.

Please let me know if you agree to this suggestion.

Yours sincerely,

Mrs J. Partridge
Accounts Supervisor

That was hardly exciting reading for you, apart perhaps from confirming the popular idea that people who write books cannot necessarily cope with household bills! But it's a good letter:

1. Its tone is an appropriate mixture of the apologetic, the pleasantly sympathetic and finally the decisive.
2. She answers all the points raised and finds a mutually satisfactory solution.
3. Throughout the voice is apt and clear.
4. Even if Mrs Partridge did not actively **enjoy** dictating the letter, I should imagine it **pleased** her, in that it did a required job efficiently and gracefully.
5. Finally, if you check the letter against the guidelines and 'rules' outlined earlier, you will find it stands up extremely well. On this occasion, incidentally, it was right to place the date in the centre, as it prevents congestion on that right-hand side.

The third example is also formal; it is an 'open' or public letter written to *The Times*. Again, please read it, and see if you agree with my comments.

Example 4
THE TIMES TUESDAY FEBRUARY 25 1986

LETTERS TO THE EDITOR

English misused by engineers

From Professor E.H. Brown and others

Sir, As professors from each of the main fields of engineering in British universities we are concerned at the near-collapse in our schools' teaching of the syntax of English.

The *power* of our language, for fine distinctions and complex arguments, results only from the systematic teaching of precision, and engineers and scientists are often dismayed to find that the present-day school-leaver cannot adequately wield that power. The emphasis in recent years on free and imaginative writing, excellent in intent, has proved no substitute for a thorough grounding in structure and grammar when exact scientific statements are to be made or when the case for a complicated proposal has to be argued.

It may be said that the modern aim is for creativity, and if so engineers will applaud it. We too admire fine writing: we know that some of the noblest achievements of man – in literature as in engineering – have sprung from the occasional genius who could see beyond the rules and create a new entity. We also know that such individuals number perhaps one in a million. The rest of us must service the civilization we have and earn its daily bread, and in engineering the task requires clear thinking and precise communication.

It may be said that usage evolves, as indeed it does: the rules are for ever shifting. We believe that the changes are slow and peripheral. There exists a rugged detailed structure of the language that enjoys general assent; it is crucial to the transfer of intricate information and it is the birthright of every Briton willing to master it.

There are moves afoot to introduce new AS-level examinations (two AS-level studies occupy the time of one A level) in Precise English, or some such title. The proper time to teach the basis of the language is in earlier years: the proper initiative is to promote an O-level/GCSE-level study, to be the heart of our secondary education.

If our schools really cannot provide it, then – and only then – we shall welcome an AS-level examination emphasizing the meticulous use of English, and we would look warmly on admission candidates who had succeeded in it.

Yours faithfully,
E. H. BROWN (Department of Civil Engineering, Imperial College, London).
J. D. E. BENYON (Pro-Vice-Chancellor and former Head of Electrical Engineering, University of Surrey).
B. N. COLE (Department of Mechanical Engineering, University of Leeds).
H. MARSH (Department of Engineering, University of Durham).
S. A. V. SWANSON (Pro-Rector and former Head of Mechanical Engineering, Imperial College, London).
J. C. R. TURNER (Department of Chemical Engineering, University of Exeter).
Imperial College of Science and Technology,
Department of Civil Engineering,
Imperial Institute Road, SW7.
February 18.

Well, I **would** choose that letter, wouldn't I! But I hope you'll agree it is a masterly performance:

1. The tone is measured and authoritative.
2. The letter is fairly long, but it develops a complex argument with admirable clarity. A lot of people reading it would want to engage the writers in discussion – perhaps to agree, perhaps to disagree, but anxious to 'talk'.
3. The voice is apparently plural, yet it has a unity and confidence that are comfortable to absorb.
4. The language is necessarily sophisticated, but the writers include from time to time a punchy phrase that stops the style from becoming over-abstract – 'earn its daily bread', 'the birthright of every Briton' and the initial, powerful 'near-collapse in our schools' teaching of the syntax of English'.
5. The letter gives real **pleasure**. The language is cogent and elegant; the style is a splendid advertisement for what they are advocating. The professors' deep concern did not prevent them enjoying the letter's composition: one can 'hear' the satisfaction in a job well done.

If we consider those letters as a trio, we see that they are all **natural**. Each writer has thought sensibly about the tone and register required: as a result each one flows easily and logically. Choice of vocabulary and sentence size are apposite; the length of each letter is just right. The writers develop their ideas properly and then sign off – a symptom of their alertness to their readers' needs and comfort.

Now let's have a little fun with two **bad** examples! The first we have encountered before in Part Three – Mr Casaubon's marriage proposal to Dorothea in George Eliot's *Middlemarch*. On this occasion I will quote only the first few lines; the fuller version is on pp. 114–15.

Example 5

My dear Miss Brooke,

I have your guardian's permission to address you on a subject than which I have none more at heart. I am not, I trust, mistaken in the recognition of some deeper correspondence than that of date in the fact that a consciousness of need in my own life has arisen contemporaneously with the possibility of my becoming acquainted with you. For in the first hour of meeting you, I had an impression of your eminent and perhaps exclusive fitness to supply that need (connected, I may say, with such activity of the affections as even the preoccupations of a work too special to be abdicated could not uninterruptedly dissimulate); and each succeeding opportunity for observation has given the impression of an added depth . . .

As I pointed out before, this is a superb performance on George Eliot's part: we are supposed to react with hostility, even cringing dislike. Casaubon's style is headache-inducing within even a few lines; one has to work very hard to decipher it, and in addition our instincts are surely chilled when we remember that this is a love letter!

Perhaps the most frightening thing about this is that it is not, in one sense, 'unnatural'. Casaubon is not being pompous: he has not adopted this tone and style in order to impress or dissemble. As we have confirmed when they are (disastrously) married, he really does think like that and in those structures. But in another sense, it of course strikes us as unnatural – grotesquely so. What is supposed to be a proposal of marriage resembles a particularly forbidding letter from a banker or solicitor, disagreeable in tone and a nightmare to understand. At the end, Dorothea responds by sobbing with joy; **we** feel that she should have 'binned' it at once! That disparity in reaction prepares us for the misery we know will overtake her later.

However, one can be **too** natural as well; or rather, a proper sense of voice must be accompanied by care and thoughtfulness. Below is a worried, somewhat irate letter from a parent to his daughter's school. Count the technical errors, and see what else you think is wrong with it. You will find my comments at the end of the letter.

Example 6

86, Peterson Road,
Milton Keynes

Dear Mrs Josephs,

I was a little surprised that I have this morning recieved the Invoice for Margarets Autumn term fees, since I was given to understand from your last letter that you felt it may be better to place Margaret at another school and this seemed to be confirmed by the school solicitor being involved to collect the outstanding £300, all this despite the fact that both I and later my wife on the telephone assured you that all will be cleared before the begining of the September term and that we were only waiting for the proceeds of of our house which had been sold. We have as you implied now made other arrangements for Margaret as we could not wait until now to find out shecould still have attended the school.

My wife and I would non the less like to thankyou for your help in the past and perhaps without knowing all the facts it must have been difficult for you to come to terms with our problems.

May we wish you and the school continued sucess,

Yours sincerely,

Not very good, is it?!

1. There are five spelling mistakes: recieve, Margaret**s** (apostrophe required), begining, no**n** the less, sucess.
2. There are three errors in composition and spacing: of is repeated in line 9 and **shecould** and **thankyou** are run together.
3. There are two technical omissions: no date, and no printed name. The latter is serious, because the signature resembles a squashed insect rather than anything legibly human.

More subtle but no less important flaws hinge on the letter's **frantic** quality.

4. Insufficient thought has been given to what he wants to say. In the large first paragraph his thoughts just tumble out and over each other. To be fair, he is confused: the school has, it seems, failed to make the full position sufficiently clear to him. But he compounds that confusion by mixing up too many separate points: notice that there is no full stop until line 9!
5. He seems to have a genuine grievance and yet abruptly switches tone in the two concluding paragraphs. One could see this as gracious; on the other hand, his penultimate sentence takes most of the sting and point away from his earlier complaints.

Incidentally, the original letter was if anything **worse**! His typewriter-ribbon was worn and he used cheap paper.

In a moment, a final pair of examples; before that, a further list of things to avoid or bear in mind.

Pitfalls
1. 'Business English' and flowery phrases
There used to be a style of writing for business letters that was ornate and pretentious. [See Example 7] It is now as outdated as the clerk's

Figure 17. 'Flowery English'.

periwig or the schoolmaster's gown, and will inspire irritation or derision rather than respect. Use modern and natural phrasing wherever possible.

2. Long Words

Writing as if you've swallowed a dictionary is equally likely to cause annoyance and ridicule. As I've stressed throughout this book, keep it simple whenever you can. Good writers seek primarily to express, not impress.

3. Gobbledegook sentences

Anyone who has ever had to complete a tax form will be well versed in gobbledegook. That lovely word refers to those seemingly endless, opaque sentences that congeal, stagnantly incomprehensible, on the page. Keep your sentences short, or at least crisp; this will ensure that your letters are quickly understood. Indeed, it will ensure that they are actually read rather than thrown away in disgust!

4. Kaleidoscope sentences

If you keep your sentences tolerably short, you are unlikely to fall into the additional trap of taking on too many ideas within a single sentence. [See Example 6 above.] Use one sentence for each specific point.

5. Jargon and 'buzz' words

Avoid these unless there really is no alternative, or unless you are certain that your reader will fully understand what you're talking about. A good rule to follow, especially if your subject is technically sophisticated, is to write as if to an intelligent layman. I admit that this will not always be possible; but just trying it will do your style a lot of good.

6. Ambiguity

It's all too easy to **think** that you've said what you mean, but it may be that you've in fact said something very different. Check this out ruthlessly: it's often a good idea to read your work through as if you were someone else seeing it for the first time.

7. The passive voice

Avoid unless you have no alternative. 'You should send the premium' is nearly always preferable to 'the premium should be sent', and in at least 90% of cases one can find a way to use the active voice. However, the passive is a wise choice if you are sure the occasion demands delicacy or diplomacy!

8. Punctuation

It would be silly to attempt cover-all advice on this in a couple of sentences. But punctuation is a fundamental skill and is no less important in letters than anywhere else. If you are not sure about your competence, consult Part Two and the relevant sections of the Grammar Primer.

Now, as a last exercise in this section, please read Examples 7 and 8. Which is better, and why?

Example 7

JOHN SMITH INSURANCE BROKERS
The Crescent
Abbeyville
Wessex

R. R. James Esq.,   19th May 1932
The Lodge,
Abbeyville,
Wessex.

Dear Sir,

Your letter of the 14th ultimo, which was received at this office on 3rd inst., does not attend to the matters arising in ours of the 3rd ultimo, and as this information is necessary for the preparation of the appropriate endorsement, we kindly request your urgent advices.

Furthermore, we regret to observe you have not yet forwarded your remittance for the additional cover requested in the aforementioned letter, so that cover cannot be enforced until such time as we are in receipt of said remittance and the responses to questions 7a and 9c from the proposal form as dealt with in our letter of 3rd ultimo.

We respectfully request you give these matters your urgent attention and await your earliest advices.

We beg to remain your most obedient servant,

J. Smith

Example 8

JOHN SMITH INSURANCE BROKERS
The Crescent
Abbeyville
Wessex
Phone: 0123 98765/4/3

Mr R. R. James   Date: 19th May 1992
The Lodge   Our Ref: AIO/PI/JS
Abbeyville   Your Ref:
Wessex   Ask for: John Smith

Dear Mr James

Policy no. MC 456789 – additional cover for Miss A. James

Thank you for your letter of the 14th April, which we received on the 3rd May.

Unfortunately, we are still missing the following:

1. A reply to questions 7a and 9c of the proposal form, i.e. the name of Miss James' previous insurers and her occupation.

2. The premium of £25 for the additional cover.

As soon as we receive the above, together with the attached remittance slip, we will send you the updated policy document.

Yours sincerely

J. Smith

I hope you agree that it's no contest – Example 8 wins by a street.

Example 7 is interesting, in that it uses the kind of language and conventions that many people think they ought to adopt when writing formally. This is a foolish myth. All that dreadful '14th ultimo' and '3rd inst.' stuff serves no purpose whatever, apart from the rather nasty (if it is deliberate) one of intimidating the reader. It's a bad letter, too, in its lofty assumption that the reader has all previous correspondence instantly to hand: the second paragraph can make no sense without reference to the firm's previous letter. Example 8 spells out identical matters in a firm but courteous way.

In addition, the **visual** effect of each is very different. Example 8 is sensibly and pleasantly spaced; that, just as much as its unfussy style, ensures rapid understanding. Example 7, on the other hand, compounds its appalling style with a cramped and stingy design. Though short, it is very hard work for the eyes and the brain – the last thing an 'urgent' letter should be.

Speaking of 'urgency', it amuses me that in both cases the correspondents took an awful long time to write, or at least post, their letters! Mr James needed three weeks to mail his letter and the brokers a further fortnight to reply. This is sloppy practice: avoid it.

Finally, don't be fooled by the 1932 date on Example 7. It is genuine, as is the letter itself; but as I've said, many people still write business letters in this way. Such presentation is silly and unnecessary, and Example 8 is a decisively superior model.

Conclusion

Despite its many hi-tech competitors, letter-writing remains a major social and commercial skill. In some respects it is also an art, for a good letter expresses a writer's personality and style: there is indeed no more direct form of writing. And although there are particular conventions and special 'rules' that you should always attend to, a good letter will achieve those qualities that characterize good writing of any kind: **clarity; appropriateness and elegance.**

Figure 18. 'One of life's pleasures'.

Letters guarantee you an audience: make the most of it. **Think** and **listen**: be precise about what you want to say and be alert as to how it will strike your reader:

If your letters say what you mean them to say, they will be read as they are meant to be read.

And they will be enjoyable, too – both to write and to read. As I said at the outset, writing a good letter does require real effort: sometimes the phone seems a much more convenient option, as does doing nothing at all. But the effort is almost always worth it. A letter is a lasting record – an important consideration whether the context is a business or personal one. In addition, writing a good letter is one of life's pleasures; so is receiving one. If you follow the guidelines and advice developed above, I'm confident that you will enjoy that pleasure from now on.

ESSAYS   11

An essayist is a lucky person who has found a way
to discourse without being interrupted.

Charles Poore

Argument seldom convinces anyone contrary to his
inclinations.

Thomas Fuller

It is one thing to write a good letter; to write a good essay is quite
another matter.

An essay is a formal, coherent and usually quite lengthy piece of
informative and/or argumentative writing, as are its 'cousins', the article
and the report, to which I devote my main attention in the two chapters
following this one.

All essays develop an argument and seek to persuade. The argument
may be pre-provided, as in a student answering a title set by a teacher
and an executive producing a study requested by the board of directors,
or it may be the writer's own idea. Whichever one applies, the activity
ought to be fun, bringing pleasure to writer and reader alike. As Charles
Poore suggests, writing an essay is an arguably unique opportunity to
hold forth for as long as you like on a topic that interests you and about
which you have plenty to say.

If those remarks strike you as wildly idealistic, I can assure you that
you're in good and large company! For while I stand by what I've just
said, the fact remains that most people find essay-writing the hardest, most
elusive and most frustrating skill to acquire, and that it takes a long time
for them to look on it as remotely pleasurable; indeed, some never do.

Writing a good letter undoubtedly requires you to make an effort,
and often puts you under a certain amount of pressure, especially if an
important matter of business or finance is at stake. However, that seems
very pale stuff when faced with writing an essay. Weeks of preparation,
discovery and sheer hard work now require a product: it's 'crunch time',
and you are aware of being under a glaring spotlight both intimate and
very public. If it is true that the single most frequent phobia is that of
speaking in public [more often cited than death, apparently!], then many
would admit that the fear of writing in public is hardly less formidable.
Moreover, the problem seems to have little to do with ability: in my
experience the very bright student encounters just as many difficulties
as does the moderate one.

If you're suffering from any or all of these symptoms, what can you do to ease matters, even cure them for good?

Writing essays: some preliminary points

1. Trust your voice

I've been stressing this matter throughout the book, but I make no apology for raising it again. For the majority of people who are required to write regularly, the essay is the longest, most complex and most ambitious genre they will use, and it is all the more important to stay as natural and individual as possible when writing it. Just because it is a formal, public and intellectually demanding task does **not** mean you need to adopt a disguise or hide behind others' views and style. On the contrary: a successful essay reveals something of the writer as well as an argument. It is ultimately a very personal form: you should bear that centrally in mind, and take advantage of it. Naturally, you need to make your language appropriate; but if you follow the many guidelines earlier in this book, there is no reason why your essay style should not be both pleasing and telling.

2. Try to start the essay in plenty of time, and on no account leave it till the last minute

Part of the pressure attending the writing of an essay or a report is *compulsion*. Students are formally required to write essays, or they risk being thrown off the course, and any rising executive who refuses to submit an important report to his or her board of directors will soon be collecting a P45. As a result, only a handful default; but many shy away from the task for too long, perhaps because shelving it gives them the illusion of a freedom that the sudden arrival of a deadline brutally explodes. As a psychological ploy, this is readily understandable: we've all done it. And we therefore also know that **as a strategy, it's very bad indeed, if not disastrous.**

If you leave an essay to the last moment, you've got no choice: you've got to do it however tired, stupid, stale or resistant you are. It is all too probable that such negative states will show through in your writing. And even if you're lucky enough to be feeling fresh and vigorous at such a time, you've still got to rush things. There's unlikely to be time for any editing or a period of careful thought to ensure that you get something just right.

All this is obvious enough, I know; nevertheless a sizable proportion of students continue wilfully to ignore such obvious facts. As a result, they put themselves under an extra and severe pressure that a little sensible planning would render unnecessary. Furthermore, there's a positive side to it: if you do start early, you'll feel much more confident about being in control, and that will increase both your pleasure and your quality of performance.

3. Pay full attention to mechanical accuracy, sentence structure and paragraphing

I am constantly struck by how many students whom I know at root to be mechanically sound seem to jettison half their competence in this respect when they write essays. [The same is true for many younger pupils when they write 'compositions'.] The reason for this is not hard to find. If one gives students an exercise on punctuation, parts of speech or whatever, they concentrate specifically on such things. There is, after all, nothing else to do; consequently, they perform very well as a rule.

But writing an essay is a multiple activity. You've got to:

(a) decode/understand the question/title;
(b) work out what you chiefly wish to say;
(c) figure out how to start;
(d) decide on how best to deploy your material;
(e) ensure you regularly substantiate your points with detailed illustration, quotation or reference;
(f) effect a satisfying conclusion

and several other things.* It is therefore not surprising if you fail to pay ordinary attention to mundane matters like spelling and grammatical accuracy. Not surprising – but very unwise and probably highly damaging. Careless errors reflect badly on you and undermine any authority your arguments may have; moreover, there is a bigger danger still.

If you don't pay enough attention to how to spell words and structure individual sentences and paragraphs properly, the chances of your essay having a clear and persuasive *overall* structure are very slim.

Good large structures consist of well-engineered and flawlessly connected small structures: that goes for essays as well as buildings, cars and domestic machinery.

4. Always pause before embarking on a fresh argument or theme

There are two good reasons for this. First, it allows you time to check that you've got all you can out of your previous focus. Very often, a few moments' reflection will lead you on to further points that lift the material from the merely satisfactory to the truly authoritative.

---

* All these matters, the six cited and the 'several other things', are covered shortly.

Second, the slight rest or change of activity will do you good, and should ensure that when you do turn to your fresh argument, you yourself are fresh and ready to tackle it with real vigour. If this does not happen, the chances are that you've become tired and should stop for a while. Note, incidentally, that this provides another reason for not leaving the essay until the last minute, when you won't be able to afford such valuable rests!

5. Read as many essays/articles as you can

You cannot become a good essayist simply by osmosis, but reading others' work will quickly make you more alert to matters of style, structure and so on. You will learn from their strengths, but equally from their weaknesses and flaws: when you come across something that is unclear or badly expressed, the chances are high that it will help you not to make the same mistake. There are many extracts from essays [good and bad] throughout this book: you could do worse than start with them.

So much for preliminaries; it is time to consider problems. And judging from my own students' experience and requests for advice, most of these hinge on how to structure an essay. The matter is large

Figure 19. 'Read as many essays/articles as you can'.

and complex, best introduced by looking at some of the more obvious areas where difficulty arises.

Essay structure: traps and troubleshooting

1. **You cannot begin to write a decent essay until you have a good command of the material concerned.**

That is such a banal observation that I almost blush to include it. Nevertheless it is remarkable how often students' alleged problems with 'structure' boil down to the much more mundane – and unflattering! – fact that they do not 'know their stuff' well enough yet. And I'm not just referring to the lazy or dilettante student who thinks a quick perusal of the source material plus recourse to some tawdry 'Study Aid' is enough of a platform for an adequate essay; conscientious and meticulous students can suffer from this flaw too.

An essay is like a good meal: it takes a lot of careful preparation and preliminary time. It makes about as much sense to attempt an essay without a clear grasp of the relevant information and ideas as it does to get out a plate and sit in front of it expecting food to materialize on it as if by magic.

If basic ignorance or incomplete knowledge isn't the problem, you may still be very low on confidence, and there can be several reasons for that.

2a. **What does the question/title ask you to do?**
2b. **Do you know what you chiefly wish to say?**
2c. **How are you going to start?**

I've listed these together because ultimately they intertwine – all exert a fundamental influence on how you deploy and structure your material. But each one also addresses a specific matter, and they're worth considering separately first.

Whether you're engaged on a 'weekly essay' or the much more pressured task of performing in an examination, your first job, before even picking up your pen, is to 'decode' the question.

Be absolutely sure that you've understood any concepts or 'targets' stated; above all, look at the instructional verbs and obey them. As an example, try this little exercise.

Exercise 27
What is the difference between these two questions?
1. **Describe the rise of Hitler.**
2. **Explain the rise of Hitler.**

Commentary

An incautious student might think there is little or no difference, and would as a result be flirting with disaster, no matter how knowledgeable and confident he or she may be. For there is a **big** difference. The first question calls for an 'objective' historiographical account, listing stages, events and what we will call 'facts'. The second question, by contrast, is much more a matter of interpretation, possibly involving a consideration of mass psychology, of the emotional appeal of Fascism, and an understanding of how mania can take hold of a nation. Of course, certain things may well emerge as common to both questions, but 1 demands an account that is essentially external, whereas 2 requires a more intuitive or internal approach. To confuse them in the heat of the moment may be understandable in a way, but it would prove a very expensive mistake.

The prime need to work out what you've got to do must **not**, in any circumstances, be taken to mean 'What do they want me to say?', which leads us to 2b.

If you don't yet know what you chiefly want to say, two possible explanations arise.

1. You haven't done enough preparatory reading, thinking, or both.
2. You're unsure about what 'line' to follow. You may have some ideas that clash with those of your teacher, or other opinions/inter-pretations you've read, and you're doubtful about whether to include them or 'play safe' instead.

I've covered 1 already, of course: if this applies, you're not yet ready to contemplate doing an essay, and should go back to your books at once!

The second reason is a much more sympathetic problem; it is nonetheless wrong-headed. In exams especially, but also in more leisurely contexts, students often imagine that their essay must be 'the right answer', that it must match what the marker thinks. **This is an absurd and extremely harmful delusion.**

It is absurd because in many cases (virtually all exams included) you will have no idea who the marker is, and therefore no knowledge of his or her beliefs, prejudices and so on. Trying to second-guess an unknown and invisible assessor is just crazy! More subtle – and also more important – is the harm done by sacrificing your biggest asset: **you**. The quest for 'the right answer' ignores the fact that it's your essay, nobody else's, and that its quality will depend on your ideas, your intellect, your prose. Provided your 'information base' and knowledge are sound, your reader/marker will be interested in what you have to say – and that will be all the stronger if it really is what you want to say, and not what you think the reader wants to hear.

I admit that you may, from time to time, be unlucky: there are teachers around who want their own views more or less reproduced in their students' essays and who penalize or are very snooty about attempted departures from them. There may also be a few such examiners at any given time – although I can assure you that they do not last long in the post if they are doctrinaire in their marking. But by and large it makes the best and most profitable sense to stick to your guns and argue the case you've worked out to your own satisfaction. And that brings us to the crucial matter of how to start.

Even to an experienced writer, a blank sheet of paper is a uniquely frightening thing. It seems to stare at you in a sneering or threatening way [possibly both], as if taunting you to get something down, however feeble! All of us succumb, at least occasionally, to such temptation, and I cannot stress too strongly that **we are *always* wrong to do so.**

There is no single good way of beginning an essay: we'll look at some of the options in a moment. Conversely, however, there are also several bad ways in which to start, and they need listing at once.

1. ***Never* allow your first sentence to be a mere paraphrase of the title/question.**

This should be obvious enough: few things are more boring than to read a [usually wordy] repetition of something already established. Yet thousands do it, time and again! It's invariably based on fear, on that intolerable need to make your mark on that blank sheet. But don't do it: it will make only a negative mark on your reader.

Figure 20. 'A blank sheet of paper is a uniquely frightening thing'.

2. **Always ensure that your first sentence does some real work.**

I'll be going into positive ways of achieving this in a little while; but as I've implied, more than half the battle is knowing the kind of thing to avoid.

A. **Don't waste time with vacuous 'general' introductions.**

These may seem to read quite well, but they will usually be flabby, however pleasantly written. [An example follows shortly.] As always, keep your readers centrally in mind: they may not object all that much if you gradually 'wind yourself up' into action, rather like an athlete warming up, but they will much prefer it if you give them something that immediately engages their full attention.

B. **Beware of confusing 'private' thinking with 'public' performing and arguing.**

That is not an easy instruction to understand, and I hope an analogy will help.

I would imagine that all of you have been to a theatre at some time. The opening moments of any production are always fascinating. One has so much to absorb: the set, the costumes, the make-up, the voices and of course the spoken lines. This heady assault on the senses is central to the unique appeal of live theatre, and it is the expectation of such imminent pleasure that accounts for the 'buzz' in the air just before the performance begins.

However, let us suppose that during those expectant minutes you not only have your chocolates, programme and the lively chatter of friends to beguile you, but also access to a closed-circuit television network that shows you what's going on backstage. You now have the opportunity to watch step by step the intricate make-up an actor needs to apply to play *King Lear, Othello, The Phantom of the Opera* or even the tramps in *Waiting for Godot*. Alternatively, you can 'tune in' to the special effects technicians and see them preparing their tricks. Or you may just see cast and stage crew chatting desultorily as they await the cue to begin. And my question is: would you make use of this new facility?

My own answer would be: yes, but almost certainly only the first time. If such a thing became available to every member of the audience, I think we all would have our curiosity too much aroused to ignore it. But I am almost sure it would diminish our overall pleasure in the performance, however initially interesting those extra insights might be. When the actors appear in role, or those special effects occur, our most likely reaction would be one of anti-climax, a loss of 'magic' or at least a reduction in excitement. On our next theatre visit, we'd firmly keep our set turned off.

Writing an essay is no less of a 'performance' than appearing in a play, albeit a less glamorous one. Just as an actor's initial impact might be seriously impaired if we had witnessed his private preparation, your impact as an essayist will be much reduced if you subject the reader to a lot of private thinking before making your first 'public' point. So I would strongly advise you not to write down this kind of thing:

Exercise 28

There follow three essay introductions. What's wrong with them?

(a) In this essay I am going to look at both sides of the proposition at issue, make a number of points about each side, and then move towards what I hope is a satisfactory and balanced conclusion.

(b) Question: Was Henry VIII a good and successful king?
I find it difficult to answer this question. It all depends on what you mean by 'good' and 'successful'. My definitions might be different from other people's, which would obviously cause confusion.

(c) Question: Are the terms 'recession', 'depression' and 'slump' synonymous?
In order to answer this question, it is first necessary to decide what is meant by the three terms 'recession', 'depression' and 'slump' cited in the title. For although they are closely linked, they are also precisely separate, and they must be distinguished between if one wishes to understand how an economic crisis can arise.

Commentary

All are quite elegantly written; none is a wise or effective way to begin.

The first is distinctly poor: indeed, it's useless. It tells the reader nothing not already implicit in the title; it is blandly vague; and it is has no 'voice'. Anyone could have written it, in answer to virtually any question. That's why I didn't in this case cite the question: it wouldn't have made any difference. The introduction spells out what one would expect as a matter of course from any answer to a two-sided proposition – and there is an almost infinite number of such questions.

So, (a) is a classic example of the vacuous first paragraph that confuses preliminary private thinking with public impact. It is very sensible to work out the structure and strategy of your essay, but it is unnecessary and boring to call public attention to them. Let your ideas speak for themselves at once and without such featureless advertising.

The second is less dull, but it still won't do. It is superficially engaging in its modesty, and a clear 'voice' is present. But it is too defensive, quickly collapsing into vagueness as a result. Sadly, the writer's instincts are sound: the words "good" and "successful" are indeed problematic, or at least need defining. Instead of doing just that, the introduction slides away into something uncomfortably close to a whine. I strongly suspect the root of the trouble is that 'quest for the right answer': a worry about 'other people' prevails at the expense of the writer's own views.

The third has a vigour and implicit independence of mind absent in the other examples; it also echoes the flaws of both. As I remarked in an earlier section (see pages 77–8), the structure 'In order to answer this question, it is first necessary to . . .' falls dully on the eye and does no real work; moreover, it can frequently decline further into a wordy paraphrase of the title, which is essentially what happens here. You might think me a little unfair, and argue that the first sentence implies that the three terms are not 'synonymous' and therefore has already begun to answer the question in a clear fashion. I wouldn't altogether disagree, but would add that the writer would have been better advised to launch into the separate definitions straightaway, which would have been much punchier. Alternatively, he could begin with his pleasingly cogent second sentence. As it is, his introduction is somewhat wordy and also not fully confident, even if it is the best of the three examples, signalling genuine promise.

So much, then, for the dangers of vacuity and confusing private thinking with public performance. These are, I hope, obvious flaws; other 'starting traps' are a little more subtle.

C. Long introductions are rarely advisable.

If essay structure worries you, it is best to keep your introductions short for the time being. Even if they are not vacuous, long introductions can be arduous to read, and your first aim should be to grab your readers' attention as attractively as possible.

Long introductions can be very impressive, I admit. I have read many good ones from students engaged upon a large task who conscientiously establish the full context and 'ground rules' of what they go on to explore. But you need a lot of confidence and a certain amount of practice to bring this off; in addition, it can tempt you into generalizations that are best left until after you've put together a detailed argument. If in any doubt, therefore, go for a short, snappy start.

D. Don't launch an attack on a question in your opening remarks.

I've already suggested you shouldn't be over-dutiful or craven when considering a title, and that you should stick to what you feel and want to say. But instant aggression is equally unwise. I don't simply mean that you should avoid openings like 'This proposition is a load of rubbish'. That kind of remark, unattractively combining stale slang and naive arrogance, nearly always bounces back on the writer, and should not be used at any time. Even if your attack is a good deal more sophisticated and elegant, however, you still risk alienating the reader if you come on too strong too early:

Question: Despite its horrors, the action of *King Lear* persuades us that 'The gods are just'.

One really doesn't know whether to laugh or cry at this proposition. The world of *King Lear* is *so* full of horror, especially at the end, when even the traditional grim comfort of tragic resolution is denied us, that any idea of divine benevolent control is just obscene. The most we can conclude is that even if the gods exist, they are indifferent to human suffering; many would argue that they seem positively to glory in it.

This was a written by a highly intelligent student of mine a couple of years ago. For what it's worth, I agree with his underlying case; but I pointed out to him that some of his phrasing was at best incautious anyway, **and especially at the start of his answer**. I also suggested, prompted by his use of **conclude**, that his remarks (suitably toned-down!) would be far more effective as his conclusion, when his undoubted knowledge and intelligence would have 'earned' him the right to quarrel fiercely with the title.

The point here is not that you should never attack a question, but that you should be sensible about doing so. The following guidelines are worth bearing in mind.

1. **You will very seldom encounter a title or question that is truly stupid or nonsensical.**

You may quite frequently come across a proposition that you disagree with, even fundamentally so; that is quite a different matter. It is a truism that there are two sides to virtually every question: academics and examiners are especially aware of this, and are chiefly interested in why and how you argue your particular case. That's why they won't set you anything obviously idiotic, and why you'll almost certainly harm yourself if you accuse them of having done so.

2. **It is best to establish your credentials before going on the attack.**

In all writing, you need to take your readers with you. If you know that you are going to ask them to consider a case to which they may be hostile, you should first establish a 'base' that persuades them that you know what you're talking about and have carefully considered a lot of evidence. If you do this well, some of your later controversial points may be gently implicit already, creating a unity and flow that will satisfy even a reader who disagrees with you.

3. Never allow your disagreement to degenerate into name-calling.

It is usually possible to respect, or at least understand, views different from your own, and that should be your strategy.* By all means attempt to demolish the opposite case, but this should be done with dignity, even courtesy. Indeed, you can often make your case more effective by praising an opposing point before demonstrating that yours is even better!

4. Be *especially* careful to demonstrate your points.

Naturally, you need to do this in any essay. But it's particularly important when arguing a contrary or controversial case: any mere assertions unaccompanied by evidence or illustration will be dismissed by those whom, perhaps against their will, you're trying to persuade.

My final 'don't' to bear in mind when seeking to ensure that your first remarks do some real work may seem puzzling at first, but it opens up a more positive approach.

E. Do not assume that an introduction is automatically necessary.

Sometimes your best policy will be to make the first 'scoring' point that occurs to you, and to move straight on from there. Indeed, it is worth developing this into a principle that applies to both the beginning and the end of an essay:

> **There is no virtue in having an introduction or a conclusion *for the sake of it*. It can be better to just start or just stop!**

I must urge caution about this: there is probably nothing better than a stylishly argued essay which has been vigorously set up and satisfyingly rounded off. But as is doubtless clear by now, writing a good introduction is a difficult skill, and to agonize about its structure can cost you valuable time, energy and confidence. Since you will be most crisp and to the point when you arrive at what you know best, it can make a lot of sense to start with that material.

Even so, having an introduction may make you feel more comfortable, or your teachers may insist on one. In that case, this next principle, which in a way is a variant of the previous one, may be valuable.

---

* There are exceptions to this. My first sentence in Part One identifies destructive criticism as 'one of life's great pleasures', and I hold to that, as several sections and exercises in this book make abundantly clear. And if you do come across a question or view that you genuinely despise, then I think you should say so. My point here, however, is that such occasions will be very rare in the writing of academic essays, and that it's poor policy to anticipate the need for ridicule.

The best time to write your introduction is last thing of all – even after the conclusion.

This is not as crazy as it looks! It has a number of strengths that may well improve an adequate essay and render a good one really impressive.

1. It will almost certainly prevent your introduction and conclusion from virtually duplicating each other – a very common flaw in essays that I read.

2. By this time you will be aware of what you have argued and why. This knowledge should allow you to write an introductory paragraph which sets up that argument in an assured and muscular way, increasing the reader's pleasure and attention.

3. As a corollary to 2, your introduction will impress by its lack of flab, uncertainty and defensiveness. You will now have filled several sides, and the shaping of your opening remarks should carry none of the normal 'blank sheet terror' syndrome!

4. Your confidence will receive a double boost. First, to start with material you're secure rather than anxious about should ensure that you write vigorously from the beginning – and you'll be beneficially aware that you're doing so, which will help to sustain your performance. Second, when you do write that introduction, you'll be sure of what you're doing and confidently aware of exactly how much to write. Furthermore . . .

5. . . . The long-term advantages of such a strategy may also be considerable. Success in any extended course hinges on confidence almost as much as on talent and industry; if this method causes you to feel less frightened about structuring your essays, and therefore confidently able to enjoy writing them more, the progress you make should be rapid and substantial.

Finally, an apparently paradoxical advantage:

6. It will no doubt have occurred to you that writing your introduction last is almost impossible in an exam, unless you can guess with uncanny accuracy how many lines to leave blank! But this shouldn't prove as much of a problem as you might imagine.

   Exams usually occur at the end of a year, or not until a good deal of the course has been covered: there isn't much point in them otherwise. By then, you will have written a number of essays, and if you've adopted good habits in doing so, you should find that you've developed a practised 'feel' for how to structure and deploy an argument. In short, by the time you sit your exams, you should be experienced enough to write your introduction first and be confident about its quality.

Summary

At the outset I listed three things that should come into play as soon as you sit down to begin an essay:

What does the question ask you to do?
Do you know what you chiefly wish to say?
How are you going to start?

We've spent a number of pages considering these separately. But as I said earlier, they are closely related in the fundamental influence they exert on your performance. Indeed, they are almost symbiotic, as these two formulae illustrate:

• **Solve the first 'problem' properly, and the second will be easier; solve that, and the third one will be**.
• **Ignore or make a mess of one of them, and the other two will suffer as well.**

Essay writing as a performance

So far I've looked at ways of ensuring that your essays are sound. If you follow the 'preliminary points' and stay mindful of 'potential 'traps', you should do a very satisfactory job. The only remaining thing to do is to consider ways of making your essays impressive rather than just solid, and I want to look at six 'advanced' skills which characterize the work of a truly authoritative writer giving a performance.

1. Keeping to the point.
2. Drawing on a proper *range* of evidence and focus.
3. Linking, digging and polishing.
4. More on introductions and conclusions.
5. Quotation and reference.
6. The strengths and limitations of 'argument'.

1. Keeping to the point

This may seem an elementary skill, and so it is in terms of obeying basic relevance and the need to answer the question. But 'advanced' writers are vulnerable to a phenomenon that rarely if ever affects their less sophisticated counterparts – that of becoming temporarily 'lost in thought'. What starts as an unremarkable idea may suddenly open up a new avenue of enquiry – a gratifying experience but also a perilous one. In your excited determination to milk this sudden inspiration to the full, you can easily make a major detour from your planned route without realizing it; sometimes it proves to be not just a detour but an elaborate dead-end.

There are times when this is entirely useful – during an 'exploratory' essay early in your course, when your essay work is as much a learning experience as a performance. But when the latter is your chief or sole aim, you need to be ruthless. Fortunately, there is a simple way of ensuring you do not get lost in this beguiling but wasteful way: keep your title and main targets in mind at all times.

How you do this is up to you. You can make regular visual checks of your first page; you can write title and targets in bold capitals on a piece of paper kept in front of you; or you can just train yourself to issue regular mental reminders. But however you go about it, make sure that your material is not just interesting in its own right but achieves an overall unity and unbroken pertinence.

2. Drawing on a proper range of evidence and focus

Most of your essays will address topics that are quite large and broad, although from time to time you will be asked to do something narrow and specific – e.g. the analysis of a scene in a play, a particular scientific reaction, or an historical document. And if the question is wide-ranging, make sure your essay is too. If you're asked to write about, say:

A. The development of a character during a large novel
B. X's foreign policy during a ten-year period
C. The strengths and limitations of Utilitarianism

you cannot afford to have a narrow or thin 'data base'. If you look at only two episodes for A, a couple of incidents for B or one example per 'side' for C, the essay is unlikely to satisfy even if the analysis you do offer is brilliant.

Good prior planning will more or less guarantee that your scope of example and detail is suitably broad. But stay alert to this while writing: as I've just pointed out during 1, it's all too easy to become so engrossed in a particular issue that earlier resolutions and schemes get forgotten.

There is a complementary danger that should be mentioned here:

Ensure a good range of evidence, yes; but don't go to the opposite extreme and sacrifice depth for quantity.

Sometimes an essay title can seem forbiddingly broad, prompting you to think that you must try to cover absolutely every relevant incident or detail. Unless you're intending to make your essay the size of a small book, you can't hope to achieve such comprehensiveness without becoming damagingly thin in your treatment of each point. Go for a muscular compromise: in a 4–5-side essay, you can focus on several key pieces of evidence and deal with them in sufficient depth to persuade the reader of their satisfying representativeness.

3. Linking, digging and polishing

Earlier I advised you to beware of boring your readers by taking them through over-obvious, unnecessary steps in the basic logic of your essay's structure. But as a writer of sophisticated essays, you must also be careful not to omit steps in the logic of your argument. It is one thing to assume that the reader knows without needing to be told that you're starting the essay, moving on to another point, finishing: such omissions are sensible and indeed essential if you don't want to irritate. But it's quite a different matter if you leave out an important link between two points, leaving the reader to do the work: that is equally annoying. As an ideal compromise:

> **Spare the reader a dull, unfruitful survey of your essay's architecture, but don't overdo it by insisting that he/she supply the bridges between your *ideas*.**

Make sure your argument progresses clearly and comfortably. It is not quite enough to put down two related points without showing that they are linked, and why. Very often you will need nothing more than a simple conjunction [which means 'linking with'], such as **so**, **thus** or even **and**.

Essays whose material is not adequately linked acquire a bland, almost unfinished quality; the same is true of essays where the writer doesn't 'dig' into the material with quite enough penetration. As a result, the points lie on the surface, as if waiting for the reader to mine them properly. So explore and develop your points as far as you can – don't, as many do, settle for the first and second useful ideas that occur to you. If you're talented enough to think of those, then a little vigorous turning over the ground is very likely to lead to a third, and a fourth – and that's one of the surest ways of transforming quite a good essay into a very good one. 'Linking' and 'digging' are closely related, in that writers who concentrate fiercely on making their points flow lucidly from one to the other will very probably find that such a clarity of focus sponsors further telling ideas.

Finally, you should read your essays over critically – that is, in the position of the reader rather than you the writer. Look them over closely: have you really said what you thought you said? Any uncertainty in your reaction, and you should clarify your material. For something to be 'more or less there' or implicit in your writing won't do: it's got to be unambiguously out in the open. Look, too, for any 'flab' or emptiness, thus ensuring that the style is as taut as you can currently achieve. To 'polish' essays in this way is a pleasant experience, and one which can make a lot of difference to their final impact and quality. Moreover, to get into the habit of 'polishing' will prove highly profitable in an exam.

4. More on introductions and conclusions

As is clear from my previous remarks on this matter, I believe that knowing how **not** to write an introduction is most of the battle. But two positive things need to be said as well.

1. **If you think the title requires you to define the terms it cites, then do so at once as your first paragraph.**

There is no need to be apologetic or diffident about this: you should not 'pussyfoot'. By all means spend some careful time composing your definition and confirming that it will sustain your argument; once you're satisfied, write it out clearly and confidently and then move onto your first point.

2. **The art of writing crisp and stylish introductions takes a lot of time and trouble to acquire, but it's worth it.**

If you can guarantee that your first few sentences will have real impact and get the reader anxious to read on, you are already well on the way to writing a successful essay. As I've said, there are times when your best policy is to leap straight in with your first detailed point; but an introduction that serves as a clear platform and is also invigorating to read will give your work that touch of class that always impresses. And as a perhaps faintly scary index of that, a friend of mine who regularly marks Finals papers for London University tells me that

In at least 80% of cases, he can guess (accurately) what overall grade the script will get by the time he's read the first page.

Taking extra care over that first page will not **automatically** ensure that the rest of the essay is good, naturally; but such good habits and sharp performance tend to be self-sustaining.

So far, I've said rather less about conclusions than introductions. The chief reason is that in several respects exactly the same points apply: if you side-step the various traps and flaws that characterize poor introductions, the likelihood is that you'll also avoid ending your essay in a lame or vacuous way. However, some separate guidelines may be valuable.

1. **Before closing your essay, always look back at your introduction and then make sure that you say something fresh and/or express yourself in a different way.**

I don't of course mean you should contradict yourself! What I'm concerned about is ensuring that your introduction and conclusion are not mere duplicates, which tarnishes a good number of essays that I read. You want to achieve unity, but that does not mean the essay should be circular.

2. **Short conclusions are usually preferable to long ones.**

Your ideal is a snappy tying-together of the main points and discussion you've recorded, leaving the reader impressed by your clarity and authority and perhaps interested in 'talking back'.

3. **If possible, conclude your argument in a way that makes explicit insights that have been implicit along the way.**

The conclusion is often the best place to register your overall reaction to the proposition at issue – better, in most cases, than at the start, when you haven't yet 'earned' your right to pass a considered judgment.

4. **As with introductions, try to avoid self-evident phrases.**

I've touched on these elsewhere, and will not weary you with a lengthy repetition. But if you observe guideline 2, it's then worth remembering that it will usually be obvious to the reader that you've reached your conclusion, because the writing stops a few lines down! You therefore don't even need the phrase **In conclusion**, let alone anything more bloated.

5. Quotation and reference

Note: if in doubt about how to punctuate quotation, please consult Chapter 22, Part Five, which covers that skill in full.

Layout and stylistic conventions
There are six chief procedures you need to follow.

1. The noun is **quotation**, not **quote**, which is a verb. The use of **quote** as a noun is becoming ever more widespread among educated people and media pundits. But don't do it: it's illiterate. And if you think that to worry about such minor confusion is tiresomely pedantic (and I can see your point), let me just say this: virtually every academic examiner I've met, dealt with or read finds the use of **quote** as a noun intensely annoying. Silly of them/me, very possibly; but if as a student you're subject to such pedantic whims, it's best to play safe!

2. There is no need to include the absurd phrase **and I quote**. All that is required is a colon after your introduction or 'set up', and to open quotation marks. (Don't forget to close them, either!)

3. Quotations shorter than two full lines may be incorporated into ordinary text. However, if quoting say 1½ lines of **verse**, you

should signify with an oblique stroke (/) where the break occurs in the original's lines.

4. Longer quotations should be isolated – i.e. treated as if they were self-contained paragraphs. In addition, they should be *block-indented* to add visual emphasis and thus impact.

5. If these longer quotations are in **verse**, always write them out in their original form – that is, in blocked lines. The oblique stroke usage identified in 3 is not appropriate in 'isolated' quotation.

6. When dealing with eponymous works [where the title of book is the same as the protagonist's name], be sure to distinguish between book and character. Underlining the former is probably the best way; thus **Macbeth** would refer to the man, <u>**Macbeth**</u> to the play.

You can use quotation marks instead – 'Macbeth' is perfectly in order. But since one tends to use quotation marks quite a lot in many academic essays, to underline may strike many as the clearer, better option.

Figure 21. 'Be sure to distinguish between book and character'.

Now for two examples that illustrate all those points. Both happen to be taken from a student assignment on *Macbeth*, but the principles they enact apply to all academic usage, not just the writing of literary essays. Numbers in brackets refer to the convention at issue in the above list.

Passage A

> Macbeth [6] never enjoys a single moment of ease throughout the play. Whether considering the murder of Duncan, hallucinating just after he has 'done the deed' [3] or bitterly reflecting on his sterile and joyless life as king, a quotation [1] from Act III, 'O, full of scorpions is my mind, dear wife!' [3] could be said to define his mental state at <u>all</u> times.

The two quotations are short enough to fit into the essayist's text while retaining their necessary punch. But in this second extract the 'isolated', block-indented quotation becomes necessary.

Passage B

> . . . The next exchange between Macbeth [6] and his wife is crucial: among other things it shows us that killing Duncan was <u>his</u> idea originally, not hers. Here he argues that such an act would be sub-human: [2]
>
> > 'Prithee, peace!
> > I dare do all that may become a man;
> > Who dares do more is none.' [4, 5]
>
> To which she retorts: [2]
>
> > 'What beast was 't then
> > That made you break this enterprise to me?
> > When you durst do it, then you were a man . . .' [4, 5]
>
> She witheringly makes him responsible for the plan, but also tempts him lovingly. The last line of that quotation [1] is full of implicit admiration, even sexual invitation – a hint that is fully developed in her next remarks designed to arouse him further: 'to be more than what you were, you would / Be so much more the man.' [3]

That is elegantly set out and easy to follow. Isolating the two longer quotations ensures their impact – partly because the reader's ease has been considered. The third, shorter quotation can fit into the ordinary text, as before, though notice the oblique stroke this time.

Following those six procedures will sharpen and clarify your presentation, which should usually have a beneficial knock-on effect on your

overall organization and style. If and when you come to write articles
for journals and so on, you may find that certain publications have a set
'house style' that may differ at times from what I've outlined; however,
I'd be very surprised if such variance is anything other than slight.

So much for the mechanics of **how** to quote; now let's look at **when**
to quote, and **why**.

Quotation: choice and timing

'Help! I've been writing this essay for half an hour, and I still haven't
quoted anything. I'd better bung one down, pronto!'

That kind of attitude or procedure characterizes an alarming number
of even good essays. As I write these words, I've just finished marking
nearly 200 A Level English Literature scripts. They ranged, as such
papers do, from awful to excitingly impressive, but only the very
best displayed an authoritative use of quotation. This is not in fact
surprising: the ability to quote with telling assurance and apposite
timing is a highly sophisticated skill, one which usually takes quite a
time to acquire. As with many other writing skills, knowing what not
to do is a great help, so let's start with a few **don'ts**.

1. **Don't quote for the sake of it**. Any quotation that does not
   illuminate a point just made or one about to be made is useless.
   Especially avoid the 'bung it down' approach our panicking student
   above seems to think advisable! Furthermore . . .

2. **. . . Don't quote in a vacuum.** Quotations hardly ever speak for
   themselves, and it is a great mistake to think that a quotation will
   automatically make your point without any further contribution
   from you. You need to show **why** you've chosen it and **how** it
   illustrates your argument.

3. **Don't quote too often.** Too many essays resemble a Jumbo Quota-
   tion-Sandwich whose 'filling' consists of increasingly indigestible
   extracts from other sources. It is very irritating to have an argument
   constantly interrupted (or indeed suspended) in such a way: be
   selective.

4. **Don't quote at great length** – or keep occasions when you do so to a
   minimum. Quoting a substantial extract can be justified sometimes,
   when the material is crucial to an argument or establishes several
   issues that are to be explored. But I find that most students who
   quote at length do not use such extracts well, providing only a
   cursory gloss before moving on. Such practice is an elaborate
   extension of the flaw cited in 1, similarly reducing quotation to
   a feat of memory, or simple copying!

5. **Don't make your quotations mere *duplicates* of the points they accompany.** It's important that quotation and point match, as observed in 1 and 2; but this kind of thing is feeble:

> . . . Lady Macbeth cannot bring herself to kill Duncan, because he looks like her father:
> > 'Had he not resembled
> > My father as he slept, I had done 't.'

The quotation adds nothing to the point already made, other than proving that the writer has read the play. Good quotation always does some real **work**.

Similarly or conversely:

6. **Don't just *paraphrase* quotations that you use.** Look at this extract from a sixth-form essay on Keats's *Ode To Autumn*:

> . . . The second stanza's last two lines are notably successful:
> > 'Or by a cider-press, with patient look,
> > Thou watchest the last oozings hours by hours.'

> Here Keats imagines Autumn as a spectator serenely observing the gradual fermentation of the cider, not concerned by the slowness of the process.

These comments are attractively written, but they don't **say** anything. Having cited the lines as 'notably successful', the writer tells us merely what they mean, not how and why they work. We might have expected a gloss on 'hours by hours', where the unusual use of the plural emphasizes the drowsy, long-drawn-out process, or some mention of the profusion of 's' sounds, which have a similar effect. As it stands, however, we have no idea why the writer thinks these lines successful or indeed why they were quoted.

Sometimes, admittedly, you will feel it is necessary to 'explain' the lines you quote, because they are difficult or ambiguous; if you're sure this applies, go ahead – it is sensible and helpful (see page 183ff). But make sure you analyse or comment upon such quotations as well as clarifying their meaning.

As may be evident, most of those **don'ts** include or imply more positive principles, which can now be listed.

1. Always ensure that your quotation matches your point.
2. Use your quotations: comment on them, show why you've chosen them.
3. Quotations are fine servants but bad masters: they should assist your essay, not run it! Stay in charge, so that it's your thinking and writing that chiefly register.

4. Your quotation must be grammatically complete in its own right and it must also fit in grammatically with whatever point of yours it accompanies.

5. Before writing out a quotation, ask yourself if it's really necessary. Is it going to do any useful work? If in doubt, leave it out. It only takes a few such 'dubious' quotations to blur or dilute your argument, or even to convince the reader that you're emptily showing off your textual knowledge to no other purpose.

In addition, or as a summary:

6. **Think** before you quote, while you quote, and after you've quoted. If you stay alert in this way, the chances are excellent that your quotation will be apt and fully integrated into your argument.

Bearing those six points in mind will make your use of quotation illuminating and pertinent. This will apply to 'ordinary' essays – those you compose in your own time – but also the 'extraordinary' ones written under pressure in exams, about which I offer this final **don't**:

> **Don't imagine there is any special or 'secret' formula concerning quotation in an examination. Success depends on good knowledge and alert thinking, not on 'tricks' or any model craftily designed beforehand. You should rid your thinking of any dependence on these false props, and treat with extreme caution any teacher who advocates them**.

Quotation: when to explain

Usually it is a waste of time and space to cite a quotation if all you then do with it is paraphrase its meaning. This is known in some circles as 'telling the story', and those who do it are nearly always guilty of underestimating the reader's intelligence and knowledge.

There are occasions, however, when meaning is ambiguous, difficult or obscure. Such instances are worth brief elucidation on your part; sometimes, as in the example that follows, the way a particular word or phrase is interpreted can be crucial.

Please read the following poem by Philip Larkin, published in 1960. It is a deceptively provocative poem – and the adverb 'deceptively' is pivotal. For the last line became instantly famous and is still much-quoted – often for absolutely the wrong reasons. I have been astonished at how many readers (including more than a few professional critics) take that line at face value. They assume that Larkin is dismissing books as enragingly useless, that in middle age he has sourly come to regard literature as a futile con-trick.

A Study Of Reading Habits
When getting my nose in a book
Cured most things short of school,
It was worth ruining my eyes
To know I could still keep cool,
5   And deal out the old right hook
To dirty dogs twice my size.

Later, with inch-thick specs,
Evil was just my lark:
Me and my cloak and fangs
10   Had ripping times in the dark.
The women I clubbed with sex!
I broke them up like meringues.

Don't read much now: the dude
Who lets the girl down before
15   The hero arrives, the chap
Who's yellow and keeps the store,
Seem far too familiar. Get stewed:
Books are a load of crap.

Figure 22. 'Get stewed'.

The truth is very different – and it hinges on a phrase in the penultimate line, **Get stewed**. Students I've taught recently, and a number of young teaching colleagues, have imagined the phrase to mean 'get stuffed'/'get out of it'/'sod off' or the like. This led them, not unreasonably, to interpret that last line in the way I've just defined.

In fact, **get stewed** means 'get drunk': in the early 1960s **stewed** enjoyed the same popular currency as do 'pissed', 'smashed' or 'legless' nowadays. Once that is grasped, the meaning of the last line is transformed – as is the poem's overall thrust. 'Get stewed: / Books are a load of crap' does not dismiss literature as unrealistic: with a mixture of pain and wry humour Larkin suggests that adult novels are all too realistic, serving only to remind him of his own inadequacies. Gone are the days when he could 'escape' from the miseries of school via Clint Eastwood-like fantasies (lines 1 to 6) or bury his 'four-eyed git' public image by indulging Gothic sexual fantasies (lines 7 to 12). Literature can no longer compensate for reality (lines 13 to 17): if you want to escape, take to the bottle, not a book.

Such a conclusion may be sadly prosaic and anti-Romantic: what it is **not** is anti-literature. On the contrary, it pays tribute to literature's uncomfortable power – a power that he would now rather avoid.

Get stewed is an excellent example of when you need to explain a line or phrase that you quote. To do so not only clarifies a particular point: it can, as in this instance, illuminate the entire piece, scene, episode or argument. Don't forget, however, to accompany such illumination with analysis of its effect and overall significance. The two tasks are not alternatives but twin essentials.

Citing references

So far my examples have been literary ones. In a way this is only to be expected: I teach English, and most of the work I encounter has a literary focus, where the ability to quote aptly from a text and make significant deductions thereby is an important skill. On the other hand, I am of course aware that the writing of history or economics essays brings other things into play. In such work you will probably make less use of quotation as such: it will be more a question of citing sources, theories and known arguments.

In fact, most of the principles and guidelines I've outlined are relevant to all subjects, especially those on pages 181-2. It makes no real difference whether you're citing an actual quotation, acknowledging a source or referring to a particular theory: you need to be sure that

1. It's necessary and relevant.
2. It does some real work, moving your essay forward.
3. It's accurate and correctly set out.
4. You're not doing it too often.
5. It is not merely a time-wasting paraphrase.

This last point is especially important when referring to a well-known source or argument, and needs a paragraph of its own.

You must of course acknowledge major sources if mobilizing them in your own argument. But it is invariably a mistake to reproduce them in detail if they're seminal or even just renowned. Let us take two examples – Elton's work on the Tudors and Friedman's monetarist theories. Any competent historian will be fully conversant with the former, and any competent economist with the latter. You may therefore take such readers' knowledge for granted, and concentrate on showing how **your** knowledge of this work influences your own thinking. Reference to such sources can and should be crisp and brief: if you know what you're talking about, there is no need to prove it with a lot of laborious 'story telling', just as there's never any need in a literary essay to recite the plot.

The mechanics of citing references are fairly straightforward – more so than the rather intricate conventions affecting quotation. A reference, whether it be the name of a writer, a well-known theory or the title of a book, can be worked into your text within brackets, or as a footnote. However:

> **Be careful about footnotes. While they are a useful device and suggest scholarly devotion, too many of them can clutter up an essay and start to irritate the reader.**

If your essay is going to contain a lot of references – and you should be aware of this before you start writing – it is probably better to use a numbering system and collate all of them at the end of the essay. Alternatively, if your use of others' work is more general, functioning as overall influence rather than the detailed citing of specific points, you can just provide an extensive Bibliography of sources used.

As a summarizing piece of advice, remember that

> **It's *your* essay. The ability to provide illuminating references and apposite quotation is a valuable part of any good writer's armoury, but such things should always be ancillary to your work and thinking. To rely too frequently on others will seriously damage your impact, no matter how superficially learned it may make you seem.**

6. The strengths and limitations of 'argument'

In this brief closing section, all I want to do is emphasize the wisdom of Thomas Fuller's remark that forms an epigraph to this chapter: your essays are unlikely to cause a major change of mind in someone with firmly established views of his or her own. That is not to say you will never do so: I have found that one of the delights of being a teacher is that I constantly learn from my students; sometimes I have significantly changed my view or interpretation of a work in the light of their insights. But on the whole I would advise you to look on your essays as a pleasurable discourse rather than a battle for supremacy, as these two admirable remarks propose:

> **The aim of argument, or of discussion, should not be victory, but progress.**   *Joseph Joubert*

> **True disputants are like true sportsmen; their whole delight is in the pursuit.**   *Alexander Pope*

If you adopt such an attitude, you will find essays more fun to write; moreover, it will stop you from using embattled or aggressive language, which can often mar an otherwise impressive case. Consider this paragraph from an essay written by a sixteen-year-old girl:

> **To a much greater extent than most of us realize and any of us wish to believe, we have become 'programmed' like computing machines to handle incoming data according to prescribed instructions. Anyone who denies this is either naive or wilfully stupid; there is nothing more dangerous than the illusion of freedom, as Orwell demonstrated with such terrifying wisdom in *1984*.**

She is clearly intelligent, and her confident tackling of a huge subject inspires admiration. But her hectoring tone is a serious flaw. Her technique of labelling anyone who does not agree with her is a decrepitly stale rhetorical trick: the idea is that readers will not want to think themselves stupid, so will meekly go along with the proposed case. In all likelihood, however, they will instead resent this approach and dissociate themselves from the argument. In addition, she offers no 'proof': she just asserts. The use of Orwell is an arresting analogy, but is less effective than intended because no attempt is made to demonstrate that Orwell's vision was accurate.

The writer's youth makes it easy to forgive her tonal misjudgments, but they offer an important warning. If you really want to persuade people of your case, courtesy and dignity are crucial ingredients; readers will follow you much more readily if you treat them as likely friends rather than probable enemies. Don't make any concessions in your material and the points you believe in, naturally; but you can stay true to yourself without being aggressive.

Always argue as if you mean it, and by all means look to persuade people to your way of thinking – it is a good ambition to have even if it is not always realized. Perhaps your ideal response from your reader should be something on the lines of 'Yes, but . . .', signifying a committed interest in what you've said but a certain degree of respectful departure from it and the desire to discuss things further with you. That is a great compliment that should satisfy most writers. What you cannot afford is a reaction on the lines of 'No, and . . .'! You may feel you're in the right, you may even **be** in the right, but all you will have achieved is to convince the reader that you match perfectly this definition:

Positive, adj. Mistaken at the top of one's voice.

Ambrose Bierce

We now move on to consider briefly the essay's 'cousins' – the article, the review and the report.

ARTICLES **12**

This is a short chapter, because most of what you need to consider when writing an article has already been covered under **Essays**. An article **is** an essay, obviously enough; however, the circumstances in which it is written and a number of technical matters make it worth investigating as a genre in its own right.

Unlike the majority of essays, articles are written for publication. They are also different from essays in that the dimension of compulsion is absent. People who write articles do so because they want to, because they're being paid for it, or both. Naturally, once you've accepted a commission or decided that you want to write a piece for submission somewhere, the pressure to get on with it is considerable; nevertheless, the original choice is yours, not imposed on you by teachers or superiors. And the choice of subject and title is also yours, which should mean that some of the agony that attends essay writing – do I know what I'm talking about yet? Do I know what I want to say? – is also absent. If it makes little sense to begin an essay before you're sufficiently knowledgeable to deal with the subject at issue, it makes no sense at all to contemplate being published on something you're not yet competent on, and I can't imagine any would-be serious writer being that foolish.

So far, so very cheering: you want to write your article because the subject matters to you, you know plenty about it, and you want to share your views with a lot of readers. These are major positives, and together with the technical strengths that I hope the previous chapter has vouchsafed, they should ensure that you do an essentially sound and vigorous job. But there are one or two constraints or special considerations when engaged on an article that do not always apply to ordinary essays.

12.1 WORD LIMITS

I have yet to meet or hear of an editor for whom space is not a permanent problem. Any magazine that survives for even a few weeks will normally have more material 'in house' than it can currently use, and the stuff it does use is always under threat of being cut, sometimes savagely. You need to bear this in mind from the start, and act on it:

A. **If the article has been commissioned, or if you're offering it to an editor you already know, establish the word limit before you do anything else.**
B. **If you're planning to send it to an editor you don't know, try to determine the apparent standard length of the pieces published and use that as your target.**

And stick to it! You often risk being cut even if you obey the word limit originally proposed; if you exceed it, the risk is very high – and you might find that something very important to your argument disappears in the carnage.

Word limits can be maddening, but on the whole they work to the writer's advantage. The discipline they impose strengthens one's work: every sentence, every word even, has to be thought about with ruthless clarity: is it really necessary? Can it be said more economically? There are times, it's true, when to keep your piece within bounds an idea or an illustration that you like very much has to go, and that can be painful. More often, however, such strict attention will render your writing more muscular and easier to read – and that should increase your chances of being published.

12.2 HOUSE STYLE

There are two separate things you need to consider here.

A. **The publication's mechanical conventions.**

Magazines and journals tend to have their own preferences as to layout, punctuation conventions, abbreviations and so on. Most of them provide their writers, actual or hopeful, with a sheet explaining all these things, and although getting to know them can be an intricate business, it is essentially trouble-free.

B. **The tone and register of its written style.**

This is a subtler matter – and also more fundamental. Any successful periodical quickly develops a 'voice' – and that voice is intimately connected with the kind of reader it imagines it is speaking to and for. It is vital that you pay at least some attention to this. I've argued throughout that you should allow **your** voice to ring clearly through all your writing, and I'm not about to go back on that. But if writing for an established publication that has a clear sense of its market and readership, you must be sure that your style is reasonably appropriate. If you can't achieve this, or feel that the change is injurious to all that is most natural and effective in your writing, it's very likely that this particular publication is not for you, and that you need to seek out one with which you're more in tune.

In addition, take careful note of the favoured length of its sentences and paragraphs, and work to that approximate model. Also, work out how often sub-headings appear. You don't usually have to provide the latter – the editorial staff will do it for you. But to be aware of the frequency of such 'trailers' will help you to organize your material accordingly.

12.3 EDITING

It is always important to read your work through carefully, but the need to do so is intense when you've completed an article. It goes without saying that you must check everything fiercely – facts and mechanical accuracy – and make sure that your work is 'clean'. In addition, you now need to do a careful word count. I can virtually guarantee that it will not match the word limit you're been given, especially if you're a comparative newcomer! If you've gone over the limit (the more common flaw), you'll need to delete certain words or phrases – perhaps whole sections if you're wildly out; if you've fallen short, you can consider inserting ideas that you originally thought must be left out.*

Your edit will also be the time when you make final decisions about the number and length of your paragraphs, the quality and cohesion of your introduction and conclusion, and (if applicable) where you'd ideally like photographs or illustrations to be placed. In short, this is when you shape your work to perfection, paying equal attention to what you most want to achieve and the likely desires of editor and readers.

There is a particular kind of article that calls into play one or two additional considerations, so before I move on to the writing of Reports, I take a look at **Reviews.**

---

* If you can't think of anything else to say, on no account fill out your piece for the sake of it; that is an unhappily certain recipe for the worst kind of **flab.** (See Chapter 7.)

REVIEWS   **13**

A review is an essay that draws attention to and passes comment on a topical matter – the publication of a book, the release of a record, the opening of a stage play or film, and so on. Reviews are usually quite short, mainly because a sizable number of things need reviewing each week, and space is at a premium in all journals and newspapers. So even if you're given a generous word allowance for a review, you need to be as concise as possible.*

Any review must do these three things:

1. **Tell the reader broadly what the book/play/film/etc. is about and what it's like.**
2. **Give a clear sense of what the reviewer thinks of it.**
3. **Say whether it's worth spending money on.**

That seems straightforward enough, but a lot of reviews fail to do one or more of these things.

The worst kind of review is that which indulges a frenzy of self-advertisement on the reviewer's part, offering little or no information about what he or she is allegedly assessing. Hardly less bad, albeit more humble, is the reviewer who is either too scared to venture a clear opinion or not interested enough in the work to care about doing so. And there is an additional complication that can threaten the quality and integrity of even well-written reviews.

Quite simply, reviewing is an **industry**, and an ever-growing one. A single, non-specialist organ like *The Sunday Times* carries thirty pages of reviews every week, on everything from books to restaurants, cars to compact discs, holidays to TV programmes. The chances of any reader experiencing all these things is nil; consequently, the review can easily become a substitute for experience rather than an inducement to it. That is a large issue, and this book is not the place to explore it fully. What I must say, however, is that because reviewing is an industry, it is not

* If being concise causes you problems [it does for all of us at times!], you may find it helpful to consult Chapter 16, Précis and Summary, where the skills involved in writing with maximum economy are analysed in detail.

Figure 23. 'Give a clear idea of what the reviewer thinks of it'.

ultimately concerned with aesthetic judgments or anything so pure: at root, it is part of a commercial process, and every reviewer forgets that at his or her peril.

That is why 3 above is so important. I am lucky enough to review records and books regularly for monthly periodicals. Every time I write a review, I try to have uppermost in my mind that I received the goods free but that readers will have to shell out a lot of money for them – £10 and upwards for most compact discs, double that or more for a hardback book. Those are not negligible sums even for well-off readers; a reviewer who blithely recommends this, that and the other as 'essential' not only does readers a disservice by ignoring the cost involved, but as a result is likely to be guilty of inflated, unreliable judgments.

One last injunction: when reviewing something, be sure that you've taken full account of it. To put it more baldly: listen to **all** the record, read the **entire** book, stay for the **whole** of the show. The reviewing world is fairly well-populated by people who don't do this; this is not only immoral in its abuse of privilege (sorry to be pompous) but, more mercenarily, carries the high risk of being exposed as a lazy fool or a charlatan – the last stigma that any writer wants.

REPORTS 14

As with **Articles,** most of what you need to consider when submitting a report is covered under **Essays,** but there are a few additional points to make, and others that need particular emphasis. The first of these has to do with **attitude**.

Writing an essay is a stressful business, especially early on in a student's career, and I've yet to meet anyone who has not at some time regarded the activity with fear and dislike. Yet a great many people come to enjoy it very much; as just noted, some become fortunate enough to derive pleasure **and** profit from something that once inspired only anxious hostility. But I've met few people who actively enjoy writing reports – even those who are good at it. Most approach the task as a matter of duty, of 'taking care of business'; they may be quietly satisfied with the result, but little or no sense of fun is present.

A cynic would argue that this makes crushingly obvious sense: reports are by definition boring, to writer and reader alike. And in our bureaucracy-infested times, it's not just cynics who believe that many reports are of dubious value if not downright unnecessary, and would be better left in their original rainforest form. Often, it is felt, reports are purely a matter of protocol: they are expected, traditional and must 'be seen to have been done', and even while we connive at such practice, we are all too aware of its underlying joyless futility.

As is I hope already evident, I am sympathetic to this point of view. I have to write and read many reports, and neither activity often fills me with energy or delight. But that is no help, either to you or to me:

> **The attitude and approach I've just outlined are very dangerous, almost a guarantee of indifferent performance**.

If you need to write a report, the only safe attitude is to believe that it **does** matter and that you need to devote your best energies to it. The sad fact that a lot of reports are poorly written should never become an excuse for doing likewise: instead, let it increase your determination to do an admirable job.

The first thing to remember is that **the chief purpose of any report** is to *inform*. The genre covers anything from a few lines to thousands of pages. It makes no difference whether it's a brief comment from a subject teacher on a school report or a massive document collating the findings of a major public enquiry: a report is useful only insofar as it is illuminating. Above all things, therefore, you need to **present your information as clearly and concisely as you can** – an 'umbrella' principle that governs all the individual points that follow shortly.

You may find that obvious advice by now: it has underscored this entire book. But a report is often a highly technical and intricate document, and one can easily get so absorbed in its sophisticated subject matter that ordinary writing skills and considerations suffer, making life very uncomfortable for readers. They will usually be prepared to make an effort, particularly if the report is long; that does not mean you should allow your writing to become irritating or laborious. Awkward, stuffy or opaque prose can always be avoided, and if you don't avoid it, your readers will quickly come to resent their task: that is not a good basis for persuading them or getting your points across effectively.

You will greatly increase your readers' appreciation – in both senses of that word – by paying close attention to these specific questions and guidelines.

1. For whom are you writing, and why?

It is always important to have a sense of your audience when writing, but it's especially so when fashioning a report. Are you writing for experts, for intelligent non-specialists, or beginners? You need to address that question – and its answer – in every sentence you write. Experienced and knowledgeable readers will quickly tire of having elementary points spelled out; conversely, a non-expert audience will soon become lost if you go too fast or fail to explain crucial things.

Of course, sometimes your audience will be a mixture, describing a perhaps considerable range of knowledge, intelligence, opinion and so on. This is always a very tricky matter, and I won't pretend I've got any easy or foolproof remedies. But I am convinced that you'll be far likelier to bring off even this delicate balance if you're firmly aware at all times of who's going to read what you've written.

2. Do you really need jargon? Will 'plain English' do?

As I've mentioned, many reports address technical or specialized matters, and it's inevitable that some of the language used will reflect that. You need to be careful, however. As 1 above advises, remember who your audience is, and be prepared to explain technical terms and other jargon. And if writing for experts, don't be any less watchful: frequent jargon is tiresome even for readers who fully understand it. As much of your prose as possible should be 'en clair': readers forced to 'decode' every second sentence will rapidly become tired and fed up. Conversely, however . . .

3. Try to avoid chattiness and trendiness

The admirable desire to keep jargon to a minimum can lead the writer astray in an opposite direction. Nobody wants you to be boring or pompous, but slang and conversational idiom are rarely appropriate to a report. Above all exclude trendy phrases: they are often as impenetrable to the 'outsider' as the severest jargon, and they tend to make the writer look like a show-off.

4. Be especially diligent about accuracy and pleasing layout

Obvious, maybe, yet many reports do not take enough trouble over such basic matters. Good reports are always dignified, and errors in spelling and presentation seriously undermine dignity. Arrange your sections, sub-sections and paragraphs with the reader's flow and convenience chiefly in mind. If a particular section is long and involved, it is both efficient and courteous to provide a short summary.

5. There is no need to be wooden or anonymous

I've already suggested avoiding both excessive jargon and over-familiarity, and that may seem to restrict your range a great deal. In fact, you have plenty of scope left. Like a successful essay or article, a good report will be a subtle blend of the soundly impersonal and the stimulatingly personal. Yes, it must be clear and logical, professional in its knowledge and dignified in its deployment of material; on the other hand, it needs a discernible voice, some kind of individuality. Nothing is more tedious than an extended piece of prose that appears to have been written by a robot – the reading equivalent of a telephone answering machine.

6. When you've completed the report, compile a single-sheet summary of your major points, and affix it to the front

This is good public relations – it eases the reader into the task, providing a clear and welcome map for what may be a very substantial journey (see page 212). You benefit also: composing the summary will automatically involve you in a close check of the material and its organization, and you may well find you can improve them. Incidentally, this practice is an intriguing variant of the idea discussed in **Essays** – the value of writing your introduction **last**.

Writing reports need not be drudgery. Within the limits outlined, stay natural as well as properly alert, and you should find that your prose is crisp, appropriate and quite pleasurable to write. If you still think report writing and fun are irreconcilable opposites, have a look at the page overleaf, adapted slightly from a piece that appeared a few years ago in *The New York Sunday Times*. It is both valuably instructive and genuinely entertaining – a combination that characterizes the ideal report.

Note: I have not attempted to offer advice on scientific or technological writing. That is partly because I believe good writing is good writing is good writing; it is often a mistake to imagine that a particular subject requires a wholly different style, approach and set of 'rules'. But it's also because I have done very little such writing myself, and advice on those specific considerations that are important would be presumptuous. There are several relevant books cited in my bibliography; here I would like especially to recommend *Effective Writing* by Christopher Turk and John Kirkman – and not just because we are all published by the same firm! It is comprehensive, practical and authoritative, and its elegant prose is a model embodiment of what it encourages.

REPORT WRITING
Some Rules of Grammar

1. Remember never to split an infinitive.
2. The passive voice should never be used.
3. Punctuate run-on sentences properly they are hard to read otherwise.
4. Don't use no double negatives.
5. Use the semi-colon properly, always use it where it is appropriate; and never where it isn't.
6. Reserve the apostrophe for it's proper use and omit it when its not needed.
7. Verbs has to agree with their subjects.
8. No sentence fragments.
9. Proofread carefully to see if you any words out.
10. Avoid commas, that are not necessary.
11. If you re-read your work, you will find on re-reading that a lot of repetition can be avoided by re-reading and editing.
12. A writer must not shift your point of view.
13. Give slang the elbow.
14. Conversely, it is incumbent upon us to avoid archaisms.
15. Don't overuse exclamation marks!!!!
16. Place pronouns as close as possible, especially in long sentences, as of 10 words or more, to their antecedents.
17. Hyphenate between sy-llables; avoid un-necessary hyphens.
18. Write all adverbial forms correct.
19. Writing carefully: dangling participles must be avoided.
20. Steer clear of incorrect forms of verbs that have snuck in the language.
21. Take the bull by the hand: always pick on the correct idiom and avoid mixed metaphors.
22. Avoid trendy locutions that sound flaky.
23. Never, ever use repetitive redundancies.
24. Everyone should be careful to use a singular pronoun with singular nouns in their writing.
25. If I've told you once, I've told you a thousand times, resist hyperbole.
26. Also, avoid awkward or affected alliteration.
27. Don't string together too many prepositional phrases unless you are walking through the valley of the shadow of death.
28. " " Avoid overuse of quotation marks. " " "
29. For Christ's sake don't offend your readers' sensibilities.
30. Last but not least, avoid clichés like the plague; seek viable alternatives.

[Adapted from *The New York Sunday Times*]

MINUTES

The taking and writing of minutes is required in a limited number of situations. It is, however, a very precise skill which can demand a different format and style of writing from normal reporting and where different criteria operate.

Companies and organizations tend to have their own preferred style of minuting meetings which should be observed. Most will follow a general pattern. A meeting will be announced by an agenda giving the date, time and venue of the meeting and listing the items to be dealt with. Usually these will formally include the reading and agreeing of the previous meeting's minutes, plus dealing with matters arising from these minutes prior to any new business. Items should be numbered for convenience, the final item being any other business which allows late items to be introduced. The chairman of the meeting will normally follow the order of the agenda for his own convenience, and this will help the minuting considerably.

The depth and detail required in the minutes will depend on the style of the company. Many will wish simply to minute final decisions taken or the major points raised; some situations demand that more detailed notes are kept to record the views of individuals present. On occasion, you could be asked to record a specific point which someone wishes to stress, and this should be given verbatim.

Tone and style are also a matter of taste and choice. The apparent cold formality of minutes can be extremely useful, in that it allows all emotion and personality to be excluded from the record. This means that the minutes will present a sober, impartial report of the meeting, which leaves out arguments and personal attacks which can occur over sensitive issues. While there are times when people insist on having their views recorded, the cooling-off period between meetings often resolves differences, and it can be with a sense of relief that participants re-read minutes that give no hint of a previous battle!

Obviously, specific dates and details need to be given, but many minutes will give the bare bones of a meeting. The actual style and vocabulary used is also formalized, and always written in the third person and in the passive voice – e.g.

The decision to re-appoint the caretaker was agreed unanimously.

The Chairman suggested that a vote be taken.

A further extended example follows on page 200, together with the complementary agenda.

To be able to write accurate minutes that satisfy all parties is a valuable skill. It is also an intriguing one: you may have noticed that several of the techniques and procedures I've just outlined depart radically from most of the advice given elsewhere. (That advice stands, naturally!) You may also have noticed that my own style in this chapter has been rather more formal and impersonal than usual. That was a deliberate attempt to match form and content, for minuting is one of the very few times when the writer seeks to be anonymous. Another such occasion, the writing of a precis or summary, is explored next.

Figure 24. 'The decision to reappoint the caretaker was agreed unanimously'.

Example A

Smith and Jenkins plc
46th meeting of the Finance and General Purposes Committee
to be held on Friday 15 May at 11.30 a.m. at Head Office.

Agenda
1. Apologies for absence.
2. Approval of the Minutes of 45th Meeting held on 19 February.
3. Matters Arising from the Minutes of 45th Meeting.
4. Budget forecast. Paper to be tabled.*
5. Departmental reports and requests for funding:
    (a) Accounts Dept.
    (b) Sales Dept.
    (c) Transport Dept.
    (d) Administration Dept.
6. Chairman's Report.
7. Annual staff outing.
8. Any other business.
9. Date for next meeting.

JS/PR
2.5.90

* This would be balance sheets of the current state of business and projected figures.

Example B

Extracts from the Minutes

1. Apologies were received from D. Brown and H. Chilcott.
2. The minutes of the 45th Meeting were agreed as a true record and signed by the Chairman.
3. [44.3.1] Salary Increases. R. Thomas (Transport) wished to know whether his Department's request for a 90% annual increase had yet been approved. The Financial Director, P. Jenkins, reported through the Chair that this oversight had been dealt with and that the increased figures were reflected in the paper to be tabled at Point 4 on the Agenda.
4. Budget Forecast.
   The Financial Director tabled a paper detailing the current state of business and giving outline forecasts for the coming year. He pointed out that in view of the drop in sales figures, it would not be possible to pay an increased dividend to shareholders in this quarter . . .

It is I hope unnecessary to go on. A complete example would illustrate little not already evident in this extract; nor would it add much to your entertainment, since reading minutes is hardly dangerously exciting! That of course is their strength and very function: important points and issues are logged in a neutral, low-key fashion.

PRÉCIS AND SUMMARY   **16**

In the 'bad old days', précis was a major and compulsory part of all O Level English Language examinations, accounting for about 20% of the overall mark. During the 1970s précis ceased to be a mandatory O Level exercise, a change upheld with the advent of GCSE. No English GCSE syllabus that I know of insists on précis competence; several do not even make any reference to it.

I think this is a shame. On the whole, those latterday changes in O Level were for the best, and GCSE has proved an exciting and imaginative replacement, allowing pupils and their teachers much greater scope than before. Far from slipping, standards have in my experience risen, and there is little doubt that English work at 16+ level – especially in syllabuses with a high proportion of coursework – is much more enjoyable now, both to teach and to learn. But the ability to précis is important; some would say it is **the** central language skill. For a start, it is a craft essential in all professions and businesses; indeed, anyone whose work includes dealing with documents at some time (and that accounts for most people) will need précis skills as a matter of course, or live to regret their absence.

Such vocational considerations, though important, are not in my view the most telling, however. The fundamental value of précis is that **it tests and exercises every aspect of linguistic competence**. To write an accomplished précis you need to have mastered eight major skills.

1. Good comprehension
To reduce a long document to its essentials requires a sound understanding of its every point and sentence. This is often more demanding [and therefore more reliable as a gauge] than any standard comprehension exercise.

2. Good prose composition
A précis should be crisp and easy to read. To achieve such at-a-glance clarity you need a muscular style, where everything is pertinent and works efficiently.

3. Discerning judgment

The prime task of précis writing is to distinguish what is really important from what is merely interesting or decorative. Regularly to achieve that requires sensitivity and discrimination.

4. An authoritative vocabulary

Although you must never invent **material** when fashioning a précis, it is entirely in order to recast ideas in your own words. In fact this is often essential, enabling you to cut down a structure of say 15 words to 5 or 6. To do that you need a vocabulary both broad and precise, supple and vigorous.

5. Literary feel

Contrary to certain prejudices, there is nothing 'airy-fairy' about good literature. Indeed, the best literature is always formidably exact; no matter how large or complex their goals, great writers are masters of nuance and precision. All good précis writers have something of such qualities; the chances are they acquired them through literary study.

6. A fierce eye for flab

Précis is a ruthless business! In most academic précis tasks, you are given an exact and mandatory word limit; in a very real sense, every word counts. And even if you are not constrained by such numerical targets, you still need to be vulture-like in your ability to tear at sentences and reduce them to their bare bones. This is closely

Figure 25. 'Vulture-like in your ability to . . .'.

analogous to the 'keyword' noting system I have described elsewhere, enabling you to 'gut' a chapter or an entire book,* and is a most valuable skill whatever your walk of life.

7. Sound logic
No matter how ruthlessly abridged, a précis has to make sense in its own right. This calls upon clarity of thinking and alertness to the distinct stages of an argument.

Finally, and obviously:

8. Accurate mechanical and grammatical English
This hardly requires a comment! Every task involving the use of English needs to be mechanically correct. None more so than précis, nevertheless: you can sabotage all the above strengths if you misspell, punctuate badly and perpetrate poor or clumsy grammar. Besides, if those things **do** disfigure your work, it's overwhelmingly probable that you will possess few if any of the seven skills just outlined, because each one depends on a sound knowledge of how language works and how it should be used.

Given that précis is a centrally important skill, how do you go about it successfully?

Well, précis is as much an art as a science, in that success depends more upon practice than upon the learning of fixed principles and guidelines, valuable though the latter can be. So let us start with an example.

> Gardeners are very frequently asked by persons interested in the cultivation of ornamental trees and shrubs to indicate to them some of the distinctive characters which mark off the common cypress from its near relative, the American *arbor-vitae*. These are two of the most widely grown ornamental conifers in the British Isles, and there is hardly a garden or park of any size in which one or other is not present.
> It is not an easy matter under ordinary circumstances to indicate to the layman the differences that exist between these two species.[†]

This passage is pleasantly written: few would accuse it of flabbiness or tedium. But while it is already tolerably concise, it can be further reduced. Let us look at it phrase by phrase.

1. **Gardeners are very frequently asked . . .** 'Very' does no real work and can safely be omitted. Perhaps, too, the simpler 'often' might replace 'frequently'.

---

* In *Brain Train* (1984) E & FN Spon, London, pp. 78–85.
† For the provision of this extract, I am indebted to Walter Shawcross, *English For Professional Examinations* (London, Pitman, 1947), p. 75 The analysis which follows is my own.

2. **By persons interested in the cultivation of ornamental trees and shrubs . . .** Fair enough – except that gardeners are unlikely to be asked anything by persons **not** thus interested! So if economy is the main criterion, the whole phrase can be jettisoned.

3. **To indicate to them some of the distinctive characters which mark off the common cypress from its near relative, the American *arbor-vitae* . . .** 'To them' has to go anyway, because we've omitted Phrase 2. Everything else that precedes 'the common cypress' can be rendered by the infinitive 'to distinguish between'; in addition the term 'its near relative' can go, as it's a mere supplementary descriptor.

The amended phrase thus reads: **To distinguish between the common cypress and the American *arbor-vitae*.**

4. **These are two of the most widely grown ornamental conifers in the British Isles . . .** The first two words can be omitted, provided a comma is placed after the preceding '*arbor-vitae*' instead of a full stop. In addition 'widely grown' can be replaced by the single word 'popular'.

5. **There is hardly a garden or park of any size in which one or other is not present . . .** 'Of any size' is weak; 'or other' is similarly inessential. And if you are feeling really ruthless – and I propose to be! – you could argue that this whole sentence is more or less implied by the word 'popular' that I've just suggested. So we can get rid of all of it.

6. **It is not an easy matter under ordinary circumstances to indicate to the layman the differences that exist between the two species.** Because Phrase 5 has disappeared completely, you can render this simply by 'This is not easy.'

The full précis thus reads:

> **Gardeners are often asked to distinguish between the common cypress and the American *arbor-vitae*, two of the most popular ornamental shrubs in the British Isles. This is not easy.**

An original total of 93 words has become 30. To be sure, some elegance, subtlety and sheer information have been sacrificed; but the new version is a clear expression of the salient 'bones' of the passage, and that is what any précis seeks to achieve.

That passage was quite well-written in the first place, which paradoxically made it relatively **easy** to précis. The sentences flowed clearly and built into an 'argument' that was comfortable to follow; to dismantle them in the interests of ruthless economy was therefore a straightforward business.

But sometimes you will have to précis material that is difficult to disentangle, where you'll have to work really hard just to understand what the main argument might be. Study this next passage carefully: I've used it before [p. 88], but on this occasion I want you just to work out what you think it means. Try to identify the key phrases that form the cornerstones of the argument:

> In the affluent society, capitalism comes into its own. The two main-springs of its dynamic – the escalation of commodity production and productive exploitation – join and permeate all dimensions of private and public existence. The available material and intellectual resources (the potential of liberation) have so much outgrown the established institutions that only the systematic increase in waste, destruction and management keeps the system going. The opposition which escapes suppression by the police, the courts, the representatives of the people, and the people themselves, finds expression in the diffused rebellion among the youth and the intelligentsia, and in the daily struggle of the persecuted minorities. The armed class struggle is waged outside: by the wretched of the earth who fight the affluent monster.

As I pointed out before, the writing here is jargonesque and top-heavily abstract, making it very difficult to identify those 'key phrases', because one is rarely sure what they actually mean! However, after (at least) two careful readings, you might come up with a list something like mine:

1. **affluent society**   An old 'buzz' term, now stale, that refers to any industrialized nation, the writer's prime focus.
2. **capitalism; commodity production** and **productive exploitation**   Capitalism is his main target; the other two phrases mean, roughly, 'the manufacture of goods' and 'the ruthless consumption of labour and resources'.
3. **all dimensions of public and private existence**   Stresses that capitalism dominates our lives in every way.
4. **available resources/have outgrown institutions**   To be candid, I still don't really know what this means: the entire sentence is an opaque mess. The suggestion seems to be that capitalism makes very poor use of the potential at its disposal, mainly because (as is implied later) its governments wish to retain power.
5. **increase in waste/destruction/management keeps system going** See my comments for Phrase 4! The idea (I think) is that the status quo preserves itself by purely negative methods, leading to . . .
6. **opposition/suppression/diffused rebellion**   . . . direct or indirect suppression. Opposition is either tyrannically put down by state machinery or ignored because it is ineffectual.
7. **struggle: wretched of the earth versus affluent monster**   The one vibrant moment in the whole piece, graphically reducing the conflict to its ultimate alternatives.

That took me a long time, both to think out and to type, which annoyed me. Nobody minds fruitful hard work: what irritated me here was that the original seems **designed** to confuse or intimidate. However, any précis writer will eventually encounter similarly poor originals, and at least that laborious 'gutting' gives us a clearer sense of what the passage is centrally about.

The next task is to 'translate' those key phrases into fluent and comprehensible English.

Phrases 1–3 present no real problem. I suggest:

> **Capitalism, the systematic consumer of all resources, dominates affluent society at every level**.

One could omit 'all' and 'at every level'; I've included them in an attempt to retain the categorical tone of the original.

Phrases 4, 5 and 6 are murderously difficult, as already noted! The core of their argument seems to be that capitalism is by turns inefficient, deliberately destructive and tyrannical, and that its primary concern is to keep the system going for the benefit of 'the haves'. So I suggest:

> **Fundamentally wasteful and tyrannical, it enlarges the range and intensity of its influence, destroying or emasculating most potential rebels**.

This takes considerable liberties, maybe; but I do not think it distorts the original's thrust or tone, and it covers all the main ideas.

Phrase 7 is blissfully easy in comparison. It makes sense to retain the powerful 'the wretched of the earth'; 'the affluent monster' is perhaps also worth preserving. However, I suggest replacing the full stop after 'rebels' with a comma, and continuing: . . . 'leaving only the wretched of the earth to fight it.'

I've sacrificed 'affluent monster' in the interests of a simple and punchy structure, but it can be reinstated if that is your taste.

The complete précis thus reads:

> **Capitalism, the systematic consumer of all resources, dominates affluent society at every level. Fundamentally wasteful and tyrannical, it enlarges the range and intensity of its influence, destroying or emasculating most potential rebels, leaving only the wretched of the earth to fight it.**

That is 42 words; the original had 120.

Incidentally, my earlier version [on page 88] was just 33 words. On that occasion I wanted to effect a working **paraphrase** that quickly revealed the original's overall meaning. Précis, as the word itself signals, requires more **precision** than paraphrase, so here I realized that one or two extra points or ideas had to be included. Remember: précis almost always involves paraphrase, but the two are not synonymous.

Now that we've thoroughly explored two very different examples, we can begin to identify some of the principles and guidelines that inform précis writing.

1. Read the original very carefully.

If it needs two readings, give it two. You should not even start to think in terms of reducing it until you're confident that you've grasped the main points and the thrust of the argument.

All that's obvious enough, perhaps, but it needs to be rigidly adhered to. Sloppy précis work invariably hinges on imperfect understanding, and that in turn derives from excessive initial haste.

2. Once you're ready to begin, isolate the key phrases.

It's up to you how you do this: you can use highlighter pens, a separate sheet of rough paper, any method you like. However, I do not recommend the savage crossing out of everything you think you can omit, for two reasons. First, it makes your 'text' look a right mess, which will not assist clear thinking. Second, you may delete a phrase that you subsequently recognize as essential, and reinstating it in your text will both waste time and be tricky anyway.

3. Start your first draft of continuous prose.

We'll assume that your 'skeleton' is sound – that you've identified and assembled the requisite 'bones'. But even a précis needs some flesh – ideally, enough to make it attractive in its own right. What else from the original should you keep or efficiently paraphrase?

Well, knowing what to omit is more than half the answer:

3a. Omit all examples, illustrations and quotations.

This is often less easy than it might sound, because such material may well be very interesting and thus memorable. However, it must be done: such things **illuminate** the argument rather than **define** it. They are **secondary**, and if you're reducing a piece to a third of its length [or even less], you can only afford to include **primary** material. That's one of the reasons why it's essential to have grasped the governing thrust of the argument before you pick up your pen.

3b. Be prepared to strike out all adjectives and adverbs.

I say 'Be prepared to strike out' rather than simply 'Strike out' because some 'qualifiers' will be necessary. If you look back at the two examples analysed above, you'll see that the adjectives and adverbs that remain really pull their weight: they are definitive, not decorative. However, if you rigorously 'interrogate' all such words as to their true value, you should find that most of them do not have a good enough case.

3c. Never repeat material, even if the original does

Be totally ruthless about this. The only concession you might make to an obsession with a particular point is to isolate it in a paragraph of its own, or make it into the précis's title.

4. In general, write in shortish, crisp sentences

Such a style may at times strike you as rigid and bare, and if you can construct longer sentences that are muscular and precise, go ahead.

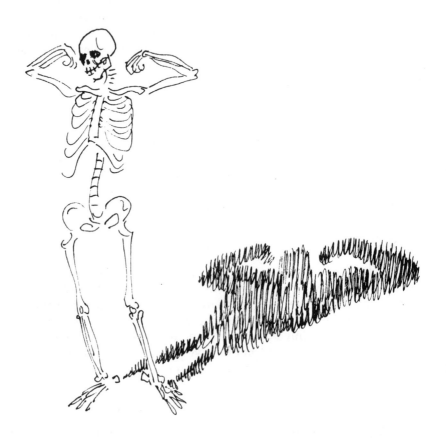

Figure 26. 'Skeleton of the original'.

But remember that you are producing a skeleton of the original, and skeletons **are** rigid and bare! Keeping your sentences short will also promote clarity, allowing you to keep a regular check on where your argument is going and whether each word is doing some real work.

5. Try to use your own words wherever possible

In truth, this is **not** always going to be possible: most passages will include some terminology or phrasing that must remain or simply cannot be improved upon. But look to paraphrase where you can: sometimes neat wording on your part will render an idea in six words that it took the original a dozen to achieve. Besides, if you stick slavishly to what you've 'gutted' from the original, it is likely that such a residue will be stilted, tending to creak rather than flow.

Now for three important **'don'ts'**:

6. **Never** invent material

Whatever you put down, especially when it's in your own words, make absolutely sure that your material exists in the original, or is at the very least strongly implied in it.

7. **Never** pass an opinion or judgment on the original

Your job is that of a disinterested scribe **and nothing else**. Your opinion is irrelevant: furthermore, expressing it will waste words that should be devoted to central points. Even if the argument you're dealing with enrages you, keep out of it!

8. **Never** bring the author's name into your text

Précis takes authorship for granted. If you really believe that who wrote the piece is of fundamental importance, then find a way to mention it in your title; do not allow it to clutter up your reduced version.

There are two views about what to do if the original is in the first person. Some authorities say that a précis should always be written in the third person, and that the original must be recast accordingly. Others argue that clarity is the chief criterion, not formalism, and that if the précis will read better in the first person, then use it. I incline to the latter view, but either is tenable. Practice, experience and 'feel' will guide you best: do what seems most comfortable, provided the resultant version is clear and apt.

Finally, three guidelines concerning shape and length.

9. Should a précis be paragraphed?

It depends on the length of the finished précis.

Anything under 100 words should be presented as a single paragraph, unless there is a major switch of topic or focus therein.

For reductions of 100–200 words, a single paragraph will often still be appropriate; but be prepared to divide into two or even three, according to the material's range and your sense of the reader's comfort.

Any final version that goes noticeably over 200 words should have at least two and probably three paragraphs; four to six if it climbs to 450 and above. If the précise is any good, it will make for fiercely concentrated reading: a single chunk of prose of 200+ words is distinctly 'user-unfriendly'.

10. If you're instructed to cite the number of words you've used, do so – and don't guess or lie about it!

People who set academic précis tasks do so very carefully. When they stipulate a word target or word limit, they are not sadistically adding a further difficulty: on the contrary, they're trying to help you, for they will already have worked out that the job can best be done in the figure they cite. So keep a regular check as you go on the number of words you've used – it will sharpen your performance.

If you're too lazy to do that, don't compound the folly by making a vague guess or, even worse, inventing a number that 'looks good'. The chances are it will look **terrible**: your assessor will not need to count the words to know that you're lying. One rapidly develops a 'feel' for a version that is too short or too long, and you are most unlikely to get away with any such chicanery!

10a. If given no such target or limit, what should you aim for?

The fraction most often mentioned in précis work is **one-third**. In the two examples explored above, I ended up reducing both originals to that length, and you'll shortly see that four of the six exercises I've included ask you to do the same.

Sometimes, however, you will be asked simply to reduce a document, a report, even an entire volume to the shortest effective summary possible. This may sound forbidding in the extreme, and I won't pretend it's a doddle! Nevertheless, to be required to precis say 5000 words on a single sheet of A4 has the advantage of **simplicity**, even if it isn't easy. Such a brief means that you can – indeed **must** – be utterly ruthless, and allows you to ignore everything apart from the most basic 'bones'. Winston Churchill used to insist that any document submitted for his perusal was prefaced by just such a single sheet outlining the

Figure 27. 'To precis 5000 words on a single sheet of A4 isn't easy'.

entire case, and this was an admirable discipline, both for him as reader and for the writer.

I've included two exercises of this type in the section that follows in a moment. In the meantime, and mainly for fun, consider the following 'brutally brief' summaries:

A. **The Plot of *Hamlet*.**
   1. Young prince hates his step-father and practically everything else.
   2. Thinks and worries a lot.
   3. Does nothing.
   4. Dies, along with virtually everyone else.

B. **The Causes of Germany's Defeat in World War II.**
   1. Signs non-aggression pact with Russia, 1939.
   2. Attacks Russia, 1941.
   3. Loses war, 1945.

C. **The Constitution of the United States.**
   1. America is the Land of the Free and the Home of the Brave.
   2. Provided you're white.

D. **The Old Testament.**
   1. In the beginning, God created the world.
   2. And spent most of history regretting it.

E. *Civil Defence Procedures in the Event of a Nuclear Attack.*
   1. Forget it.

Précis exercises

Six passages follow. Four require you to reduce them to about a third of their original length; two [B and D] ask for a much shorter summary. They are arranged in what I think is an ascending order of difficulty, but you may not agree! In any event, I hope you will find Passage A a gentle start; I'll also be very surprised if you don't find F the hardest, for it is **the** most difficult précis exercise I've ever encountered.

Take your time: remember that a rushed précis is invariably poor. Don't start noting or writing until you're sure you've grasped the main gist of the original. You will find my suggested versions at the back in Appendix: Answers to Exercises. And as a brief 'rehearsal', can you reduce this 28-word sentence to 5 words?

> If we look carefully into this matter, gentlemen, we cannot fail to see that the action of the Government has been justified in every particular by the event.*

Figure 28. 'Forget it'.

* Answer: 'The Government's action is justified.'

Passage A: Exercise 29
Reduce this extract of 72 words to 25.

His plan, which was clearly very ingenious, was to throw a weighted rope over a branch of a tree not twenty feet from his window, to jump out with the other end attached to his waist, and, trusting to the friction of the rope, to be lowered safely the sixty or so feet to the ground. This desperate plan he put into execution, and by means of it effected his escape.

Passage B: Exercise 30
(i) Summarize this argument in no more than 140 words
(ii) Summarize this argument in a single sentence of about 20 words.

As reported in last week's *Times Educational Supplement*, a movement against inter-school fixtures has been gathering momentum for some time in the school sports world and its proponents have mustered some convincing-looking arguments.

Now I am not against the individual sporting activities which have begun to make inroads against the traditional team games – squash, badminton, trampolining. There is a place for them. But they must always be subordinate to the major team games for moral and philosophical reasons to which the 'away with fixtures' lobby has paid insufficient attention.

I was not educated at a public school. Nevertheless I think some of their ideals are more than ever necessary now in our state schools.

Team sports inculcate discipline in an individual; first of all, of course, this is imposed by a teacher in charge but it gradually leads to self discipline, responding to the demands of the game, co-operating with team mates and never better exemplified than by a scrum half and a fly half working harmoniously together. It is accompanied by the discipline of the two or three hours training after school in cold and rain.

I can point to lads in my school, a mixed comprehensive, who would have been in the hands of the police now had it not been for the moral uplift they gained from playing in a team. And I am not just talking about a school side. We run three rugby sides from the first-year boys alone and that is in addition to other sports such as hockey and cross country.

The other value team sports impart is pride. In today's larger-scale schools, many on split sites, there's no feeling of being part of that corporate body: the school. A team gives the school a name in which all members of that body can take pride. To understand what I mean, the scoffers would have had to see the 300–400 pupils and parents who turned up to wave goodbye to our rugby party setting off for a month's tour of Australasia in 1981.

Moreover, the pride generates a response in the local community. Some of our home fixtures attract gates of over 1,000. More importantly shop owners and businessmen identify with the teams and respond generously when approached for help.

The effect on the staff is nothing but beneficial. At my school, the sport has never been regarded as an extension of the PE department. Up to 20 regularly help with school sides, some nowhere near the touchline but doing posters or helping with refreshments. The discipline of the field is carried over into other areas of school life and relationships between pupils and staff are qualitatively better.

To finish on the plane of argument from which too many of the opposing camp never rise: material cost. A rugby team needs one ball, price £20, and the players only a pair of boots apiece when they go along to the local club – and that matters when unemployment is rife. But when you start encouraging squash and golf it costs far more to continue after school than rugby. Is this really a 'broad curriculum provision'?*

Passage C: Exercise 31
Reduce this piece [800+ words] to about 275, and title it.

GATTING'S CAREER IS LAUNCHED INTO OBLIVION
Mike Selvey offers sympathy but no excuses for an old colleague as he sets off today to play in South Africa

This is by nature of an obituary: not for a person but for a Test career cut off in its prime. For in effect that is what will have happened once Mike Gatting plonks his bulk into a seat on a South African Airways plane today. In opting to tour South Africa this winter and next, he and his fellow rebels will rule themselves out of Test cricket until the spring of 1998. In June this year Gatting will be 33, no age for a quality batsman. But 41? That is a different matter. It is a pound to a pickle sandwich that the best Middlesex batsman since Compton will never again wear the lions and crown of England.

* Written by Ray French in 1985.

For one who has followed and admired his career since he rolled noisily into the Middlesex dressing room to begin his career in 1975, it is desperately sad. For there has been no one, in my experience, who has valued playing for his country more. He weeps at patriotic music and at great deeds by other British sportspeople. He is a very proud man.

He is also a pretty good player, a high-quality butcher who deals in biffs and bludgeons rather than the wand – although he can be surprisingly delicate at times. When the Test bio-rhythms were right he could be devastating, as for instance in Faisalabad when for little more than an hour he harnessed a blazing temper to score 79 breathtakingly brutal runs to reduce the Pakistan attack to ineptness after others had struggled.

It took him 52 goes to make a century for his country – from Karachi in 1978 to Bombay in 1984. The longer he went without that hundred, the harder mentally it was to achieve. When he finally carved the runs through extra cover that took him to three figures, it was like casting off chains. Even the English press contingent recognized it for what it was, and in an unprecedented gesture rose and applauded. The irony of that will not be lost on him today.

Rarely has he stinted since. But the past couple of years have been painful to watch, as the cheerful, beaming barrel of a lad has become a sad grey-beard, old and weary before his time. The pinnacle of his career had come when he marched his troops magnificently round Australia, cleaning up trophies wherever they went. His downfall was swift and systematic. Within the Australian triumph had been the first evidence of the breakdown of discipline in the English camp, and it was to cost them dear. Not only did the team performances become poor, but petulance was rife – led, it has to be said, by the captain.

Later, in Faisalabad, following that defiant innings and in one of the most notorious sporting incidents of the decade, he confronted the umpire Shakoor Rana when he should not have done so, as he knows and admits. Gatting's stand, and his virtual condoning through his own actions of the team's behaviour on the tour of New Zealand which followed, might justifiably have cost him his job, and had it done so he might, curiously, have not been doing what he is today. Instead they sacked him for the tabloid exposure of an alleged affair with a barmaid which the Test and County Cricket Board thought unbecoming in an England captain.

Since then Gatting has become increasingly disillusioned with the way Test cricket has been run. A broken thumb, loss of form and the death of his much-loved mother-in-law added to the troubles last summer; yet to the last he has maintained that he did not really want the South African trip, that England would always be more important. Even after he had accepted a touring contract he could have been talked out of it, and he approached the authorities to see how the land lay. All he wanted, it seems, was a little love. But none, apparently, was forthcoming, and so off he goes.

It would be good to think that in years to come it will be for his cricket that Gatting is remembered: for the dismissive power of his strokeplay; for the wide-brimmed old sunhat and his waltzing yards down the pitch to smack some hapless spinner over long-off, or winding up to crunch square a seamer who has strayed just a fraction off line. Sadly, it is more likely that he will be remembered as a rebel, a pawn, as someone who confessed to not knowing much about apartheid when he did not really mean that. He allowed himself to be dragged into another game beyond his scope.

Mike Gatting, who by the spring of next year will be a reported £200,000 richer, does not need and would certainly never seek or expect my sympathy. But that is exactly what he has today.*

Passage D: Exercise 32
Summarize this 600-word passage† in 100 words, and title it.

In our time it is broadly true that political writing is bad writing. Where it is not true, it will generally be found that the writer is some kind of rebel, expressing his private opinions and not a 'party line'. Orthodoxy, of whatever colour, seems to demand a lifeless, imitative style. The political dialects to be found in pamphlets, leading articles, manifestos, White Papers and the speeches of ministers do, of course, vary from party to party, but they are all alike in that one almost never finds in them a fresh, vivid, home-made turn of speech. When one watches some tired hack on the platform mechanically repeating the familiar phrases – **bestial atrocities, iron heel, bloodstained tyranny, free peoples of the world, stand shoulder to shoulder** – one often has a curious

---

* *The Guardian*, Thursday, January 18, 1990
† From George Orwell's 'Politics And The English Language', in *Inside the Whole* (1946)

feeling that one is not watching a live human being but some kind of dummy: a feeling which suddenly becomes stronger at moments when the light catches the speaker's spectacles and turns them into blank discs which seem to have no eyes behind them. And this is not altogether fanciful. A speaker who uses that kind of phraseology has gone some distance towards turning himself into a machine. The appropriate noises are coming out of his larynx, but his brain is not involved as it would be if he were choosing his words for himself. If the speech he is making is one that he is accustomed to make over and over again, he may almost be unconscious of what he is saying, as one is when one utters the responses in church. And this reduced state of consciousness, if not indispensable, is at any rate favourable to political conformity.

In our time, political speech and writing are largely the defence of the indefensible. Things like the continuance of British rule in India, the Russian purges and deportations, the dropping of the atom bombs on Japan, can indeed be defended, but only by arguments which are too brutal for most people to face, and which do not square with the professed aims of political parties. Thus political language has to consist largely of euphemism, distortion and sheer cloudy vagueness. Defenceless villages are bombarded from the air, the inhabitants driven out into the countryside, the cattle machine-gunned, the huts set on fire with incendiary bullets: this is called **pacification**. Millions of peasants are robbed of their farms and sent trudging along the roads with no more than they can carry: this is called **transfer of population** or **rectification of frontiers**. People are imprisoned for years without trial or shot in the back of the neck: this is called **elimination of unreliable elements**. Such phraseology is needed if one wants to name things without calling up mental pictures of them.

Inflated, abstract style is itself a kind of euphemism. A mass of Latin words falls upon the facts like soft snow, blurring the outlines and covering up all the details. The great enemy of clear language is insincerity. When there is a gap between one's real and one's declared aims, one turns as it were instinctively to long words and exhausted idioms, like a cuttlefish squirting out ink. In our age there is no such thing as 'keeping out of politics'. All issues are political issues, and politics itself is a mass of lies, evasions, folly, hatred and schizophrenia. When the general atmosphere is bad, language must suffer. I should expect to find that the German, Russian and Italian languages have all deteriorated in the last ten or fifteen years, as a result of dictatorship.

Passage E: Exercise 33
Reduce this 1100-word passage to 300 maximum, and title it.

There is an interesting ambiguity in the words ambition and ambitious. Sometimes when we praise a man we say he is very ambitious. Sometimes when we condemn him we say he is very ambitious. Is being ambitious a virtue or a vice? Probably it is both, because ambition contains the urge to be excellent in your field or discipline. It also contains the urge to get ahead of other people! Academics, and probably also clergy, are apt to be critical of politicians who are obviously ambitious. We are all ambitious, and we are all jealous of somebody else who has greater eminence. The politician happens to display his ambition more publicly than anybody else. Always, it comes back to accusing or excusing ourselves.

In our collective life, there will be more accusing and less excusing, for we cannot deny that however virtuous and unselfish we are as individuals, collectively we are and have been selfish. Collective egotism, particularly the collective arrogance of the races, is tremendous. Even that, however, is not pure evil, when one recalls what the white man's civilization has done for Africa, for example, which is now forgotten by the black African states. But why do we taint these creativities of our Western civilization with obvious arrogance that has made the white man odious on the black continent?

In our collective activities there is egotism in regard to race and perhaps to class, and certainly in regard to our own nation. Not only our enemies or detractors, but our friends and allies, are inclined to say that we think too highly of ourselves. Collectively we excuse and do not accuse ourselves, because from the day of our founding we have had the idea that we are a peculiarly virtuous nation. Other nations are selfish, but we are not. We stand for justice and freedom, not for self-interest. It is basically impossible for a nation to do so. Nations more than individuals think about their own interests and we ought to realize that if we have any virtue, it is not pure unselfishness but the virtue of a relative justice that finds a point of concurrence between our interests and those of the larger world.

This is the situation in human nature. Whether in the family or in the nation, there is always a mixture of good and evil, of self-regard and self-giving, of self-obsession and self-forgetfulness.

There are many answers to this problem. One is the answer of complacence which says, 'Well, that's the way we are. We are all selfish – what of that?' Montaigne, the great Renaissance philosopher said, 'I know my nature. I want to be just as I am . . . I don't strive with my nature.' Did he mean to say – 'I do not strive with my nature of self-regarding. I want to be just what I am'?

If you don't strive with it at all, your self-regard gets to be so consistent that it borders on neurosis. A more popular answer is to pretend that we are not self-regarding, that we really are interested in other people. Since we are always interested in others to some degree, we can make that point. Pretension is one of the evils of all good people. A brilliant English philosopher in a book that has not been widely enough read, *Principles of Power*, declared: 'If people deceive their fellowmen about their motives, they are doing it just because they first want to deceive themselves and use their fellowmen as allies of their self-deception.' This again is the curious business of accusing and excusing ourselves. We have a deep suspicion that we are more concerned with ourselves than we ought to be, therefore, we try to make ourselves a little better.

The third answer involves an ascetic position, which has a great tradition. We **are** self-regarding. Very well, we will do everything to **root** out this self from itself. We will be selfless, utterly selfless. The Protestant Reformation revolted against these disciplines of unselfish asceticism. Mystic asceticism is the self trying to get rid of itself. There is the well-known mystic saying, 'The self is like an onion with layer upon layer of self-regard that has to be peeled off.' But others have pointed out that it is impossible to get rid of the self by peeling off layers of self-regard, for the self, like the onion, only becomes more and more pungent.

Finally, there is a healthy, but not cynical, realism about our selfishness. Martin Luther said – and this is frequently misunderstood – 'Sin bravely, if you also have great faith.' This means, don't be so morbid about the fact that you're selfish; don't deny that you are self-regarding, but work in life and hope that by grace – this perhaps is the door to the real answer – you will be redeemed. **By grace.**

Today even Christians do not emphasize common grace enough.

We do not become unselfish by saying so. But, thank God, there are forces in life and history that draw us out of ourselves and make us truly ourselves. This is grace: a common grace, prevenient grace.* Grace is every impulse or power which operates against the pull of my self-regard, and makes me truly a self by helping me to forget myself. This is the basic answer of the Christian faith.

Certain other answers follow. One is that if this is a permanent situation, then there is a chance that you can change. It may be a change wrought by some destiny of history, of affection and responsibility, whether in family, in community, or in state. Perhaps we should draw the conclusion that our common life, particularly among the nations, is made tolerable by the knowledge of all this. We are sufferable only when somebody has the power and the courage to stand against us.

The history of Western democracy and the pageant of its development rest upon this insight about common grace. An English historian once said: 'Modern democracy rests upon the insight that what I think to be just is tainted by my own self-interest. I have just enough residual virtue to know that it is tainted, and that someone has to stand against me, and declare his different conviction.'

Passage F: Exercise 34
Reduce this 900-word passage to 250 maximum, and title it.

Resistance, therefore, being admitted in extraordinary emergencies, the question can only be among good reasoners, with regard to the degree of necessity which can justify resistance, and render it lawful or commendable. And here, I must confess, that I shall always incline to their side, who draw the bond of allegiance very close, and consider an infringement of it as the last refuge in desperate cases, when the public is in the highest danger from violence and tyranny. For, besides the mischiefs of a civil war, which commonly attends insurrection, it is certain that, where a disposition to rebellion appears among any people, it is one chief

---

* 'Prevenient grace' is a theological term, meaning: 'the grace of God which precedes repentence and conversion, predisposing the heart to see God, previously to any desire or emotion on the part of the recipient.'

Shorter Oxford Dictionary

cause of tyranny in their rulers, and forces them into many violent measures which they never would have embraced, had every one been inclined to submission and obedience. Thus, the **tyrannicide**, or assassination, approved by ancient maxims, instead of keeping tyrants and usurpers in awe, made them ten times more fierce and unrelenting; and is now justly, upon that account, abolished by the laws of nations, and universally condemned as a base and treacherous method of bringing to justice these disturbers of society.

Besides, we must consider, that as obedience is our duty in the common course of things, it ought chiefly to be inculcated; nor can any thing be more preposterous than an anxious care and solicitude in stating all cases in which resistance may be allowed. In like manner, though a philosopher reasonably acknowledges, in the course of an argument, that the rules of justice may be dispensed with in cases of urgent necessity; what should we think of a preacher or casuist, who should make it his chief study to find out such cases, and enforce them with all the vehemence of argument and eloquence? Would he not be better employed in inculcating the general doctrine, than in displaying the particular exceptions, which we are, perhaps, but too much inclined of ourselves to embrace and to extend?

There are, however, two reasons which may be pleaded in defence of that party among us who have, with so much industry, propagated the maxims of resistance; maxims which, it must be confessed, are, in general, so pernicious and so destructive of civil society. The **first** is, that their antagonists, carrying the doctrine of obedience to such an extravagant height, as not only never to mention the exceptions in extraordinary cases [which might, perhaps, be excusable], but even positively to exclude them; it became necessary to insist on these exceptions, and defend the rights of injured truth and liberty. The **second,** and, perhaps, better reason, is founded on the nature of the British constitution and form of government.

It is almost peculiar to our constitution to establish a first magistrate with such high preeminence and dignity that, though limited by the laws, he is, in a manner, so far as regards his own person, above the laws, and can neither be questioned nor punished for any injury or wrong which may be committed by him. His ministers alone, or those who act by his commission, are obnoxious* to justice; and while the prince is thus allured by the prospect of personal safety, to give the laws their free course,

---

* 'Obnoxious' here means 'answerable, liable to'.

an equal security is, in effect, obtained by the punishment of lesser offenders; and, at the same time, a civil war is avoided, which could be the infallible consequence, were an attack at every turn made directly upon the sovereign. But, though the constitution pays this salutary compliment to the prince, it can never be reasonably understood by that maxim to have determined its own destruction, or to have established a tame submission, where he protects his ministers, perseveres in injustice, and usurps the whole power of the commonwealth. This case, indeed, is never expressly put by the laws; because it is impossible for them, in their ordinary course, to provide a remedy for it, or establish any magistrate, with superior authority, to chastise the exorbitances of the prince. But as a right without a remedy would be an absurdity; the remedy, in this case, is the extraordinary one of resistance, when affairs come to that extremity, that the constitution can be defended by it alone. Resistance, therefore, must of course become more frequent in the British government, than in others which are simpler and consist of fewer parts and movements. Where the king is an absolute sovereign, he has little temptation to commit such enormous tyranny as may justly provoke rebellion. But where he is limited, his imprudent ambition, without any great vices, may run him into that perilous situation. This is frequently supposed to have been the case with Charles the First; and if we may now speak truth, after animosities are ceased, this was also the case with James the Second. These were harmless, if not, in their private character, good men; but mistaking the nature of our constitution, and engrossing the whole legislative power, it became necessary to oppose them with some vehemence; and even to deprive the latter formally of that authority, which he had used with such imprudence and indiscretion.*

Note: Passages E and F are taken from the General Paper that forms part of the Entrance Examination for the Colleges of Oxford University. E was set in 1987, F in 1985.

* From David Hume's 'Of Passive Obedience'

REPORTAGE   **17**

Reportage refers to day-by-day – even hour-by-hour – journalism. Some authorities insist that an account must be first-hand to qualify as genuine reportage; others deny that 'I was there' stipulation, arguing that the term can cover any news story based on eye-witness testimony. The purist in me makes me incline to the former view, largely because John Carey makes it the governing principle of his excellent *The Faber Book Of Reportage*. For the purposes of this brief chapter, however, I shall favour the looser or broader definition: a news story that incorporates eye-witness evidence (the writer's, others', or both), in-coming reports and background information.

Any newspaper story seeks to answer these six questions:

Who? What? When? Where? Why? How?

It could sensibly be argued that all writing seeks to satisfy the reader's curiosity in a roughly similar way; what makes reportage distinctive, even unusual, is the way this is done.

Please read the following story, taken from the Birmingham *Evening Mail* of December 13, 1986. Does it provide answers to those six questions? If not, can you think of any reason why [discounting the possibility that the journalist was incompetent!]? And what do you notice about its structure?

PLANE IN PLUNGE ON HOME
Special correspondent

A woman passenger was killed and the female pilot seriously injured when a light plane crashed on to the roof of a private house in a London suburb today.

The plane bounced off the roof and came to rest in a field near St John's Road, Walthamstow, East London, where 40 firemen battled to free the pilot from the cockpit.

The two women were the only occupants of the plane.

Rescuers battled for over an hour to release them from the cockpit while another team searched the damaged house for occupants.

The passenger was certified dead by a doctor at the scene. The pilot was taken to Whipps Cross hospital where her condition was said to be stable.

BOTH TRAPPED

A neighbour said the single-engined plane skimmed across roofs, and crashed into the wall of a factory.

She said: 'Both the women were trapped in there. One of them was dead – that was pretty obvious. The engine had come right through the plane into the pilot's seat.

'It was horrendous. We were probably 30 feet away so we're feeling a touch lucky. They were very unlucky – there is a large field on the other side of the house.'

Another witness, Mr Adrian Pietryga, 37, said: 'I heard a bang first of all. One of them was still alive, shouting: "Get me out, get me out!"'

The plane was a Tomahawk TA38 two-seater on a flight from a pilot training school at Panshanger, near Welwyn Garden City, Herts.

Commentary

Four questions are answered: the missing ones are **who?** and **why?**

We are not told the names of the two crash victims. There are two possible reasons: either the writer didn't yet know the names, or (as often happens in such cases) they were not being made public until relatives had been informed. We also don't know why the plane crashed – a fact that may not be known for months, when the Accident Research team has completed its investigations.

The story was clearly 'hot' news: the very fact that the 'Special Correspondent' is unnamed suggests that the paper received the report not from one of its staff but an outsider who happened to be on the scene shortly after the crash. On the whole, I would say that he or she did a fine job, crisply giving all the information available and letting the incident's hideous drama speak for itself. The missing pieces stimulate our curiosity rather than irritate us: we know that in such 'Late Extra' circumstances, new information is coming in all the time, and that a later edition would probably find the story amended somewhat.

That leads us neatly to the writing's structure. The paragraphs are short – forgivably so, given the high drama of the episode. However, much more significant than their length is their **order**.

Each paragraph is progressively less important than its predecessor.

This is radically different from nearly all other kinds of writing – especially the essay and its related genres. A typical newspaper story describes the following structure.

The first paragraph, in harness with the headline, seeks to encapsulate the whole story.

Very often, as in this example, that first paragraph will also be set in heavy type, to increase its impact.

The second paragraph looks to outline most if not all or the important details.

In a really major story*, that task may require two of three paragraphs of more or less equal 'status', but the principle remains.

Successive paragraphs will flesh out the above skeleton.

Such material need not of course be negligible: in our example, the revelation that a large field lies on the other side of the house the plane hit comes pretty late. But although that information is horribly poignant, it is still secondary to the primary facts: hence its position.

The belief that major information should be given first to ensure clarity and impact is one reason why newspaper reportage is structured in this way. The other concerns space and the 'hour-by-hour' nature of the business. Editorial staff need constantly to shift material around, to enlarge this piece and therefore cut that one, to find room for new information or entire new stories. The easiest way to effect this is to cut paragraphs – starting at the bottom and working upwards. If you study a selection of newspaper stories, I think you will find that the last paragraph is often of marginal value: usually, it can be sacrificed without doing any noticeable damage to the piece as a whole.

Longer works of reportage, or those that deal with something less immediate than our example, may not exhibit these structural characteristics in quite so obvious a way; there can even be times when

---

* See for example the account of the dropping of the first atomic bomb on Hiroshima in Chapter 8, Part Three, pages 128–9.

there seems to be little difference, so far as procedure and shape are concerned, between a substantial piece of reportage and an essay. The criteria are different, nevertheless: in reportage, no matter how lengthy, complex and detailed, facts and information are at an absolute premium, and the structure and organization will always reflect that.

That completes this 'horses for courses' section. It has not been exhaustive: I have not, for instance, offered specific advice on how to write instructions and technical explanations, although it is implicit in a good deal of the material and is addressed elsewhere in the book. And I haven't looked at all at descriptive or 'creative' writing – mainly because I do not believe you can instruct someone in creativity, which depends on imagination and essentially private compulsion. However, I hope that whatever your writing needs or desires may be, these chapters have made them easier to fulfil. I now move on to my most difficult task – that of making grammar enjoyable!

GRAMMAR PRIMER

PART FIVE

'Why care for grammar so long as we are good?'
Artemus Ward

Try this simple game.

Take a piece of paper and write **GRAMMAR** at the top. Then beneath it write down the first few things that come into your head as you consider that word.

I'd be surprised if your associations do not include something suggestive of boredom, hostility, impatience or dread, or possibly all four! For grammar has a very poor image at present. It conjures up pictures of dusty arid classrooms or of tedious struggles with the mechanics of a foreign language. Grammar seems to be the preserve of dull pedants who delight in taking you to task for a momentary slip or who write crusty letters to *The Daily Telegraph* and suchlike, bemoaning the illiteracy of contemporary life.

Now this is very sad – mainly because it is unnecessary. There is no reason why grammar need be any of these negative and irritating things. Grammar ought to be **fun** – not side-splittingly uproarious, perhaps, but quietly satisfying and enjoyable. And the first thing to remember is

> **Language – including and especially everyday usage – does not serve grammar: it is the other way round.**

Mere grammatical competence is less important than quality of response and imagination, creative energy and proper clarity. However, no one should imagine that grammar is the enemy of those things: it is their partner and help-meet. The true value and purpose of grammar has been well defined by S. H. Burton:

> 'Grammar is not a collection of hard-and-fast rules. It is more flexible (and, therefore, more useful) than that. Grammar gives an account of the way in which a language is used by those who use it well.'*

A good working knowledge of grammar will unquestionably help you to become a better writer and speaker. The more you are aware of how

---

* *Mastering English Language* (London: Macmillan, 1982) p. 128.

language works, the better placed you will be to take full advantage of its resources.

I do not claim to offer an exhaustive guide to every conceivable grammatical point; what follows, however, does cover most things that students and writers will need to know in the course of their normal work. If you require a comprehensive treatment, there is still nothing finer than Fowler's *Modern English Usage*, and I list other recommended works in the bibliography.

AN OUTLINE MENU

It is highly unlikely that all readers of this section will have identical needs. Some may be comfortable about the various parts of speech but experience difficulty with any kind of syntactical analysis; some may be entirely sound apart from the odd confusion or 'blind spot'; some may be beginners. I've divided the material accordingly, allowing you to skip the bits you don't need, or to go first to the section where you need most help.

1. **Parts of speech**   The jobs words do.

2. **Inflections**   Changes in the form of words according to the job they are doing.

3. **Syntax**   How words operate in groups, as parts of sentences.

4. **Parts of Speech (Advanced)**   A further, more sophisticated look at the jobs words do.

5. **Punctuation: Speech and Quotation**

6. **Spelling and Confusibles**   A list of words that cause trouble, because of their spelling, their meaning, or both.

Regular practice exercises are included.

18.1 PARTS OF SPEECH

Introduction

It should be stressed at once that

> **A Part of Speech does not define a word exhaustively; it merely describes its *current* function.**

The distinction is important, because a host of English words can operate as several different parts of speech, depending on the circumstances of their use.

Take for example these two very common words: **table** and **fast**.

Most people would say that 'table' is a noun and that 'fast' is an adjective; they would of course be quite right, as these simple sentences illustrate:

(a) **The table is brown, rectangular and polished**.
(b) **He caught a fast train to London**.

However, **table** can also be used as an adjective or as a verb:

(c) **She bought a beautifully carved table lamp**.

Here **table** describes the lamp, as does **beautifully carved**.

(d) **The MP for Derby tabled a motion in the Commons.**

And here **tabled** denotes an action, something done.

Similarly, **fast** can have other functions – an adverb:

(e) **She ran fast**

where **fast** modifies (gives more information about) the verb **ran**, telling us how she performed the action.

It can also be a noun:

(f) **The pilgrims observed a twenty-four-hour fast in recognition of those starving in the Third World**.

And as a verb:

(g) **Jesus fasted for forty days and forty nights**.

Figure 29. 'Tabled a motion in the Commons'.

Those seven examples are I hope clear enough when examined. But that is the point: very often one cannot tell what part of speech a word is unless its context is closely examined.

Words are as versatile as certain more concrete objects. One can buy 'all-purpose' cleaning substances that are just as effective for wood as they are for metals, glass, linoleum or fabrics. Many foodstuffs are similarly versatile. Vegetables can be used to complement meat or fish; they can be the central constituent of a dish (as in all vegetarian cooking); they can be primarily decorative; they can be adjuncts for dips or soups, and so on. In each case, the cleaning substance or the vegetable has its function adjusted according to the needs and wishes of the user. Words work in a very similar way; indeed, there may be occasions when you legitimately 'invent' a new function for a word, as did Ted Hughes in the opening stanza to his poem 'Pike':

'Pike, three inches long, perfect
Pike in all parts, green tigering the gold.
Killers from the egg . . .'

Strictly speaking, there is no such verb as 'to tiger'. But Hughes's daring invention is totally successful – 'tigering' suggests both the colouring of the fish and its innate ferocity (which is followed up in the next line). Such linguistic suppleness and imagination are founded on an alert sense of the work words do and can be made to do.

The eight parts of speech

verb	a word (or group of words) used to denote actions, states or happenings.
noun	a word used to name something.
adjective	a word that qualifies (describes) a noun.
adverb	a word used to modify (tell us more about) a verb, an adjective or another adverb.
conjunction	a word used to connect one part of a sentence to another.
preposition	a word placed before another word to locate the latter in time or space.
pronoun	a word used to stand for a noun.
interjection	a word used to express mood or reaction.

You may acquire a clearer idea of these terms if you group them in this way:

Group A	Group B	Group C	Maverick
noun	verb	conjunction	interjection
pronoun	adverb	preposition	
adjective			

Group A	consists of words which name things or give more information about the things so named.
Group B	consists of words that denote actions, states and happenings and words that describe those actions, states and happenings.
Group C	consists of words that connect or pin down other words or groups of words.
Maverick	simply means 'odd one out'. Interjections have no grammatical connection with the rest of a sentence.

Let us look at each term in detail.

18.2 VERBS

Introduction

Most surveys of Parts of Speech begin with the noun and the adjective. I have placed the verb first because it is the most important part of any sentence. In addition, I'm convinced that once you understand the various forms and functions of the verb, all other Parts of Speech will be easier to comprehend.

Thirty years ago verbs were often referred to by primary-school teachers as 'doing words'. A lot of people came to sneer at this, pointing out that many verbs do not denote any 'doing' at all – every verb of being and becoming, for instance. But while that term had its shortcomings, it is much more helpful than subsequent alternatives such as 'process words' or 'active signifiers'. If you are even occasionally unsure which part of a sentence is the verb, this description may help:

> **In any sentence, the verb is the word (or words) which tells you what is happening, whether it be an action (something <u>done</u>) or a state of being (something <u>felt</u> or just something <u>existing</u>).**

Here are three simple examples.

1. The boy kicked the ball.
2. His strength surprised him.
3. The ball landed over a hundred yards away.

In Sentence 1, **kicked** is, evidently enough, a physical action – a genuine 'doing word', if you like!

In Sentence 2, **surprised** is not an action as such; but it still tells us what happened – in this case that a powerful feeling affected the boy.

In Sentence 3, **landed** again tells us what happened – in this case a statement concerning the ball's destination.

Now try the following elementary exercise.

Exercise 35
Identify the verb in these sentences. 1–7 are 'simple' [i.e. one-word] verbs; 8–10 are compounds [2 or more words].

1. The anxious householder telephoned the police.
2. The wind's strength appalled him.
3. Hitler was arguably this century's most evil genius.
4. Lightning destroyed the chapel.
5. To everyone's surprise she became the school's best cricketer.
6. The chef cautiously tasted the soup.
7. The kitten savaged the ball of wool.
8. No one has ever vanquished death.
9. She will be returning shortly.
10. This result will disappoint him greatly.

Answers in the Appendix.

Figure 30. 'She became the school's best cricketer'.

Transitive and intransitive verbs

In any sentence, a verb is either **transitive** or **intransitive**.

Transitive means 'passing across': if you think of **transfer, transmitter** or **trans-Atlantic**, you'll get the general idea.

If a verb is transitive, it means that the action passes from the 'do-er' [the **subject**] across to something or someone else [the **object**].

For example:

1. The police **captured** the fugitive.
2. The ball **smashed** the window.

In each case there is a transfer of action. **The fugitive** and **the window** are on the direct receiving end of actions by **the police** and **the ball**. So the verbs are **transitive**.

Intransitive simply means 'not transitive': there is no 'passing across'. The action of an intransitive verb refers solely to the subject.

For example:

3. The lion **roared**.
4. The tide **receded**.

These are complete sentences making complete sense. Nothing other than the subject [**lion, tide**] is involved or even implied.

As you'll gather, identifying a verb as transitive or intransitive involves working out what is happening and whether anyone or anything else is involved. It is important to be able to do this, because many English verbs can be **either** transitive **or** intransitive, depending on how they are used.

Take the verb **run**, for instance. Most commonly it is a verb of motion, and as such it is intransitive.

5. You **run** exceptionally fast.
6. They **ran** down the street.

No 'transfer of action' occurs. In 6, **down the street** is a phrase telling you **where** the action took place: it is an adverb.

But take a look at this sentence:

7. The car **ran down** the pedestrian.

This **is** transitive. The word **down** 'belongs' to **ran** rather than to **the pedestrian**, forming a compound verb that means 'rammed'.

These uses are transitive also:

8. She **runs** her own business.
9. The huntsmen **ran** the fox five miles.

Both involve a 'passing across': 8 means that the woman **manages** a commercial enterprise, 9 that the huntsmen **chased** the fox for a distance of five miles. Each verb has a direct impact on a separate thing or creature, and thus is transitive.

It might help you to remember that

A. *All* sentences have a subject and a verb.
B. **Only sentences whose verb is transitive have an object.**

Now try this brief exercise.

Exercise 36
Pick out **subject, verb** and, *if there is one*, **object** in these sentences. Answers in the Appendix.

1. The bomb destroyed the house.
2. The dog bit the postman.
3. Then the postman bit the dog.
4. The man walked as if crippled.
5. The children walked the dog.
6. The cheetah ran over the field.
7. The lecturer ran over the main ideas.
8. The bulldozer ran over the hedgehog.

The infinitive

Don't be put off by this apparently forbidding term. The **infinitive** is the most basic form of a verb, the root from which grow all other forms. It is not **defined** by a subject or made **finite** by being placed in time – hence, **in finite**.

In its classic form the English infinitive is preceded by the word 'to':

to behave; to eat; to die; to desire; to mow; to kiss.

In practice, the 'to' is not always used. Look at these two linked examples:

I ought **to go** now.
I should **go** now.

They mean the same thing; in each case **go** is an infinitive. It's simply that in certain cases English usage over the years has led to the dropping of the 'to'.

Slightly more complex, but still a 'root form', is the **past infinitive**:

to have lived; to have eaten; to have betrayed.

These structures are clearly placed in the past, but they remain undefined by subject.

Infinitives are the **undeveloped** form of the verb; to develop them one needs to select **person, number** and **tense**.

Person and number

All verbs can be placed in one of three **persons** [1st, 2nd, 3rd] and one of two **numbers** [singular, plural]. Taking as models the two infinitives **to drive** and **to mend**, the full list, or conjugation, runs:

1. 1st person singular   **I drive**
    I mend
2. 2nd person singular   **you drive**
    you mend
3. 3rd person singular   **he/she/one/it drives**
    he/she/one/it mends
4. 1st person plural   **we drive**
    we mend
5. 2nd person plural   **you drive**
    you mend
6. 3rd person plural   **they drive**
    they mend

Both models are called **regular** verbs, which are relatively straightforward in English, unlike several other languages. In addition, however, English has several hundred **irregular** verbs – that is, verbs that deviate from the forms defined by **drive** and **mend**. One such verb is **to be**, the commonest and most fundamental verb of all:

Figure 31. 'They drive'.

1. **I am**
2. **You are**
3. **He/she/one/it is**
4. **We are**
5. **You are**
6. **They are**

Generally speaking, person and number only present problems when questions of grammatical agreement arise. This matter is covered in Chapter 20.

Tense

In essence, **tense** means 'time': a verb's tense establishes the time in which it is set. There are three main tenses:

past	**present**	**future**

For example:

I ate	I eat	I shall eat

Each of these main tenses can have modifications. The form of these depends on whether the action is **complete** (known grammatically as a **perfect** tense) or **incomplete**, part of a process still in operation (known as **imperfect** or **continuous** tenses).

Thus:

A. I **ate**
   I **have eaten**   are past tenses in the **perfect** form.
B. I **was eating**   is the **past imperfect** or **past continuous**.
C. I **eat**   is the present tense in the **perfect** form.
D. I **am eating**   is the **continuous present**, occasionally known as the **present imperfect**.
E. I **shall eat**   is the future tense in the **perfect** form.
F. I **shall be eating**   is the **future continuous**, sometimes called the **future imperfect**.

Finally, there are two other tenses, more complex than the rest.

G. The **pluperfect** is a past tense one stage further removed in time:

I **had** eaten

Its value lies in allowing a writer to distinguish between different times in the past:

[A]   [B]
After I **had eaten**, there **was** a sudden explosion.

In that little narrative sequence, it is clear that Event A occurred **before** Event B. And while a term like **pluperfect** may seem intimidating and confusing, if you are alert to its function, it can give your writing valuable increased range.

H. The **future perfect** looks forward to a time when a proposed action or event has been duly completed.

By the time you've finished shopping, I **shall have eaten**.

As with the pluperfect, this tense affords you greatly increased range in your writing and speech, allowing you to establish 'time zones' that are more subtle and precise than those offered by basic past, present and future tenses.

Note: This section has been introductory rather than comprehensive. Additional tenses – for example, the **conditional** and the **future in the past** – are studied on p. 299–300, which also explains how to 'translate' tenses from direct speech into reported speech and other complex matters.

Voice

I've talked about 'voice' in the ordinary sense a good deal in this book; the grammatical term **voice** is separate, although like its ordinary cousin it affects the way a sentence sounds and comes across.

Verbs are cast in one of two voices: **active** or **passive**. The choice depends on whether you wish the subject to **act** or **be acted upon**. That rather ponderous explanation is best amplified by some examples.

1. The audience cheered the conductor with wild enthusiasm.
2. The union fined the man £100.
3. Lightning destroyed the chapel.

Those sentences all have **active** verbs. The subjects [**audience, union, lightning**] are 'in charge' of the relevant actions [**cheered, fined, destroyed**]. The other nouns mentioned [**conductor, man, chapel**] are directly 'on the receiving end' of those actions.

Supposing, however, you want to re-design those sentences and place the **object** first. You cannot do this simply by switching the nouns' position, because that would utterly transform meaning:

1a. The conductor cheered the audience with wild enthusiasm.
2a. The man fined the union £100.
3a. The chapel destroyed lightning.

1a and 2a still make sense, although their information is so surprising as to become almost comic. 3a is of course absurd.

So merely reversing the position of the words is no good, because you reverse the meaning as well. But you can place **conductor/man/chapel** at the head of the sentence, *provided you alter the form of the verb*:

1b. The conductor **was cheered by** the audience with wild enthusiasm.
2b. The man **was fined** £100 **by** the union.
3b. The chapel **was destroyed by** lightning.

The verbs have been recast in the **passive voice**. Grammatically speaking, what has happened is that words that were originally the **object** of actions have become the **subject** that is **acted upon**. There is no significant change in meaning; there is an observable difference in **emphasis**.

Elsewhere in this book I have argued that passives should be used sparingly. You should normally use the **active** voice: it is simpler, more direct, more efficient. But there are times when the passive is the better choice, and such times usually involve a question of emphasis. Let us take a last look at the three sentences we've been using.

In 1, it makes little difference in emphasis whether you choose active or passive. Therefore the active form is better. But in 2 and 3 there is a genuine difference. If you choose the active voice –

> The union fined the man £100.
> Lightning destroyed the chapel

– you give the 'star role' or major emphasis to the two subjects (**union, lightning**). That does not mean that **the man** or **the chapel** are unimportant or uninteresting, but it does mean that the reader's strongest visual attention is focused on the thing carrying out the action. However, if you wish instead to fix that attention on **the man** or **the chapel**, you need to introduce that focus **at once**, and the passive voice becomes the better choice:

> The man was fined £100 by the union.
> The chapel was destroyed by lightning.

People sometimes use the passive voice to 'soften' the impact of an order, especially in business letters. Look at these two pairs of examples:

1a. You should send us a cheque in payment immediately.
1b. A cheque should be sent in payment immediately.
2a. I would appreciate an early reply.
2b. An early reply would be appreciated.

It could be argued that 1a and 2a are somewhat hectoring, even threatening, and that 1b and 2b are therefore safer and more courteous structures. Well, yes; but it could also be argued that 1b and 2b are simply timid, 'wrapping up' a direct requirement in a needlessly elaborate, fudging way. It all depends on how urgent the writer considers the matter to be, or even how annoyed he/she is! If 1a's firm really needs that cheque, or has been waiting an unreasonably long time for it, the added 'pressure' that the active voice embodies is fully justified; similarly, if the writer of 2a is thoroughly fed up with having letters ignored, that is the right choice rather than 2b.

Such tonal matters are important, and you must be the judge of them when you write. In general, though, I suggest trying to limit your use of the passive to those times when **emphasis** is the criterion. To use it to soften or dilute may seem sensible, but it's worth bearing in mind that writing that hedges its bets, is worried or simply *scared*, will invariably be bad writing.

As I pointed out earlier, 'calling a spade a spade' need not cause offence or become impolite. On the contrary, your readers will thank you for making things as clear and direct as you can.

The terms **active** and **passive** are hardly fascinating in and of themselves, and even a full understanding of their function is not of much use on its own. But I hope you can see from this section

Figure 32. 'An early reply'.

that such an understanding plus the always-crucial facility to think clearly about the effect you wish to make adds up to a most valuable tool. Grammatical terms may seem arid as words on a page, but a sharp sense of how they can be used will quickly lead to a significant improvement in your writing and powers of expression. The same goes for the next topic – the **mood** of a verb.

Mood

Verbs are placed in one of three moods: **indicative, imperative** and **subjunctive**. Once again, these are tricky-looking terms, but in practice only the last is at all problematic.

Most of the verbs we use are in the **indicative** mood, which is employed when we make statements or ask questions.

1. **She drives me crazy.**
2. **Why are you bothering with a tablecloth? They're all so drunk that they won't even notice.**
3. **He disappeared one day, and nobody understood why.**
4. **What are you talking about?**

All seven verbs in that collection are in the **indicative** mood. They **indicate** information, or the desire for information, in a straightforward, unqualified fashion.

The **imperative** mood is used for commands or entreaties.

5. **Stop that at once.**
6. **Give me your badge.**
7. **Please don't do that again.**

The imperative is easily recognized because, as you can see, the subject (**you**) is rarely included, being 'understood'.

There is also a **first person plural imperative**, which is as much a suggestion as a command:

8. **Let's go.**
9. **Let us pray.**
10. **Let's play Trivial Pursuit.**

The **subjunctive** is regularly found in Latin, French and German, but its use in English is rare. It is important nonetheless, because it is used in remarks where **supposition** or **condition** are implied, and thus it can play a subtle part in establishing precise meaning.

For example, probably the commonest subjunctive in English:

11. **If I were you** . . .

It is, obviously, impossible for anyone to be someone else. When we

Figure 33. 'If James were to give up smoking'.

use this popular expression, we are imagining what we would do if we found ourselves in that other person's position. The advice that we give may well be valuable, but it is wholly suppositional, and the subjunctive 'telegraphs' that fact.

Sometimes the use of the subjunctive is more delicate in terms of meaning. Consider this pair of sentences:

12a. **If James gives up smoking, he'll be fit in no time**.
12b. **If James were to give up smoking, he'd be fit in no time**.

On the surface, they say the same thing. But 12a is, don't you find, more **positive** than 12b? The speaker seems to be fairly confident that James **will** give up smoking. In 12b, however, the tonal implication is that James **won't** give up smoking, or that he is unlikely to do so. By casting the remark in the **subjunctive** mood, 12b suggests a lack of confidence in James's willingness or will-power.

The subjunctive resembles the passive, in that it is a neat way of altering tone and impact. Used sparingly, with that precise aim in mind, it is a vital part of a writer's armoury; it is also important to be able to recognize its use by others, in order to judge their tone correctly. But just as you should usually stick to the active voice, you'll find that most of your verbs are indicative ones. If the subjunctive occurs in your writing more than occasionally, you're probably hedging your bets too much and are not sufficiently certain of what you think or want to say!

Auxiliary verbs

An **auxiliary** means a 'helper' or a 'secondary aid'. **Auxiliary verbs** are used to help another verb form one of its tenses, moods or voices. There have been many examples in this section already – for instance, all those verbs listed under **imperfect** or **continuous** tense forms.

Altogether there are sixteen such verbs. Three are **primary** –

be   do   have

– used to form compounds of ordinary verbs:

1. I **am** going to London.
2. I **do** not think that is true.
3. I **have** been for a long walk.

The other thirteen are **modal** – that is, they express grammatical mood* or, to an extent, tense.

4. I **shall** resign tomorrow.
5. It looks as if it **may** rain.

Modal auxiliaries are examined in detail in Chapter 21. The full list is:

can	**must**	**should**
could	**need**	**used (to)**
dare	**ought (to)**	**will**
may	**shall**	**would**
might		

Participles

There are two kinds of participle:

A. **The past participle** is usually formed by adding **-d** or **-ed** to the infinitive:

decided   denoted   depar**ted**   discus**sed**

There are however a sizable number of exceptions – for example:

sung   brought   been   had   run   learnt

I'm afraid there is no 'rule' I can offer to guide you through such irregularities: they just have to be **learnt** (!) one at a time.†

The past participle combines with an auxiliary verb to form a past tense:

---

* If uncertain about this, consult the section on **Mood** above.
† The case of **learnt** (past participle of learn) is complicated by the fact that there **is** a word **learned**. It is an adjective meaning 'well read, erudite' and is pronounced with two syllables: **learn-ed**.

1. I have decided
2. They had departed three hours earlier.
3. Why haven't you brought your pyjamas?
4. She was run off her feet.

The past participle also has a separate function as a simple adjective: this is examined on page 261.

B. **The present participle** always ends in **-ing**. It combines with an auxiliary verb to form a continuous tense:

5. In a few hours, thank God, I shall be **sleeping**.
6. They were **waiting** patiently in the bitter cold.
7. If I were **writing** this in longhand, I'd go mad.

Like the past participle, the present participle has a separate life as an adjective. Again, you will find this covered on page 261.

That concludes our preliminary look at the verb. There is more to say about the work verbs can do and the forms they take, but if you've understood all the material in this section, you should now have a sound grasp of this most central part of speech; as a result, you should find the rest of this section progressively more comfortable to master. The verb is the most complex, the most far-reaching and the most muscular device in language, compared with which all other parts of speech will, I trust, seem straightforward. Before we move on to **nouns**, therefore, try the next two exercises, which test all the material so far. If you can score well on them, you should have no fear of anything else that grammar can throw at you!

Exercise 37

A. Pick out the verbs in these sentences, and identify which of them are **transitive**, and which **intransitive**.

1. The sun was shining.
2. The sun burnt the grass.
3. The word-processor exploded.
4. He bought a new word-processor.
5. The tennis coach hit the ball very hard.
6. This record will be a big hit.

B. Put these sentences into the **tense** designated.

1. I go to the shops. [continuous present]
2. The floods were devastating. [pluperfect]
3. They appear on 'Blind Date'. [past imperfect]
4. He passed his driving test. [future perfect]
5. Julian sees Susan every day. [future continuous]

C. What **mood** are these sentences in [indicative, imperative or subjunctive]?

1. How are you?
2. Put yourself in my place.
3. I'd be amazed if that were to happen.
4. I'll be happy if that happens.
5. Please make an effort this time.
6. Let's have a party.

Exercise 38

A. Change these sentences from the **active** to the **passive voice**.

1. The snake swallowed the bird.
2. The gale blew the slates off the roof.
3. The band did not satisfy the large audience.

B. Change these sentences from the **passive** to the **active voice**.

1. An early settlement of your account would be appreciated.
2. The charity's funds were embezzled by the treasurer.
3. All travel-arrangements have been taken care of by your Sunshine Tours representative.

C. Provide the correct **past participle** of the verb given in brackets to make the sentence grammatically accurate.

1. Have you [bring] the flowers?
2. She had [commit] herself to three years' work.
3. Where has my car [go]?
4. He had [hop] off the field, nursing his injured foot.
5. I have [cut] my finger badly.

D. What's the difference in meaning or effect between these two pairs of sentences?

1a. The organization was destroyed by its own inner corruption.
1b. Its own inner corruption destroyed the organization.
2a. If you do that, you'll regret it.
2b. If you were to do that, you'd regret it.

18.3 NOUNS

There are four types of noun:

1. **Common** or **concrete**
2. **Proper**
3. **Collective**
4. **Abstract**

Over thirty years ago, just as verbs were often called 'doing words', so nouns were referred to as 'naming words'. This primary school term was useful when thinking about types 1–3 but far less successful when type 4 was under consideration. Nouns do 'name' things, yes; it is nevertheless forgivably hard for pupils to regard such words as **grace**, **happiness**, **misery** or **stupidity** (all abstract nouns) as 'things'. So if the concept **noun** does not yet make complete sense to you, a better way of defining and identifying all kinds of noun is needed. We can best do this by looking in turn at each type.

Common or concrete nouns

(**Note**: grammarians would argue that in suggesting that **common noun** and **concrete noun** are synonymous I am combining two quite separate terms. They would be perfectly correct, and I address the matter in Chapter 21. At this stage, however, I am concerned with assisting anyone who is unclear about this most basic of nouns and what differentiates it from other types, especially the **abstract noun**. My procedure here may be eccentric, but it is designed to clarify and make comfortable a concept that many students find difficult and confusing. Those who already have a sound understanding can afford to skip this section and consult instead the more sophisticated later explanations.)

Let's start with some examples.

millionaire   **earthquake**   **comet**   **rhinoceros**   **lord**   **silk**

Those six words are all **common nouns**, but the term is useless (or worse) unless its exact meaning is understood:

> *Common* **here has nothing to do with** *ordinariness, frequent occurrence* **or** *vulgarity.*

Millionaires and **earthquakes** are hardly ordinary; **comets** are not an everyday phenomenon and the **rhinoceros** is threatened with extinction; **silk** is far from being 'cheap and nasty', nor is a **lord** likely to be 'common as muck'.

   Common can also denote 'belonging equally to', and that is the meaning that applies here.

A common noun is the name common to all members of or items in the class named by the noun.

That is a good, precise definition*, but I still don't like it much – mainly because, as you'll have gathered, I dislike the term itself. In my experience it confuses rather than illuminates, and I much prefer the term **concrete noun**.

Concrete means 'physically substantial' or 'existing in material form'. A **concrete noun** is one that can be apprehended by the senses – any, several or all of them. This point is very important when it comes to deciding what an **abstract noun** is, as we'll see shortly.

Some further examples:

man   desk   ashtray   leopard   pump   book

All are **concrete**. We identify these things through our senses: they have physical properties. And all are **common**: each one signals a set of characteristics that define all **men**, all **desks**, and so forth. Of course, individuals can and will vary greatly: men can be short or tall, good or evil, black or white and a host of other things; desks can be metal or wooden, bare or cluttered, and so on. But the nouns make immediate sense to us because they produce a standard image in our minds, one which identifies the essence of a man, a desk, et cetera. That is what **common** in the grammatical sense really means, and it is easier to visualize that essence because of its **concreteness**.

Proper nouns

Proper nouns always begin with a capital letter. They name a particular person, thing or place. For example:

1. **Mario** is a **Catholic**. He is a trainee priest at **St Peter's** in **Rome**. He used to be engaged to **Giulietta**, but had to renounce marriage when he entered the **Church**.

Notice that the words **Catholic** and **Church**, capitalized here, could in other circumstances be correctly spelt with a small **c**. **Catholic** is always capitalized when its reference is to the Church of Rome, but it takes a small **c** when used as an adjective meaning 'broad-minded' or 'wide-ranging', as in:

2. His tastes in music are remarkably **catholic**: he has an equal enthusiasm for Puccini, Oscar Peterson and Pink Floyd.

---

* Furnished by S. H. Burton, *Mastering English Language*, p. 131.

Similarly, **Church** is only capitalized when it refers to an ecclesiastical body. Look at these two sentences:

3. He entered the church.
4. He entered the Church.

The only visible difference is the lower/upper case **c**; the difference in meaning is nevertheless considerable.

Sentence 3 means that an unspecified male stepped inside a building designed for and symbolizing religious worship. It could be any such building, anywhere in the world, and he could be entering it for any reason – to pray, to attend a service, to change the flowers, to rob the collection box, and so forth.

Sentence 4 is much more specific, telling us that an adult man took Holy Orders: he committed himself to becoming a priest of some kind (the meaning in sentence 1).

Those four examples make a point that has a broader significance than the consideration of **proper nouns**. They show that tiny differences in the visual presentation of words can make a major difference to their meaning. This is a good place to stress the matter nonetheless, because capitalization – the obvious hallmark of a proper noun – is a device that can on its own radically change the function of a word, and that's why it is important that you learn to recognize what proper nouns are and to spell all of them correctly.

Collective nouns

A **collective noun** names a group or collection of things, persons or creatures. Such nouns are easy to recognize because they are always followed by, or imply, the word **of**:

   a **herd** of cattle   a **bunch** of daffodils   a **class** of students

The collective noun is singular in **grammatical number** even though it stands for a plural aggregate, and must therefore be used with a singular verb. This may seem obvious enough, but it can easily be forgotten when using words like **army, library** or **galaxy**, whose 'members' may add up to millions.

Incidentally, one of the most delightful aspects of English is its taste for the exotic when deciding upon collectives. Do you know these?

   a **charm** of goldfinches   a **murmuration** of starlings
   a **school** of porpoises   a **whoop** of gorillas

Figure 34. 'A whoop of gorillas'.

Abstract nouns

Abstract nouns name qualities, feelings, notions – anything strictly non-physical.

I stress 'strictly' because a large number of people err in this area, perhaps because they've been taught this popular formula:

If you cannot see it, hear it or touch it, it's abstract.

This works most of the time: ultimately it won't do. I once had an argument with a fellow-teacher about the status of the word **air**. She maintained – observing that formula – that **air** is abstract. Was she correct?

Well, you cannot **see** air, you cannot **hear** it [unless and until it becomes **wind**, which is a separate concept] and you certainly cannot **touch** it, as anyone who has tried to grab a handful of air will confirm. The fact remains that if air were an abstract noun, we'd all be dead: indeed, no human, animal or plant could ever have survived for more than thirty seconds! Air contains life-giving oxygen and a host of other gases, and is basic to all existence.* In view of this, one must argue that **air** is amongst the most fundamental concrete nouns in existence.

---

* In the same way, all gases are concrete nouns, even if our physical awareness of them is infrequent.

The above formula is thus inadequate, and needs replacing with something more comprehensive and precise:

An abstract noun names something devoid of all physical properties and which can only be apprehended by the *mind* rather than through any of the five *senses*.

Of course, **all** words are inventions: they have evolved through human thought and humans' need to signify things to other humans. **Concrete** nouns are straightforward inventions, in that they do not often promote argument or misunderstanding. Words like **table, banana, dustbin, television** or **water** are unlikely to cause problems between any two people competent in English. But **abstract** nouns are more intricate: they are **doubly** inventions. They perform not only the creative act of naming, but also the creation of a non-material concept. That is why they seem (and often are) harder to understand than other types of noun, and it's also why they can occasion so much confusion.

Take the abstract noun **morality**, for example. Now I might be completely confident that I understand its meaning; but you might have a very different understanding. We'd soon find that any discussion we might have on the subject would either become very difficult to pursue or simply break down; at the heart of an exchange of views conducted in a language apparently common to us both would lie two separate and probably conflicting ideas of what **morality** means. Such

Figure 35. 'Abstract noun'.

occasions are frustrating enough: just imagine what life would be like if all words were as slippery! Suppose that every time I used the word **tree**, some of my audience imagined I meant **lawn mower**, some **umbrella**, some **handkerchief** and others **avocado**. Communication would be impossible, life absurd.

On the other hand, potential ambiguity and elusiveness make abstract nouns interesting as well as difficult. This is as it should be: they are ideas, and ideas interest most people. Few would find such words as **umbrella**, **handkerchief** or **desk** endlessly invigorating in and of themselves; but concepts like **grace**, **happiness**, **oppression** and **politics** have fascinated men and women since civilization began.

This brief detour into the philosophy and practice of language may not seem to have a close bearing on functional grammar; nevertheless, it once again has emphasized the need for clarity and successful communication. The more you are aware of the considerations that attend abstract nouns, the better your grasp of English will be.

Noun phrases and noun clauses

I've so far concentrated on nouns as single words. But a phrase or clause can also fulfil the function of a noun, as in these four examples.

1. **Starting the race** is no problem: the finish bothers me a lot.
2. The entire assignment depends on your **ability to enter the building unnoticed**.
3. Tell me **what you were doing**.
4. According to **what we hear**, there is no evidence against him.

In each case, the highlighted words combine to perform a single function – that of a noun.

In 1, you might think that **starting** is a verb; but notice that the phrase **starting the race** could be replaced by the simple noun **The start** without any real change of meaning and no change in grammatical function: both choices form the subject of the verb **is**.

In 2, all the highlighted words are dependent on the preposition **on**. Prepositions can only govern nouns or pronouns; since the structure is not a pronoun, it must be a noun. Again, the phrase could be replaced by a single-word noun, even if such a substitution would make for a less precise statement:

2a. The entire assignment depends on your **invisibility**.

In 3, **tell me what you were doing** is the **object**. It is a clause, not a phrase, since it includes a finite verb; but otherwise it is just like 1 and 2 in fulfilling the function of a noun. As in those two, the clause could be replaced by a simple noun-plus-preceding adjective:

3a. Tell me **your actions**.

In 4, as in 2, the highlighted words are dependent on a preposition – **according to**. As in 3, we have a clause here, not a phrase, because of the finite verb **we hear**. But the function is again that of a noun, as this single-word noun replacement shows:

4a. According to **rumour**, there is no evidence against him.

That concludes this preliminary look at nouns. For a more sophisticated examination of their form and function, please consult Chapter 21. In the meantime, try this exercise.

Exercise 39

A. Ten nouns follow. Identify each one as common/concrete, proper, collective, or abstract.

1. hearth.
2. Belgrade.
3. army.
4. misery.
5. depression.
6. flock.
7. cigarette.
8. Caesar.
9. ink.
10. gravity.

B. In this passage there are four concrete/common nouns; three proper nouns; two collective nouns; and three abstract nouns. Can you find them all?

The man looked with indifference at the vast gathering of eagles landing on Big Ben. A fleet of traffic, including countless buses and taxis, had stopped in Parliament Square to watch in fascination; but his only interest lay in finding the nearest McDonald's and buying a huge hamburger.

C. Pick out the noun phrases (1–3) and noun clauses (4–6) in these sentences.

1. Catching the last train home always tires me out.
2. The old man's delight in painting was infectious.
3. Can you tell me the name of that well-dressed woman?
4. That your writing style is improving shows how hard you have worked.
5. The reason for choosing Simon as captain is that he has the most experience.
6. He refused to say what they were looking for.

18.4 PRONOUNS

Please read this passage:

> 1. Richard Palmer and all the readers of *Write In Style* are looking at pronouns. Pronouns stand in place of nouns; the job of nouns is done neatly and quickly by pronouns. When Richard Palmer and all the readers of the book have finished with looking at pronouns, Palmer and all readers will move on to adjectives. Adjectives are used to qualify nouns rather than replace nouns.

It contains just four sentences, but it's hard work, isn't it? It's clumsy, tedious and slow, and one shudders to think what it would be like to read **pages** of such a style.

When I composed that passage, I behaved as if there were no such things as **pronouns**. Here is how it reads in 'normal' English, with the eight pronouns highlighted:

> 2. **We** are looking at pronouns, **which** stand in place of nouns, whose* job **they** do neatly and quickly. When **we**'ve done **that,** **we** shall move on to adjectives, **which** are used to qualify nouns rather than replace **them**.

I hope you agree that 2 is infinitely better than 1. Seven lines have been reduced to four, and four sentences to two: it reads comfortably and fluently. And it demonstrates how enormously useful pronouns are.

In essence, the pronoun is a straightforward device. The term combines the word for naming a thing or person (**noun**) with the Latin preposition **pro**, which means 'on behalf of' or 'standing in place of'.

There are six types of pronoun.

1. **Personal**
2. **Demonstrative**
3. **Relative**
4. **Interrogative**
5. **Pronouns of Number or Quantity**
6. **The Indefinite Use of 'it'**

One important general point before we look at these in turn:

Every pronoun must have a definite *antecedent* – that is, it must be unambiguously clear which noun the pronoun refers back to.

---

* You might think this is a pronoun, but it is a **relative adjective**, describing the noun **job**. This is explored in the next section.

Failure to ensure this can lead to sentences like:

> Susan and her mother went shopping: **she** bought an expensive jewel case.

The reader has no idea which of the two women is denoted by **she**. Other examples of careless ambiguity are provided as we go: I hope there are no **un**intentional ones!

Personal pronouns

Personal pronouns stand for people – **I**, **we**, **you**, **they** and so on – and we use them a great deal. Their only complexity is that they are **inflected** – that is, they take, according to how they are used, one of four different forms:

nominative   accusative   possessive   reflexive

In the case of the pronoun **I**, these work out as follows:

nominative: I
accusative: me
possessive: mine
reflexive: myself

One could construct a perfectly accurate sentence where all four were employed:

> **I** want the money owed **me**: it is **mine**, and the rightful property of only **myself**.

This is rather clumsy, yes, and also somewhat repetitive or insistent! But all four pronouns are used correctly and show the four forms available. The complete list runs:

nominative	accusative	possessive	reflexive
I	me	mine	myself
you [sing.]	you	yours	yourself
he	him	his	himself
she	her	hers	herself
we	us	ours	yourselves
you [pl.]	you	yours	yourselves
they	them	theirs	themselves

People make mistakes over personal pronouns, mainly because to choose between those four forms is sometimes tricky. Here are five sentences which use pronouns: they each contain at least one mistake. Can you spot them all? Answers on page 351.

Exercise 40

1. Between you and I, I think he's going crazy.
2. She and me are going to the cinema.
3. Pass me them socks: they need a wash, pronto.
4. They think her is the only one what can do the job.
5. The rich don't care about we poor people.

Demonstrative pronouns

The term **demonstrative pronoun** may seem long and intimidating, but it need not be if you associate it with the verb **to demonstrate**. For these pronouns **point** to things: they put a demonstrating focus on a particular object or concept:

> I like **this** very much: it's a lot better than **that**, and it's far superior to **those**.

Demonstrative pronouns need to be used with care, however. Always be sure you obey the **antecedent** rule defined above, and guard against vagueness, which the following sentence fails to do:

> He left her without saying a word, although he smiled shyly. **That** made her angry.

This isn't a bad effort in most respects – it's intriguing and quite dramatic. But it is not clear what **that** refers back to. Is it the fact that he left, that he left without saying a word, that he smiled shyly, or a combination of all three? We need to know, and we can't tell as it stands.

Relative pronouns

Relative pronouns **relate back** to a noun just used:

1. The book **which** I am reading is full of mistakes.
2. The woman **who** values her sanity will take no notice of soap-powder advertisements.
3. The man **whom** I ran over in my car has made a miraculous recovery.

Again, always be sure you've made it clear to which noun you wish to refer back; in addition, always respect:

A. Any necessary **inflection** – as in **whom** (accusative) in 3.

B. The **human** status (or otherwise) of your antecedent:

who should only be used of humans, or occasionally such loved creatures as pets.
which is used for everything else – all objects and all other beings.

Finally, take great care when punctuating. Here is 2 again, but re-punctuated:

4. The woman⌐ who values her sanity⌐ will take no notice of soap-powder advertisements.

Those commas make a big difference. 2 means that **any** woman who values her sanity will ignore soap-powder advertisements. It is a **recommendation** to all women. 4 speaks of **one** woman who will ignore those advertisements and who happens also to value her sanity. It is an **observation** about a specific woman.

In 2 there is a direct and intimate connection between women ignoring advertisements and preserving their sanity. There is no such connection in 4, because the commas make the two points quite separate, thereby also changing the focus from the generic to the particular. More on this in Chapter 21.

Interrogative pronouns

I would suggest that this term is the easiest of the lot. An **interrogative pronoun** is simply one that introduces a question:

1. **What** is that appalling noise?
2. **Who** is that idiot on the balcony?
3. **Whom** do you wish to see?
4. **Which** would you prefer – keeping quiet or having your face re-arranged?

Notice that with interrogative pronouns, you do not for once have to worry about **antecedents**. That is because a question naturally embodies some suspense: it needs an answer. It is quite in order for the reader to be kept waiting to find out what the pronoun refers to, since the questioner is similarly awaiting information. However, **inflections** must still be obeyed, as in 3.

Of number or quantity

These do the standard pronoun job of replacing a noun while also offering information as to amount or extent. They are quite straightforward, but care needs to be taken over **agreement**, since some such pronouns are singular, others plural:

1. Beware of buying second-hand clothes: **all** may be cheap, but **many** are of poor quality.
2. There is not **much** to be said.
3. Sorry, there is a big demand for tickets: we've only a **few** left, and you can have just **two** each.

The third sentence might puzzle you a little, in that **few** and **two** are normally thought of as adjectives, not pronouns. But both refer back to **tickets** and in effect take the place of the unnecessarily longer phrases **a few tickets** and **two tickets**. Thus in this instance they are pronouns.

The indefinite use of 'it'

When used in such expressions as

it is raining   it is midnight   How far is it to Babylon?

it requires no antecedent. Do not, however, confuse this **indefinite** use with those occasions when **it** refers, or should refer, to something specific:

It bothered him   They were attached to **it**

In these instances, unless each **it** refers back clearly to an established creature or thing, the reader will be confused and possibly annoyed.

   As signposted along the way, further material on pronouns can be found in Chapter 21.

18.5 ADJECTIVES

Adjectives qualify [give more information about] nouns. There are six types:

1. Descriptive
2. Possessive
3. Demonstrative
4. Relative
5. Interrogative
6. Adjectives of number or quantity

Descriptive adjectives

All the following highlighted words are descriptive adjectives:

a **scruffy** man   a **brilliant** intellect   **red** cabbage
rose-coloured glasses   the **wooden** horse   the **damp** cloth

Actually the term descriptive adjective is pretty fatuous, not to say tautologous. **All** adjectives have a descriptive function: **basic** or **ordinary** would be a more helpful term, since the other five types do a special, prescribed job. No matter: such adjectives should present no problems either of recognition or use.

Adjectives of this type can also be constructed from verbs:

1. the **astonished** policeman
2. the **borrowed** book
3. the **dancing** bear
4. the **leading** athlete

Both 1 and 2 use past participles, 3 and 4 present participles. In other circumstances, of course, each one could be used as verb or part of a verb:

1a. The riot **astonished** the policeman.
2a. He **has borrowed** the book from me.
3a. She **was dancing** for hours.
4a. He **is leading** the field.

Figure 36. 'Dancing bear'.

As I said at the beginning of this section, a host of words have a multiple potential function. But they can only be one Part of Speech at a time, and in the original examples, **astonished, borrowed, dancing** and **leading** are all adjectives, since they both qualify the relevant nouns and grammatically depend on them.

Possessive adjectives

These closely resemble the **personal pronouns** studied a few pages ago – a fact that makes them both easy and difficult! The complete list of possessive adjectives is:

> **my   your   his   her   its   our   your (pl.)   their**

His takes the same form as adjective and pronoun, and its function can only be determined by context:

1. Are those **his**?
2. Yes, those are **his** clothes.

In 1 **his** stands on its own, and is thus a pronoun. In 2 **his** is dependent upon the noun **clothes**, and is thus an adjective.

In all the other instances, the possessive adjective is distinct from the pronoun despite any superficial similarity:

Adjective	*Pronoun*
This is **my** money.	It's **mine**, O.K.?
Is this **your** book?	No, it's **yours**.
I'm **her** husband.	I'm **hers**.
That's **our** house.	It belongs to **us**.
They were obliged to share **their** profit.	However, the expense had been all **theirs**.

Demonstrative adjectives

These are the same as **demonstrative pronouns**, except that they accompany a noun rather than stand on their own:

> Give me **that** gun   Hand over **those** bullets   Sit in **this** chair

Like their pronoun cousins, **demonstrative** adjectives 'point to' a noun, as if spotlighting it.

Relative adjectives

These work very like relative pronouns, but they accompany a noun:

> He's a man **whose** behaviour is notorious.
> I'll return at six, by **which** time the work must be finished.

For the most part relative adjectives are unproblematic. But watch out for two things, one elementary, the other subtle.

A. Do not, as many people do, confuse **whose** with **who's**. The latter is short for **who is** (pronoun + verb) and cannot be used adjectivally.
B. As with relative pronouns, punctuate with great care. An incautious pair of commas can transform meaning:
   1. The man, whose work is successful, takes a break from time to time.
   2. The man whose work is successful takes a break from time to time.

Sentence 1 tells us of a particular adult male who works well and takes the occasional holiday. The two things are not directly linked even if some connection may be inferred.

2 is intended as a **maxim**: it argues that **all** men who want to succeed in their work **must** take occasional holidays.

Both sentences are perfectly satisfactory, of course, but you need to be clear about which meaning you want and whether that's the one you've chosen. Keep this subtle matter in mind at all times.

Interrogative adjectives

The easiest type of all, I think. With their accompanying nouns, **interrogative** adjectives introduce questions:

What time is it?
Whose coffin is that?
Which suit would you like to wear?

Adjectives of number or quantity

Number refers to **how many**, used with plural nouns; **quantity** refers to **how much**, used with singular nouns.

Few people get to read their own obituaries.
Twenty minutes remained when Clench scored the winner.
Much heartache was caused by the Council's decision.
Half her time was spent clearing up after others.

Be careful not to confuse, as many people do, **much** and **many**, and **less** and **fewer**:

Much and **less** should only be used with **singular** nouns.
Many and **fewer** should only be used with **plural** nouns.

Figure 37. 'Read their own obituary'.

For example:

1. There was **less** trouble this time because **fewer** hooligans were present.
2. We haven't **much** time left – so **many** weeks have been wasted.

If in doubt about this, a moment's thought about the noun's status – is it singular or plural? – should ensure that you get it right.

The three forms of adjectives

In addition to being divisible into six **types**, adjectives also have three **forms**:

simple   **comparative**   **superlative**

There are two **regular** ways of forming 2 and 3. The first is to preface the adjective with the adverb **more** for 2 and the adverb **most** for 3:

simple	comparative	superlative
difficult	more difficult	most difficult
ridiculous	more ridiculous	most ridiculous
terrible	more terrible	most terrible

You'll notice that the three root adjectives chosen are all quite long words, and in fact all adjectives of three or more syllables take this form in the comparative and superlative. So do all participles, even if they are of only one syllable:

confusing	more confusing	most confusing
thrilling	more thrilling	most thrilling
bored	more bored	most bored
torn	more torn	most torn

Almost all other adjectives of one syllable take a different form in the comparative and superlative, adding the suffix **-er** or **-est** instead of using the adverbs:

thick	thicker	thickest
fast	faster	fastest
bright	brighter	brightest

Many **two**-syllable adjectives use the suffixes too –

easy	easier	easiest
tricky	trickier	trickiest
severe	severer	severest

– but not all:

absurd	more absurd	most absurd
dreadful	more dreadful	most dreadful
compact	more compact	most compact

Why some two-syllable adjectives follow the suffix pattern while others add the adverb is hard to explain, and certainly not something one can codify in the form of a 'rule'. The most helpful guide is **euphony**. To my ears **absurder, dreadfuller** and **compactest** sound clumsy and odd, something not true of **easier, trickier** or **severest**. However, you might think **severer** is rather awkward, as is its close counterpart **cleverer**, and prefer **more severe** and **more clever**. Those last two alternatives are perfectly correct, and often such choices are more a matter of taste and style than of formal accuracy.

In addition there are four **irregular** forms.

good	better	best
bad	worse	worst
far	farther/further	farthest/furthest
old	elder	eldest

Figure 38. 'She was the fairer of the two'.

Old is only 'semi-irregular', because of course the forms **older** and **oldest** are entirely correct.

Beware: there are certain adjectives whose meaning is **already absolute** and which therefore cannot assume comparative or superlative forms. Obvious examples would include:

dead   unique   eternal   circular   absolute

Nor can any number used as an adjective take the comparative or superlative form: it would be absurd to talk of

eigh**ter** hours   twent**iest** minutes   **most** thousand years

Finally, remember that the comparative can only operate when **two** things are being compared, and that **three or more** must be involved for the superlative to be used.

1. He was the **best** in the class.   Correct
2. He was the **tallest** of the pair.   Incorrect
3. She was the **fairer** of the two.   Correct

Now try the following exercise, which 'tests' grasp of pronouns and adjectives.

Exercise 41
A. In this passage, can you identify three **relative**, four **demonstrative** and three **interrogative** pronouns?

'What's that?'
'What?'
'The book which you're reading.'
'Oh, that. It's a thriller by Gabriel Spiggott.'
'Who?'
'A guy whom I knew at school.'
'Those were the days, eh?'
'You must be joking. Anyone who thinks that must be potty.'

B. Explain the difference in meaning between these sentences:

1. Students who plan their work sensibly tend to be more successful than others.
2. Students, who plan their work sensibly, tend to be more successful than others.

C. Choose the correct alternative from the words given in brackets in these sentences:

1. Mozart wrote an astounding number of compositions: (all, each) are good, and (much, most) are sublime.
2. There are (less, fewer) people here than I expected.
3. We haven't (much, many) funds left: so (much, many) has been wasted.
4. Not one of us (is, are) prepared to put up with this.

D. These sentences contain one mistake each. What are they?

1. Do you know who's briefcase that is?
2. Mind where your going.
3. Spurs and Arsenal met in the semi-final: they won 3–1.
4. Salvador Dali was quite unique.
5. I'll have the smallest half, please.

18.6 ADVERBS

Adverbs do an analogous job to adjectives: they give more information about other words. Whereas adjectives qualify nouns, adverbs modify verbs, adjectives or other adverbs.

A. He drove **stupidly**   She screamed **loudly**
B. **remarkably** careless   **highly** intelligent
C. **very** well   **quite** quickly

In **A** the two adverbs modify the verbs **drove** and **screamed**, in **B** the adjectives **careless** and **intelligent**, and in **C** the adverbs **well** and **quickly**.

There are seven types of one-word adverb.*

1. **Manner**
2. **Place**
3. **Time**
4. **Degree, Quantity or Extent**
5. **Number**
6. **Relative**
7. **Interrogative**

Adverbs of manner

These give us information about **how** the verb is performed:

1. He ate his food **rapidly.**
2. **Gingerly** she stepped into the pool.
3. They greeted the news **joyously.**
4. He read the document **conscientiously** but **slowly.**

All those examples end in **-ly**, as indeed do the majority of adverbs of manner. Quite a few take a different form, however: **fast** and **well** are two obvious examples.

Adverbs of place

These tell us **where** the verb is performed.

1. He visited Amsterdam and had a wonderful time **there.**
2. Come **hither.**
3. You cannot smoke **here:** the smoking area is **nearby.**

---

* There are several further types of **adverb phrase** and **adverb clause**; for a full treatment of these, see Chapter 21.

Adverbs of time

These tell us **when** the verb is performed.

1. It poured with rain **yesterday.**
2. I **often** eat sweets and I want one **now**.
3. The train arrived **late.**

Adverbs of degree, quantity or extent

These all have to do with **amount** or **proportion,** answering the implicit question 'how much?':

1. You've **nearly** finished it.
2. He's said **enough**.
3. They were **very** annoyed.

Adverbs of number

These are separate from types 3 and 4, referring to an **exact** number:

1. The postman always rings **twice.**
2. He increased his savings **fourfold.**
3. Robert tried heroin – **once.**

Notice that 3 could, by being repunctuated or rearranged, take on different meanings. As it stands the sentence stresses that Robert tried heroin **on a single occasion.** This next version –

3a. Robert tried heroin **once.**

– means that he did so **in the past** (as in 'once upon a time'), and that **many** individual occasions may have been involved. And in this version –

3b. **Once** Robert tried heroin . . .

– **once** has the force of 'From the moment that', and we need a further clause to complete the sense, as in:

3c. **Once** Robert tried heroin, his whole life collapsed.

As I've said, adverb **clauses** are covered in Chapter 21; in addition, matters of word order and word placing (**syntax**) are examined in Chapter 20.

Relative adverbs

These connect two clauses, like relative pronouns and relative adjectives:

1. He found out **where** the party was.
2. November is the time **when** everyone feels lethargic.
3. Tell me **why** you're upset.

Interrogative adverbs

Like their pronoun and adjective cousins, these are entirely straightforward, introducing direct questions:

1. **Where** is my drink?
2. **When** are you going to do some work?
3. **Why** are we waiting?

The three forms of adverbs

Just like adjectives, adverbs have three possible forms:

simple	comparative	superlative

The majority of adverbs – including all those ending in **-ly** – follow this pattern for the two modified forms:

quickly	more quickly	most quickly
rarely	more rarely	most rarely
often	more often	most often

As with adjectives, however, one-syllable adverbs use suffixed forms:

soon	sooner	soonest
fast	faster	fastest
hard	harder	hardest

There are also two **irregular** adverbs:

well	better	best
badly	worse	worst

In general, forming the comparative and the superlative is an easier matter with adverbs than it is with adjectives, and if you understand how the latter work, you should have no trouble with single-word adverbs. But please read the brief section that follows before we move on to **prepositions**.

Interim summary

It may occur to you that compared to the other Parts of Speech covered so far, I have rather 'breezed through' this study of adverbs. That is because I have only looked at **simple**, one-word adverbs. **Adverbials** – words or groups of words that have an adverbial function – are the most frequently-used structures in English, and many of them are highly complex. You stand a much better chance of using them well if you first master the basic functions that adverbs perform. Hence the elementary approach that I've chosen here: it furnishes, I hope, a sound platform from which you can build a full understanding of the advanced material in Chapter 21.

18.7 PREPOSITIONS

As its formation suggests, **preposition** means 'placed before'. Prepositions are words placed before a noun or pronoun to show relationship between persons or things or actions.

1. They live **in** the country.
2. She sat **beside** me.
3. Tell me **about** yourself.
4. Keep **off** the grass.

There are some fifty English prepositions. A full list would not serve any useful purpose; what **is** important is that you take note of these two points:

A. All prepositions take the accusative case.

In English the accusative case is 'invisible' most of the time; as we've seen, however, such inflection comes into play with several pronouns, and the accusative form must always be used:

5. He sent a letter **to me**.
6. We don't know anything **about her**.
7. They could see the roaring torrent **beneath them**.
8. The house **opposite us** is being renovated.

B. Many prepositions can 'double' as adverbs.

By definition a preposition must operate with a noun or pronoun. If the latter is omitted, the preposition changes function, becoming an adverb:

9. He stood **outside** the building   **preposition**.
10. She went **outside**.   **adverb**
11. Above us the waves.   **preposition**
12. See **above**.   **adverb**

Prepositions help form **phrases**; these can be adjectival, adverbial or noun phrases, structures studied in Chapter 20.

18.8 CONJUNCTIONS

Junction means 'joining'; **con** is Latin for 'with'. **Conjunctions** are words which join a word, phrase or clause with another word, phrase or clause.

1. Whisky **and** water   [word to word]

Figure 39. 'Shaken but not stirred'.

2. Shaken **but** not stirred   [word to phrase]
3. Do you want the cassette tape **or** the compact disc?   [phrase to phrase]
4. Do it, **and** as soon as possible.   [clause to phrase]
5. I can't go to the concert **because** I'm broke. [clause to clause]

Strictly speaking, conjunctions are divided into two types – **co-ordination conjunctions** and **subordinating conjunctions**. This distinction is explained in Chapter 20; from an ordinary writer's point of view however, the key thing with conjunctions is not to overdo them! Even sophisticated writers can easily fall into the trap of cluttering up their sentences with too many **and**s, **but**s, **or**s and **because**s. The deft use of punctuation – particularly colons and semi-colons – will often preclude the need for a conjunction, and you should try to use **every** joining device in the course of your work to prevent boredom, both on your part and the reader's.

18.9 INTERJECTIONS

Well, I reckon this sentence takes care of the whole topic!

Interjections are 'verbal tics'. Some of them should be avoided at all costs anyway, and must certainly never contaminate formal writing:

er/um   **you know**   **I mean**   **sort of**

Other interjections are however perfectly permissible, although they should be used sparingly and isolated via punctuation:

oh   **well**   **oh well**   **O.K.**   **yes**   **no**

1. **Oh**, you've changed!
2. **Oh well**, if you won't do it, there's no more to be said.
3. **O.K.**, so I'm lazy.
4. **Yes**, you're intelligent; **no**, you're not studious.

In each instance, the highlighted interjection has no **grammatical** connection with the rest of the sentence. It is a mild exclamation or introductory message whose omission would not alter the **sense** of what is said. But interjections do add **tonal colour** – nowhere better demonstrated than in oaths:

Goddammit!   **Strewth!**   **Crikey!**   **Blast!**

Those examples are remarkably restrained on my part, but I hope you get the general idea!

An inflection means a change in the form of a word according to the job it is doing. English is not highly inflected, especially compared to several European languages, but there are still many times when inflection is required. This section looks at all of them, although it is not an exhaustive treatment. Occasionally my remarks will be brief, as we have come across some of these instances of inflection during the previous chapter on Parts of Speech.

Irregular verbs

A regular verb is one whose forms are determined by rules and is thus predictable. If we take the three verbs **look**, **listen** and **perform** we find they all behave alike when changes are required:

1. They add **-s** to form the 3rd person present singular.
2. The past participle and simple past tense are formed by adding **-ed**.
3. The present participle is formed by adding **-ing**.

There are well over 300 verbs which do not obey one or more of these procedures. Space precludes listing them all; besides, I think that would be tedious rather than helpful – both to read and to write. What **is** worthwhile is to look at the various **kinds** of irregular verb, with examples of each.

The eight classes of irregular verb

A. A number of verbs seem to be entirely regular, but they incorporate a change of spelling in one or more of their forms. For example:

(a) **stop** takes a double **p** in both participle forms and in the simple past:

stopping   **stopped**   **they stopped**

(b) So does hop:

| **hopping** | **hopped** | **she hopped** |

It is especially important to get (b) right, because you otherwise confuse it with **hope**, whose same forms are:

| **ho̲ping** | **ho̲ped** | **we ho̲ped** |

(c) **panic** adds a **k** to all three forms; the hard **c** of the original would otherwise be softened by the **i** and **e**:

| **panicking** | **panicked** | **you panicked** |

(d) **die** is regular in past participle and simple past forms, but changes spelling in the present participle:

dying*

Such verbs are, arguably, **minorly inconsistent** rather than **irregular**. Pedantically, that may be so; but they cause writers a lot of trouble, and in my view thus earn their place here!

B. Verbs whose only irregularity is the ending used for the past participle and simple past. For example:

have: had   learn: learnt   burn: burnt   send: sent

C. Verbs whose simple past is regular but whose past participle takes a different form:

He mowed the lawn   They were mown down
The crowd swelled   Her face was swollen

D. Verbs whose ending for the simple past and past participle is the same but irregular. In addition, there is a change of vowel or vowel number:

teach: taught   seek: sought   sell: sold   keep: kept

E. Verbs whose past participle ends in **-n** and which also have an irregular simple past form. The base vowel is affected as well:

break	broken	He broke cover
take	taken	We took stock
blow	blown	She blew her top
see	seen	I saw a ghost
run	run	I ran a mile

---

* If you use the verb **dye** in present participle form, the **e** must be retained to avoid confusion: **dyeing**.

F. Verbs whose forms do not change at all:

infinitive	past participle	simple past
cut	cut	He cut his finger
let	let	She let them in
cast	cast	He cast off the ship
broadcast	broadcast	She broadcast the news

N.B. **All** verbs are inflected in the third person singular, adding **-s**, which prevents confusion between present and past. (**She lets them in/She let them in.**) In the other five persons, however, present and past forms are the same:

present	simple past
I cut my finger	I cut my finger
You let him get away	You let him get away
We cast caution aside	We cast caution aside
They broadcast daily	They broadcast daily

Context will normally establish whether the writer intends the present or the past; if you find, when writing yourself, that the context doesn't resolve ambiguity, select a different form of the tense you require that is fully clear.

G. Verbs which have no discernible ending and whose past participle and simple past forms are the same. A base vowel change also occurs.

sit	sat	They sat down
stand	stood	He stood up
lead	led	She led him astray

H. The most irregular type of all. These verbs have no discernible ending; the past participle and simple past forms differ; the vowels change.

come	come	It came to me
go	gone	They went away
begin	begun	She began to read
lie	lain	He lay down

That last one is important, because **lie** seems to cause a lot of problems. For a start, it has two different meanings, and they follow quite separate grammatical forms. The above example uses **lie** in the sense of 'to be prone'; if the meaning of 'to tell an untruth' is required, the verb becomes **regular**:

| lie | lied | He lied to me |

The matter is further complicated by the fact that **lay** is not only the past tense of **lie** but a verb in its own right. It is **transitive** (**lie** is *in*transitive) and has several meanings:

Figure 40. 'Hens lay eggs'.

1. To deposit   **He lays his life on the line.**
2. To present   **Let me lay my cards on the table.**
3. To impose   **They're laying the blame on me.**
4. To produce   **Hens lay eggs.**
5. To arrange   **Lay the table, would you?**

That is not a comprehensive list: it omits amongst others a somewhat
raunchy meaning. However, if you ever refer to **laying around the house**,
don't be surprised if you incur a few giggles and/or odd looks! More
seriously, take great care not to confuse **lie** and **lay**: few things look or
sound more illiterate. Incidentally, the past participle of **lay** is **laid,** as
is its form in the simple past.

Irregular verbs can infuriate. There are so many types, and their
formation often seems quite irrational. Fortunately, the vast majority
of them are frequently used, so one quickly learns, if only through error.
In addition, the inflections occurring in irregular verbs are the trickiest,
most complicated there are: get a good working grasp of those and the
others should be plain sailing.

Contracted negative verbs

Quite a mouthful, that term! Happily, the usage it defines is a fairly
simple matter.

In the previous chapter we looked at the sixteen **auxiliary verbs** [p. 246]. All of them can be contracted in the negative form – something never possible with any main verb:

verb	standard negative	contracted negative
can	cannot	can't
do	do not/does not	don't/doesn't
ought	ought not	oughtn't
shall	shall not	shan't
will	will not	won't

And to prove that you can't do this with ordinary* main verbs:

discuss	not discuss	**discussn't**
eat	not eat	**eatn't**

The negatives in bold type are self-evidently absurd.

Other inflections affecting verbs

Apart from contracted negatives and all the inflections that occur in irregular verbs, there are three other instances when the verb changes form:

1. The third-person indicative singular of all verbs adds **-s** or **-es** to the root.

he departs   she leaves   he discusses   it goes

2. Present participles are formed by adding **-ing**. Normally this is straightforward, but sometimes the spelling changes:

lie: lying   die: dying   come: coming   judge: judging

As the last two examples indicate, nearly all verbs ending in **-e** drop that letter when forming the present participle. There are exceptions, however – designed to prevent the confusion of similar words with separate meanings:

sing: singing	**singe: singeing**
die: dying	**dye: dyeing**
swing: swinging	**swinge: swingeing†**

* The three **primary** auxiliary verbs – **be**, **have** and **do** – can also operate as main verbs. **Be** and **have** can be contracted in either function; the need to contract **do** as a main verb never arises:

Auxiliary	Main
It isn't raining	He isn't rich
I haven't been there	We haven't time
She doesn't smoke	–

† The verb is archaic; the participle/adjective means 'huge'. The recently popular word **whingeing** follows the same principle.

3. Past participles are formed by adding **-d** or **-ed** [see page 246].

4. Both present and past participles are also used to form different **tenses**. [see pages 239–40].

5. Verbs can change form in their different **moods** [see page 244].

Noun plurals

Most nouns have a singular and a plural form. [We look at the exceptions shortly.] Normally the plural is formed by adding **-s** to the singular noun:

eggs   cows   televisions   waters   saxophones

Words whose singular already ends in **-s, -sh** or **-ch** add **-es** in the plural:

kisses   masses   brushes   fishes   marches

Irregularities

1. Common, collective and abstract nouns whose singular ends in **-y** preceded by a consonant drop the **-y** in the plural and add **-ies** instead:

family/families	**party/parties**	**city/cities**
aviary/aviaries	**misery/miseries**	**pity/pities**
[Cf. boy/boys	guy/guys	jay/jays]

2. Proper names ending in **-y** preceded by a consonant simply add **-s** in the plural:

Kennedys   Marys   O'Reillys

3. Seven nouns change their vowel in the plural form:

man/men	**woman/women**	**foot/feet** **tooth/teeth**
goose/geese	**mouse/mice**	**louse/lice**

4. Three nouns add **-en** to form their plural:

ox/oxen   child/children   brother/brethren*

5. A number of nouns change their final **-f** to **-v** and add **-es**:

wife/wives	**knife/knives**	**leaf/leaves**
half/halves	**wolf/wolves**	**loaf/loaves**

---

* In religious contexts only – e.g. The Plymouth Brethren. In ordinary contexts **brothers** should be used.

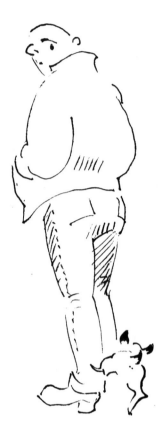

Figure 41. 'My favourite trousers have been ruined'.

6. Foreign words

English has 'borrowed' thousands of words from other languages. Sometimes they obey their original plural form [**crises**]; sometimes they assume an 'English' plural [**syllabuses**, not **syllabi**] and sometimes either is possible [**cactuses** or **cacti**].

Naturally, a full list is out of the question. But take particular care with the following, which many people get wrong:

singular	plural
criterion	criteria
phenomenon	phenomena
curriculum	curricula
medium	media

7. Invariable nouns

Some nouns are used only in the singular:

music   homework   snow   stuff

They should always be used with a singular verb even if the implicit 'sense' is plural:

1. Music in every form delights me.
2. Snow has fallen, snow on snow.

Other nouns are used only in the plural:

shears   thanks   people   trousers*

Similarly, they must be accompanied by a plural verb, even if the implicit 'sense' is singular:

3. That's wonderful: thanks are in order.
4. My favourite trousers have been ruined.

And a few nouns have the same singular and plural form:

sheep   partridge   aircraft   innings

Such words should always be used in close conjunction with a word that clearly establishes **number**:

5. Your sheep is missing.
5a. Your sheep have escaped.
6. The aircraft is damaged.
6a. They've grounded all aircraft.

The genitive of nouns

We've come across the genitive in Part Two in the section devoted to the use of the apostrophe [pages **43–51**]. I pointed out then that **all** apostrophes denote omission and that the notion of a 'possessive apostrophe' is erroneous. In simple genitives like **John's book** or **the girls' clothes** the apostrophe denotes the **omission** of letters that were included in the original Anglo-Saxon structures: **Johnes book** and **the girlses clothes**. As the years went by, the extra syllable was elided: hence the apostrophe.

The genitive case, then, is formed in the singular by the addition of **-'s** and in most plurals by the addition of the apostrophe only.

the man's tie	**the woman's salary**	[singular]
the boys' playground	**the employees' canteen**	[plural]

---

* You will sometimes hear the noun **trouser** used by assistants in men's outfitters. I'm sorry, but I think it's ridiculous, managing to be both tacky and pretentious. However, it can be used sensibly as an adjective – **trouser suit, trouser-leg**.

Take care with irregular plurals [see the previous section]:

men's handkerchiefs   **the media's influence**
the Kennedys' tragedy   **geese's migration**

Singular nouns ending in **-s** seem to be somewhat problematic, in that a lot of people make mistakes when forming the genitive. Strictly speaking, singular nouns of one or two syllables ending in **-s** should add an apostrophe and a further **s**:

The class's behaviour   Jesus's life

This principle has been much disparaged of late; many authorities find it needlessly meticulous, if not downright pedantic. I would defend it on the grounds of pronunciation: when we speak the above phrases we add the extra syllable – **class's** and **Jesus's** – and I think it makes sense to signal that fact when writing them down. However, the point is a minor one and largely a matter of taste; certainly it is now accepted usage to employ the apostrophe only.

For all longer words ending in **-s** the addition of a further **s** looks and sounds awkward, so only the apostrophe is used:

Coriolanus' mother   the hippopotamus' grin

N.B. Take great care over placing the apostrophe. I shudder to think of the number of times I've encountered this kind of thing:

Dicken's books   Henry Jame's novels

Such apparently minor errors are not just comic: they suggest someone who is just not thinking.

Not all genitives denote possession as such. Study these:

St Mark's Gospel	**the man's story**	[origin]
a winter's night	**a Ploughman's Lunch**	[description]
in three hours' time	**one day's respite**	[measurement]

None of those six phrases denotes belonging in the strict sense. Indeed, the first is often expressed as **The Gospel <u>according to</u> St Mark**, which is distinct from any notion of ownership. And **a Ploughman's Lunch** does not signify a midday meal belonging to a tiller of the soil: it's a pretentious marketing phrase for 'bread and cheese'!

The genitive can also be used to express the role of **subject**:

the client's claim   [i.e. **the client claimed**]
the wrestler's submission [i.e. **the wrestler submitted**]

Or as **object**:

the thief's pardon   [i.e. **someone pardoned the thief**]
the discs' reissue   [i.e. **someone reissued the discs**]

The genitive's inflections remain the same whatever their function. Sometimes, however, it is better to use a different structure to express the genitive. In these examples –

> **His misery's worst part was the loneliness.**
> **The course's single most attractive feature was the year spent abroad.**

– the genitive structures are somewhat bloated and would be better expressed using **of**:

> **The worst part of his misery was the loneliness.**
> **The single most attractive feature of the course was the year spent abroad.**

In general the **-s** genitive is used for personal and animate nouns and the **of-** genitive for inanimate and abstract nouns. But such things are finally matters of taste and style rather than 'rules': if, as always, you **listen** to what you write, you will invariably make the right choice.

Prefixes and suffixes

These are morphemes* added to the front of words (**prefix**) or to the end (**suffix**) to form new meanings.

1.   noble: **ig**noble
2.   interested: **un**interested/**dis**interested†
3.   face: **pref**ace
4.   late: **trans**late
5.   happy: happi**ness**
6.   rely: reli**able**
7.   captain: captain**cy**
8.   relation: relation**ship**

Strictly speaking, I suppose, the majority of prefixes and more than a few suffixes are not **inflectional** devices, since they do not alter the grammatical function or structure of the words to which they're added. Of the eight examples above, only 4, 5 and 6 effect such a change of function:‡

---

* **Morpheme**: the smallest divisible speech element having a meaning or grammatical function.
† The two prefixed words are **not** synonyms! **Uninterested** means 'bored'; **disinterested** means 'impartial'. See p. 333, Chapter 23.
‡ It could be argued that 7 also embodies a functional change, since the suffix changes the noun from concrete to abstract. Obviously, though, both words are the same basic Part of Speech.

4   changes an **adjective** into a **verb**
5   changes an **adjective** into a **noun**
6   changes a **verb** into an **adjective**

But all prefixes and suffixes have to do with morphology [the study of word structure] and all, as noted, alter meaning. Whether genuine inflections or otherwise, they are a valuable resource for any writer, even if several are easy to confuse. You will find a substantial guide to those in Chapter 21.

Additional inflections

All **personal pronouns** are inflected, as are some forms of the **relative, demonstrative** and **interrogative** pronouns. This has been covered in full on pages 257–59.

Adjectives and adverbs are inflected in the **comparative** and **superlative** forms. This too has been dealt with, on pages 264–5 and 270.

Try the exercise on inflections that follows; the next section looks at **syntax**.

Exercise 42

A. In these sentences, put the verb in brackets into the form designated on the right.

1. Two minutes into the interview she (panic). [**past tense**]
2. His left knee was dreadfully (swell). [**past participle**]
3. We are (begin) to get somewhere. [**present participle**]
4. He (lie) motionless on the bed. [**past tense**]
5. They (lie) to the police throughout. [**past tense**]

B. As economically as you can, add something to these two sentences to ensure that the **past tense** is signalled:

1. TV-AM broadcast daily.
2. We let them off with a caution.

C. Change the highlighted nouns (and, if necessary, their accompanying verbs) from singular to plural:

1. I prefer **a kiss** to **a march**.
2. It almost seems as if **Kennedy** was doomed from the start.
3. The **party** did not please the **guy**.
4. What is your **criterion** when judging intelligence?

D. These sentences all include one mistake. Can you put each one right?

1. Are you telling me you dislike **all** Mahler's musics?
2. Would you pass me that shears?
3. Paul Gascoigne was once Spur's most talented player.
4. Many people find the medias' intrusiveness objectionable.
5. I want to talk to you tonight about childrens' rights.

E. Form the opposite meaning of these words by adding a prefix.

1. normal.   2. opportune.   3. spell.   4. array.   5. associate.

F. Add a suffix to change these words into the form designated.

1. uneasy [adjective into abstract noun]
2. detest [verb into abstract noun]
3. joy [noun into adjective]
4. urgent [adjective into adverb]
5. depend [verb into adjective]

The word **syntax** bothers a lot of people – including me, I might add! I find it slippery: it is difficult to pin down exactly what it means or can mean – an elusiveness confirmed when consulting *The Shorter Oxford English Dictionary*:

syntax:
   A. The arrangement of words (in their appropriate forms) by which their connection and relation in a sentence are shown . . . Also, the constructional uses . . . characteristic of an author.
   B. The department of grammar which deals with the established usages of grammatical construction and the rules deduced therefrom.

There is a fundamental difference between the two definitions. The first limits **syntax** to matters of word relationship and word order – a significant issue, certainly, but much narrower than **B**, which almost makes **syntax** synonymous with **grammar** itself.

Figure 42. 'Syntax'.

It is definition A that governs the material here. The two previous chapters have already dealt with much that definition B encompasses, and there is further such material in Chapter 21 hereafter. Indeed, in a sense this entire book has been about syntax, and not just in the terms prescribed by B: the last sentence of A defines the crucial determinants of the quality that has centrally concerned me throughout – **style.**

So this relatively short section looks at how words operate in groups – in phrases, clauses and various types of sentence – and how you can best arrange them to ensure the meaning required.

Phrases

So far in this Primer, we have focused on individual words. To be sure, this has occasionally involved looking at compounds, as in tenses (**we have eaten**), comparative adjectives (**more difficult**) and the like; nevertheless, each topic has looked at an individual part of speech and the various forms it may take.

A **phrase** is a structure that may employ several parts of speech in the expression of a single idea:

1. on the table
2. All things considered
3. parts of speech
4. Behind every successful man

Phrase 1 uses a **preposition,** an **adjective** [the definite article* **the**] and a **noun.**

Phrase 2 uses an **adjective,** a **noun** and another **adjective** formed from a **past participle.**

Phrase 3 uses a **plural noun,** a **preposition** and a **singular noun.**

Phrase 4 uses a **preposition,** two successive **adjectives** and a **noun.**

Phrases are thus plural constructions and quite complex when compared to individual words. However, although all the above make **some** sense, none of them makes **complete** sense. A phrase is never an **independent** structure: to acquire complete sense it needs to become part of a larger structure that identifies **subject, action** and **time.**

1a. He threw up on the table.
2a. All things considered, the tour was a disaster.
3a. I've had enough of parts of speech for the time being.
4a. Behind every successful man there's a good woman – or an understanding bank manager.

---

* This term and its 'brother' the **indefinite article** [**a, an**] are fully explained in Chapter 21.

Each original phrase has been placed in a context which makes complete sense. The subjects and verbs define and illuminate the phrases – and vice versa. Four intriguing **sentences** result.

Before we proceed further, try this little exercise.

Exercise 43
Which of the following six are sentences, and which are phrases? Answers below.

1. Cabinets full of records.
2. It is raining.
3. Given your considerable abilities.
4. This year I'm not going to be lucky.
5. Underneath the resplendent sweep of the bridge.
6. The dilapidated old shed with the chicken-coop next to it.

Only 2 and 4 are sentences: all the others require a verb if they are to make complete sense.

The exercise, simple enough, visually stresses an important point: **sentences** can be very short, and mere **phrases** can be quite long. The shortest structure in those six is the three-word 2, but it's a complete **sentence**; 6 already has eleven words but will need even more to become independent. That neatly sets up our next topic.

The simple sentence

This term means a sentence that has just one **finite verb**. That is the **only** criterion: in this usage **simple** has nothing to do with length or 'easiness'.

1. It **is raining**.
2. The council **condemned** the dilapidated old shed with the chicken-coop next to it.
3. The highlight of the evening, and in my view one of the greatest performances ever heard in this country, **was** his scintillating rendition of Liszt's B Minor Sonata.

Sentence 1 could hardly be shorter or easier; 2 is quite substantial; 3 is long and involved. But each one is a **simple sentence**, as the highlighted single finite verb confirms.

Double and multiple sentences

These next examples consist entirely of **simple sentences**.

1. It is raining. I am fed up.
2. The doorbell rang. He rose eagerly to his feet. The dog started barking ferociously.

If you were to write like that for any length of time, the resultant jerkiness would soon irritate or bore your reader. That danger can easily be averted, however:

1a. It is raining **and** I am fed up.
2a. The doorbell rang **and** he rose eagerly to his feet, **but** the dog started barking ferociously.

Sentence 1a is a **double sentence**: simple sentence + simple sentence. Sentence 2a is a **multiple sentence**: simple sentence + simple sentence + simple sentence.

Theoretically, there is no limit to the number of simple sentences you can include in a multiple sentence. However, frequent and lengthy multiple sentences are just as irksome to read as a string of simple sentences, if not more so:

2b. The doorbell rang and he rose eagerly to his feet, but the dog started barking ferociously so he gave it a biscuit and shut it in the kitchen to prevent trouble, and then he was able to admit his visitor.

Reading that sentence is hard, unrewarding work: even replacing some of the conjunctions with appropriate punctuation wouldn't make it much better. The writer crams too much into the sentence, rendering it breathless and blurred. In addition, greater structural variety is required, which is where the use of **clauses** comes in.

All sentences within a double or multiple sentence have equal **status**. In all the examples looked at so far, each sentence could stand on its own, making complete sense: that is indeed the definition of a sentence. Another way of putting it is that a simple sentence consists of a **main clause**, a double sentence of **two main clauses,** and a multiple sentence of **three or more main clauses.** However, clauses can also be **subordinate,** helping to form **complex sentences**, which is our next topic.

Clauses and complex sentences

The difference between a clause and a sentence is not easy either to understand or define. I have addressed the matter already in Part Two [pages 18ff] and offer this summary here:

All sentences have a subject and finite verb and make complete and independent sense.

All clauses have a subject and main verb, but do not *necessarily* make complete and independent sense.

You may forgivably find this unclear unless you *knew* the difference anyway, and some examples should help:

1. The man was frightened.
2. The man was frightened: the dog looked vicious.
3. The man was frightened, because the dog looked vicious.

Sentence 1 is a **simple sentence** consisting of one **main clause**.

Sentence 2 is a **double sentence** consisting of two **simple sentence/ main clauses**. The colon signals a connection between them, but they are grammatically independent.

Sentence 3 is a **complex sentence**: it has a **main clause** and a **subordinate clause**. Let's analyse it briefly.

Although the sense of 3 is virtually identical to that of 2, the sentence works in a grammatically different way. The first clause can stand on its own, of course, as in 1; but if the second clause is isolated it fails to make complete sense:

3a. Because the dog looked vicious . . .

I put in those dots to show how the clause 'hangs in the air'. **Because** is a **subordinating conjunction**: here it signals a link between the dog's vicious appearance and . . . well, what? As 3a stands, it could be anything: it must be specified for the structure to make full sense – i.e. for it to become a **sentence**. Intriguingly, we can achieve that by **adding** the clause that originally started the sentence:

3b. Because the dog looked vicious, the man was frightened.

Some purists say you should never begin a sentence with a conjunction; as I've said earlier, this is a 'phony rule' that I find just silly.* The only real criterion here is which is more effective – the word order in 3 or 3b? What is **your** view? Think about it for a moment, and see if you agree with my remarks that follow.

I don't think there's much in it, is there? Nonetheless, I prefer 3, which I find punchier than 3b. The dog's vicious appearance is the most dramatic thing in the sentence, and has greater impact, I think, if left till the end. In 3b, the main clause is rather anti-climactic, almost as if we could have guessed it after such an opening. But my argument is a subtle matter of taste and style: if you prefer 3b, fine – it's a clear and accurate sentence.

* See above, Part Two, pp. 102–3.

Sometimes, though, the positioning of clauses makes a decisive difference to meaning or tone or both. Study these two sentences carefully:

4. The record **which John wanted** was out of stock.
4a. The record was out of stock, **which John wanted**.

Sentence 4 means that a particular record that John wanted was unavailable.

Sentence 4a is tricky. **Either** it's a rather incompetent attempt to say the same thing as 4 **or** it's a deft way of saying something else entirely – **that John wanted the record to be unavailable**. Maybe his kid brother/ sister/wife/father was planning to pollute the home's aural atmosphere with something he found excruciating, and was thus delighted that the purchase couldn't be made!

Similarly, how do these sentences differ?

5. Although I understand you've not been well, this work is inadequate.
5a. This work is inadequate, although I understand you've not been well.

If you were the student concerned, which one would you prefer to hear? They seem to say exactly the same thing . . .

I hope you agree that 5a is far more sympathetic. The speaker suggests that the student's recent illness explains and indeed mitigates a poor performance. Sentence 5 regards the recent illness as an irrelevance: the speaker wants the student to realize that such work won't do and that no excuses are admissible.

The differences in word order primarily affect **tone**, but you can see that tonal qualities can in turn affect **meaning**. Certainly, listener 5 would go away from the interview in a very different frame of mind from listener 5a!

Interim summary

I've called this an 'Interim summary' because there is a lot of additional material on clauses in the next chapter. But I hope you can already see that **complex sentences** – i.e. those that consist of a main clause and one or more subordinate clauses – are the writer's most valuable friend.

I've stressed from the outset of this book that your writing should always be **clear**, and I am certainly not urging you to write complex sentences for the sake of it. Whatever your task and whatever its length, you will regularly need to 'spell things out' in as direct a fashion as possible; on those occasions the simple sentence and its 'elder brothers', the double and multiple sentence, will probably be your best choice. But they have their limitations. As we've seen, in even a six-clause multiple sentence, each clause has the same status. Gradations of tone and meaning are very hard to effect in such sentences: this is indeed as it should be, because they aim at directness, not subtlety.

But on many other occasions the success of your writing will depend on **nuance** – i.e. subtle shades of tone and meaning, the kind of precision that simple, double and multiple sentences ultimately cannot achieve on their own. That is why **syntax** is a fundamental and genuinely creative matter. In the 'simple sentence family', word order is not significant, provided basic rules of logic and grammatical sense are obeyed. Complex sentences allow you to build meaning and effect in a fashion both aesthetically pleasing and pithily exact, and they do so because their placing of words is hardly less important than the choice of the words themselves.

Finally in this section, a brief look at how the placing of individual words, rather than phrases or clauses, can alter meaning.

The right word in the right place

During the study of adverbs of number in Chapter 18, we saw how the word **once** could have a different function or meaning according to where it was placed. In the same way, see how the exact location of **only** in these three sentences effects three separate meanings:

1. Mark **only** wanted to see Ginny.
2. Mark wanted **only** to see Ginny.
3. Mark wanted to see **only** Ginny.

Sentence 1 is fairly casual, or possibly defensive/apologetic. It means that Mark **merely** wanted to see Ginny.

Sentence 2 is extremely forceful. It means that Mark had just one thing in mind – **seeing Ginny**. Nothing else mattered.

Sentence 3 means that Mark wanted to see Ginny **alone**. Presumably someone else turned out to be present, and the implication is that Mark was fed up about this! Alternatively, it could mean that Mark wanted to see Ginny and **no one else**: maybe she wasn't there, or maybe he single-mindedly went in search of her. Both versions are also forceful, but with different meanings from 2.

A second, final example. In these three sentences, the varying position of **even** radically affects meaning:

4. **Even** Bert offered money.
5. Bert **even** offered money.
6. Bert offered **even money**.

Sentence 4 puts the chief stress on **Bert**. The implication is that Bert is a notorious skinflint, but that in the circumstances he is (unusually) prepared to cough up!

Figure 43. 'Even Bert offered money'.

Sentence 5 puts the chief stress on **money**. This too might imply that Bert is mean; alternatively, it could signal **desperation** or **extreme determination** on his part.

Sentence 6 is both less dramatic and more technical than 4 and 5. Here Bert is a **bookmaker**, trying to deter the punters by quoting stringent odds on the favourite for the Derby/The World Cup/the next Pope/whatever.

As I said at the beginning of this section, all of this book has concerned itself with **syntax**, whether in terms of choosing the right word at the right time or of grammatical structures in general. Syntax is the writer's 'signature': like all good signatures, it should be both clear and stylishly individual. Proper attention to rudimentary sense and crisp exactness of word order should ensure that your own 'signature' satisfies both criteria.

PARTS OF SPEECH (ADVANCED)   **21**

Chapter 18 covers the eight Parts of Speech in considerable detail, but its range is restricted. Although some of the material on verbs, adjectives and adverbs looks at compounds – structures of more than one word expressing a uniform linguistic concept – on the whole its focus is on **single words**. This section is mainly devoted to the further study of compounds – phrases and clauses that do the work of verbs, nouns and so on. In addition, it covers certain other sophisticated matters 'postponed' from the earlier section.

I stressed at the outset that this Primer is not a fully comprehensive work, and I do not claim to cover every matter pertaining to Parts of Speech. But I do hope that between them Chapters 18 and 21 take care of most of the things that you need to know or will find useful.

21.1 VERBS

Direct and reported speech

Please read these elementary sentences:

1. I am going into town.
2. He drives like a maniac.
3. They all detest pasta.

In each case there is an implicit sense of speech: as we read we **hear** the words as well. And to make that sense of speech explicit doesn't require much effort or ingenuity:

1a. 'I am going into town,' he told them.
2a. 'He drives like a maniac,' she observed.
3a. 'They all detest pasta,' the waiter explained.*

* At this juncture the difference between writing direct speech and reported speech is my chief concern, not the mechanics and conventions of speech punctuation. I deal fully with the latter in Chapter 22.

It would not be quite accurate to call those examples of **dialogue**, because that word presupposes an exchange of speech, and the above sentences are all 'one-offs'. But the principles of dialogue are the same as exist here – indicated direct speech plus an identification of the speaker. You will of course frequently come across direct speech and dialogue in novels, short stories and several other genres, and almost certainly most of you will have had occasion to use them yourselves.

But supposing you don't want to use direct speech, or feel it is inappropriate? After all, direct speech is either taboo or irrelevant in a number of written tasks – most reportage; the writing of minutes; précis, summary and report work; reviewing; instructional and technical writing. How do you keep the **sense** of the direct speech you'd use in other circumstances while changing the **form**?

Let's return to my three examples. To put them into **reported speech** – that is, speech that you **report** rather than **quote** – is quite a complex process even in such elementary sentences:

1b.   He told them that he was going into town.
2b.   She observed that he drove like a maniac.
3b.   The waiter explained that they all detested pasta.

Sentence 1b changes the original **I** to **he**; 2b and 3b retain the original pronouns. But – and this is the most important feature of reported speech – all three have changed the tense of the direct speech verb. Reported speech is as it were 'one stage removed' from direct speech, and this is usually reflected by moving 'one tense back'.

But not always. Before we go on to other examples, look at these versions of 2 and 3:

2c.   She observed that he drives like a maniac.
3c.   The waiter explained that they all detest pasta.

Here the original tenses have been retained. In this form 2c and 3c suggest that what the verbs represent is a matter of **permanence** – i.e. that he always drives like a maniac and probably always will, that their detestation of pasta is unchangeable. Both notions are highly plausible, and the sentences are perfectly correct. But they are, obviously, different in meaning from 2b and 3b, and when fashioning reported speech, make sure that your version means what you really want it to.

To recast direct speech already in the past tense, follow the principle of moving back one tense. If the direct speech is in the perfect tense, use the pluperfect; if it's in the past imperfect, use the continuous pluperfect:

Direct	Reported
4. 'I have been out,' he admitted.	He admitted that he had been out.
5. 'I have never done such a thing,' she maintained.	She maintained that she had never done such a thing.
6. 'I was going to resign,' he revealed.	He revealed that he had been going to resign.
7. 'I was just having a drink,' he said.	He said that he had just been having a drink.

Notice, however, that the reported speech version of 7 is ambiguous in a way that its direct speech counterpart is not. The latter means:

All I was doing was having a drink.

But we can interpret the former in two ways:

He said that all he had been doing was having a drink
or
He said that he had just **finished** having a drink.

Once again, you need to be completely sure that you've rendered the original accurately, both in meaning and in grammar. On this occasion, the ambiguity can be prevented by substituting **merely** for **just**:

He said that he had merely been having a drink.

Judging from the number of mistakes people make, the **simple past** tense is a misnomer when it comes to translating it into reported speech! In fact, the 'one tense back' principle still applies, but it's very easy to be careless. Study these little sentences:

8. 'I was lonely,' he said.
9. 'We did it,' they admitted.

In reported speech these must go into the pluperfect:

8a. He said that he had been lonely.
9a. They admitted that they had done it.

If you incautiously were to leave them in the simple past –

8b. He said that he was lonely.
9b. They admitted that they did it.

– you suggest that the original words were in the present:

8c. 'I am lonely,' he said.
9c. 'We do it,' they admitted.

So take special care!

Dealing with 'you'

So far all my examples have been in the first or third person. The second person is sometimes tricky to render in reported speech:

1. 'You are ridiculous,' she remarked.
2. 'Are you ready?' he asked.

As each stands, we cannot tell whether the **you** is male or female, singular or plural. Normally, the context and surrounding material should solve the problem, and you can select the appropriate pronoun:

      1a. She remarked that he/she was quite ridiculous.
or 1b. She remarked that they were ridiculous.
      2a. He asked if he/she was ready.
or 2b. He asked if they were ready.

Figure 44. 'Are you ready?'

However, if the context does not clarify things, you need to use an impersonal noun rather than 'guess' at the appropriate pronoun:

    1c. She remarked that the addressee was ridiculous.
    2c. He asked if the auditor was ready.

Both sound pompous and awkward, I freely admit – and they are forced to choose between singular and plural. All they do is make the best of a bad job: let's hope you never have to do the same!

So far I have made no mention of future tenses and their forms in reported speech: that is because they need a section to themselves. Four modal auxiliary verbs are involved in their construction, and the function of those needs to be precisely understood before reported speech matters can be tackled.

Shall or will?

What is the difference between these four uses of the future?

    1. I shall do the essay tomorrow evening.
    2. I will do the essay tomorrow evening.
    3. They will return at six o'clock.
    4. They shall return at six o'clock.

Many people think that **shall** and **will** are interchangeable, but strictly speaking they are not. Moreover, the ways in which they differ are highly complicated.

In the **first person**:

I/we **shall** expresses the **simple future**.
I/we **will**, though still expressing the future, additionally conveys **intention** or **determination**.

Thus 1 is an unadorned statement, while 2 is more in the form of a promise.

But the position is reversed in the **second** and **third persons**:

You, he, she, it and they **will** express the simple future.
You, he, she, it and they **shall** are almost **directives**. They still express the future, but there is an additional sense of determination or even command conveyed.

Thus it is 3 above that is the unadorned statement; 4 is in effect issuing an order, or at least expressing the speaker's belief that the words will come true.

All this seems somewhat pedantic, no doubt. After all, in speech and in writing we often contract these verbs, and when we do the form is the same whether **shall** or **will** was at issue:

I'll; you'll; he'll; she'll; it'll; they'll

Given this obliteration of the distinction in much ordinary usage, why does the distinction matter at all? Well, anything that preserves shades and distinctions of meaning should be honoured – not out of reverence for the heritage of the language but because such nuances aid precision and clarity. And those who don't know or care about the difference between **shall** and **will** invariably land themselves in serious trouble when trying to render those verbs in **reported speech**, which is where their 'cousins' **should** and **would** come in.

Should or would?

This pair of words is used in two quite separate constructions. We shall shortly see how they help form **conditional tenses**; first, a look at how they create a tense known as the **future in the past**.

The future in the past

This tense is formed when you change direct speech with a future tense verb into reported speech. Let's look again at two sentences studied earlier:

1. I shall do the essay tomorrow evening.
2. They will return at six o'clock.

These simple statements about the future are translated into reported speech form thus:

3. I said that I should do the essay tomorrow evening.
4. He said that they would return at six o'clock.

For statements about the future that additionally indicate a promise or an implied order, the procedure is different. Remember these earlier sentences?

5. I will do the essay tomorrow evening.
6. They shall return at six o'clock.

In reported speech they become:

7. I said that I would do the essay tomorrow evening.
8. He said that they should return at six o'clock.

When dealing with the future in the past, then, **shall** always becomes **should**, **will** always becomes **would**. However, there remains a small problem, best illustrated by a return to sentence 3:

3a. I said that I should do the essay tomorrow evening.

On reflection, we can see that the sentence is ambiguous. **Should** is not only the form **shall** takes in the future in the past: it can also, independently, be synonymous with **ought to**. As a result, 3a could imply that the speaker felt under an obligation to do the essay – a different matter from a simple statement about when it would be done. If that sense of obligation is what you wish to communicate, the best thing to do is use **ought to** and leave **should** for those simple statements.

Summary

Translating direct speech into its reported form always strikes the beginner as extremely complex. It is certainly never an easy task, because it requires fiercely clear thinking: you need to be quite sure about what the original says or is seeking to say before you can render it accurately in a different form. [The same is true if you are translating reported speech 'back' into direct speech.] However, this premium on clear thinking is also to your advantage: if you take care of that adequately, the transposition should not present any problems, since the procedure is based on watertight, logical principles. Proper attention to those principles, together with a vigilant eye for any possible ambiguity, should ensure that you perform the task successfully and with a minimum of pain.

The conditional tense

This tense is similar in some ways to the subjunctive mood [see above, pp. 244–5]. Both are used to refer to theoretical rather than actual states. In this pair of examples, notice the difference that changing to the conditional tense makes:

1. I **shall** react to any change in the programme with extreme disapproval.
2. I **should** react to any change in the programme with extreme disapproval.

Sentence 1 is essentially a threat. The speaker implies that such change is likely, and that he will duly complain with great vigour. Sentence 2 is markedly different in **tone**. The speaker remains firm and prepared to speak out, but his use of **should** implies that it will probably not be necessary: his words express the hope that wisdom will prevail and that no change will be made.

In the conditional tense, one uses **should** in the first person and **would** in the second and third persons. Thus:

3. If you cared about us, you **would** be home more often.
4. They **would** have made a mess of it regardless.

In informal and oral usage, **should** and **would** are considered interchangeable. That is comfortable and perfectly acceptable; for formal

Figure 45. 'If you cared about us you'd be home more often'.

usage, however, you should attempt to stick to the 'rules' and conventions I've outlined, mainly because not to do so will eventually, as we've seen, cause ambiguity or confusion in your writing, a blemish you should always seek to avoid.

Phrasal verbs

A phrasal verb consists of a main verb combined with another word to make a new main verb. There are three ways of forming such a structure:

A. **Verb + adverb**	take off	break down
B. **Verb + preposition**	look at	hit on
C. **Verb + adverb + preposition**	put up with	get stuck in

In all these cases, the additional word or words become part of the verb rather than operate as a separate part of speech. Thus the sentence

He got stuck into his work

consists of three basic components – subject [**He**], verb [**got stuck into**] and object [**his work**].

As that example suggests, phrasal verbs are often less complicated than they might appear. But some are transitive, others intransitive; in addition, transitive phrasal verbs can pose subtle problems of word order. Both these matters require a separate look.

Transitive and intransitive phrasal verbs

Type A [verb + adverb] can be either transitive or intransitive, as this brief list of examples shows:

Transitive	**Intransitive**
to break something up	to break down
to catch somebody up	to give up
to close something down	to go away
to leave something out	to get about

Type B [verb + preposition] are always transitive.

He asked for more money.
He arrived at St Pancras.
I believe in God.
I came across a fascinating article.

Some such verbs can be **doubly transitive,** in that both the verb and the preposition take an object:

He asked his boss for more money.
He referred the complaining woman to the manager.

Type C [verb + adverb + preposition] are also always transitive.

We are looking forward to your performance.
I am fed up with writing essays.
She walked out on him.

Word order in transitive phrasal verbs

As I've stressed throughout this book, listening to what you write should normally allow you to achieve the best word order, in terms of both clarity and elegance. But the three types of phrasal verb are worth a detailed look in this respect, for they follow varying conventions.

Type A [verb + adverb]
If the object is a **noun,** it may appear either before the adverb or after it, as this pair of [perfectly correct] sentences demonstrates:

1. He caught up **the leader** during the final lap.
1a. He caught **the leader** up during the final lap.

If the object is a **pronoun,** however, it must appear **before** the adverb:

1b. He caught **him** up during the final lap.*

Type B [verb + preposition]
No real problems here: whether noun or pronoun, the object comes after the preposition:

2. I believe in **democracy.**
2a. I believe in **it.**

But, as noted, one needs to be quite careful if a phrasal verb is used in such a way that both the root verb and the preposition take an object:

3. The secretary checked the agenda with the chairman.
3a. The secretary checked it with him.
3b. The secretary checked it with the chairman.
3c. The secretary checked the agenda with him.

Notice that the word order does not in fact change whether nouns, pronouns or a mixture of the two is used. But if my experience as a reader/marker is anything to go by, many people get into a surprising tangle with such structures, perpetrating things like:

3d. The secretary checked with the chairman the agenda.
or 3e. The secretary checked with him the agenda.

Perhaps such stilted phrasing is a spin-off from the notion that one should not end sentences with prepositions or, by extension, prepositional phrases. As I've already pointed out (see pages 103–4) this is a mistaken belief that can often damage good English rather than guarantee it; so stick to structures 3–3c.

Type C [verb + adverb + preposition]
Potentially complicated, but in fact straightforward: in every phrasal verb of this type, all parts of the verb come before the object, be it noun or pronoun:

4. Don't put up with bad manners.
4a. Don't put up with them.

Conclusion

Phrasal verbs are a particular kind of compound verb – that is, a verb consisting of more than one word. These can seem very forbidding, especially when they run to four, five or even six words:

---

* I hope you can see/hear that 'He caught up him during the final lap' is clumsy and ugly.

1. I **have been looking forward to** your visit.   [5]
2. I **am not putting up with** this any longer.   [5]
3. He **should not have got out of** that so easily.   [6]

But I hope they seem far less formidable once you understand that even verb 3 expresses **one idea.** Remove one of the six words, or attempt to break them down into sub-sections, and meaning collapses. To be sure, several components and complex aspects are involved:

(a) the subtle use of **should** in the sense of **ought to**;
(b) a compound tense [here, the perfect];
(c) an adverb and a preposition as part of the verb;
(d) the addition of a negative.

Nonetheless, all four components end up doing a single job; all six words are as it were hyphenated, forming a single Part of Speech. If you are able to look at words in that **conceptual** way, and not as separate, necessarily one-off entities, these verbs should cause you minimal trouble, either in writing what you want to say or arriving at an exact understanding of others' writing.

The same conceptual principle underlies all other 'advanced', apparently complex Parts of Speech. Our next focus is the noun.

21.2 NOUNS

The six classes

In Part One I divided nouns into four **types:** concrete, proper, collective and abstract. However, that is not the full story: nouns also divide into six **classes** – a more sophisticated matter, though overlapping with that earlier material:

1.   Nouns are either **proper** or **common.**
2.   The latter are then further divisible into **count** and **noncount** nouns.
3.   And both count and noncount nouns can then be divided into **concrete** or **abstract.**

The diagram which follows* may help to clarify these divisions:

---

* I am indebted for this to David Crystal, *Rediscover Grammar* [Longman, 1988], p. 93.

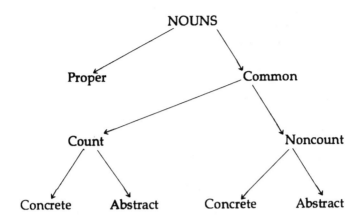

Proper and common nouns

This first pair of classes is problematic, but not because the division itself is difficult: indeed, most pupils/students find proper nouns easy. There are two major reasons for this:

1.   Proper nouns are names of specific people, places, events, publications, times and so on; as such they are always capitalized, and thus easy to recognize and use correctly.

2.   The **behaviour** of proper nouns is limited and simple.

   (a)   They are always able to stand alone –

   Washington   Whitsun   Marmaduke

   – in a way denied to the majority of singular common nouns. Thus it makes perfect sense to say

   (i)   I found Washington frightening.
   (ii)   Marmaduke has caught a mouse.

   but something is clearly wrong with

   (iii)   I found book frightening.
   (iv)   Cat has caught a mouse.

   (b)   They usually do not take a plural form. **Some** can –

   Fridays   Christmases   Cup Finals

   – but most are meaningless and unconvincing in plural form:

   Cambridges   Sallys   Niagaras

   (c)   They are not normally used with determiners: it is obviously absurd to speak of

Figure 46. 'Marmaduke has caught a mouse'.

      a Cambridge   **the** Sally   **some** Niagara

As I said in Part One, I find it is the term **common noun** that causes difficulty. A formal definition might run:

> **A common noun is one which refers to something or someone as a member of the <u>set</u> of similar things.**

Thus **a dog** is a member of the set of all dogs. However, for the (I suspect) many people who do not find that explanation very illuminating, it's probably easier to make a virtue of the fact that proper nouns are easy to recognize and thus say:

> **All nouns that are not proper are by definition common.**

Count and noncount nouns

In truth, I find these terms rather ugly, but they are useful in distinguishing between individual or **countable** entities –

    books   **players**   **desks**   **animals**

– and nouns that refer to an undifferentiated mass or notion –

    milk   **earth**   **music**   **luck**

If ever in doubt about whether a noun is count or noncount, try to remember these three characteristics:

1. Count nouns cannot stand alone in the singular. There is obviously something wrong with:

    Book is damaged;   animal is wounded

2. Count nouns allow a plural; noncount nouns do not. Thus the above

    books   players   desks   animals

    are fine, but it sounds and looks odd to refer to

    milks   earths   musics   lucks

3. Count nouns occur in the singular with the indefinite article **(a, an)**, noncount nouns with **some:**

    a book   an animal   some music   some luck

    Both count and noncount nouns can be used with the definite article **(the)**:

    the book   the player   the music   the luck

Finally: quite a number of nouns can be count **or** noncount, according to their precise meaning or use. For example:

1a. I refuse to eat meat.	[noncount]
1b. There was a splendid selection of cold meats.	[count]
2a. I'd love some tea.	[noncount]
2b. Do you serve afternoon teas?	[count]
3a. He writes literary criticism.	[noncount]
3b. Do you have any specific criticisms?	[count]

Concrete and abstract nouns

This distinction has already been covered in detail on pages 249–54, and not much need be added here. Abstract nouns refer to intangible items – anything that cannot be seen, heard, touched, tasted or smelled. Many are easy to recognize because they end in **-ness** –

happiness   cleanliness   ugliness   faithfulness

– but there are numerous other forms:

joy   precision   remark   intensity   evil

The key thing to bear in mind is that all abstract nouns are **mental constructs**: they are ideas, notions, judgments and so on, created by the human mind and having no physical existence. If in doubt about whether a noun is concrete or abstract, try imagining whether it could be physically isolated or transferred as an entity: could you photograph it or give it to someone? You could if it's a mountain or a sweet, but you cannot take a snap-shot of music or give someone a chunk of intensity!

Gender

Many languages divide all their nouns into masculine or feminine forms. English does not do this, but there are still many occasions when gender has to be observed.

In essence, the gender of a noun is determined or signalled by the pronoun or possessive adjective that goes with it:

> I admire that **man**: **he** is superb at **his** job.
> **She** is a girl **who** worries too much about **her** weight.
> The **table** is in the wrong place: move **it**, please.
> I'm offering you some **advice**, and I suggest you take **it**.

Those examples illustrate two of the three 'groups' in which gender operates – **personal animate** nouns and **inanimate** nouns. The third group, **nonpersonal animate** nouns, is used of animals and occasionally machines. An animal can of course be referred to as **it**, but most animals have specific male/female forms:

> **bull/cow   dog/bitch   cock/hen   cob/pen   dog/vixen**

'Lower' animals and fish [e.g. flies, ants, plaice] are not distinguished in such a way, however.

One of the more delightful – or ridiculous, according to your point of view! – eccentricities of English is its tendency to give cars, aeroplanes, ships and the like the **feminine** gender:

> **She is** a lovely car – fast and elegant.
> The plane was damaged but the pilot landed **her** safely.

Personally I have a lot of sympathy with the character in Ian Fleming's short story *The Hildebrand Rarity* who 'corrects' James Bond's remark 'She's your ship' with:

> '*It's* my ship . . . That's another bit of damned nonsense, making a hunk of steel and wood female.'*

He seems to be in a minority, however; such practice, sentimental 'nonsense' or not, is still widespread, and you should bear it in mind. In addition, countries are often referred to in the feminine form, despite some nations' fondness for the term '**Father**land'!

---

* In *For Your Eyes Only* (Pan, 1962), p. 163.

21.3 ADJECTIVES AND ADVERBS

The articles

There are two kinds of article – **definite** and **indefinite**.

definite article   =   **the**
indefinite article   =   **a, an**

The terms may seem rather imposing for words that are the simplest adjectives of all! But articles are far from inconsequential: their omission can make a significant difference to meaning.

1. **A man** walked into the shop.
2. **Man** is the most recent of the planet's species.
3. Pass me **the books**, please.
4. **Books** are one of life's great pleasures.

In 1 and 3 the highlighted articles make their nouns **specific**, whereas in 2 and 4 the absence of an article makes the nouns **general** or **universal**. All four are quite correct; but when writing, stay alert to whether you need an article or not. **The** and **a/an** may not seem to matter much one way or another, but they are crucial aids to precision and do a surprising amount of work.

Adjective order

On the whole it is not good writing practice to string together a lot of adjectives: even three will often seem excessive, let alone six or seven! But on those occasions when you do employ several determiners at once, you should follow this order:

1. Adjectives describing **feelings** or **qualities**   [pleasant]
2. Adjectives of **size, age, temperature**, or **measurement**
                                                          [big, young, cold]
3. Adjectives of **colour**   [pink]
4. Adjectives of **nationality** or **origin**   [Welsh]
5. Adjectives denoting **substance** or **material**   [iron, linen]

Thus:

(a) I met a **pleasant young black American** miner.
(b) She bought a **large old Irish linen** tablecloth.

I hope you agree, however, that those examples are dangerously top-heavy; such four-adjective constructions should be kept to an absolute minimum.

When adjectives precede the noun, you do not need separating commas, as (a) and (b) illustrate; neither should you normally use **and**, except for adjectives of **colour**:

(c) The large **red and white** linen tablecloth.

Certain adjectives **cannot** precede nouns:

    asleep   **afraid**   **afloat**   **alive**   **alone**

It sounds [indeed **is**] wrong to say:

    the **asleep** boy   I saw an **afloat** body

You need to change either the construction or the adjective:

    the boy was asleep or the **sleeping** boy
    I saw a body afloat or I saw a **floating** body

Further matters of order and punctuation

One of the commonest errors in both speech and writing follows this kind of pattern:

    As a novelist, she admires Hardy, but not as a man.

That sentence does not actually say what it intends: **as a novelist** goes with **she**, not **Hardy**. That's perfectly possible, of course – she could very well be a novelist herself – but it's obviously ridiculous to imagine that she can also operate **as a man**, which is what must be implied if that first interpretation is maintained! The sentence suffers from a **'hanging' descriptor** or **displaced nominative** – two rather stuffy terms that merely indicate that the words need to be better arranged:

    She admires Hardy as a novelist but not as a man.

Taking real care over such matters will bring two benefits. First, it will mean that you're in no danger of looking or sounding foolish! This is less trivial than it might seem: time after time I'm irritated by male interviewers who say to their female guests:

    As a woman, I'd like to ask you . . .

to the extent that I fail to concentrate on the question that follows. That may be pedantic and just silly of me, but I know that many other people react in a similar way, and such moments are not conducive to good communication.

    Second, and more important, it will prevent ambiguity. For displaced nominatives can lead to weightier problems than mere absurdity, as a return to a shortened version of that first example shows:

    As a novelist, she admires Hardy.

Strictly speaking, this can *only* mean that **she** is a novelist herself. But, as noted, that may not be the meaning that is intended; furthermore, even if that meaning is intended, many readers – whether they be ignorant, unalert or suspicious – are likely to assume the alternative. You may think that you've got quite enough to take care of without legislating for bad or suspicious readers, and I do very much see your point! However, in this case the solution is simple. When using a descriptor like **as a novelist**, try this little test:

> **If you immediately add the relevant reflexive pronoun [myself, herself, etc.], will the sentence still make sense?**

For example:

A. [Male] 'As a woman **myself**, may I ask you . . .'

The addition immediately confirms the absurdity; the descriptor is obviously in the wrong place.

B. [Pianist] 'As an instrument **myself**, I prefer the Steinway.'
As for A.

C. [Pianist] 'As a pianist **myself**, I prefer the Steinway.'
Perfectly correct, and clear.

D. [Novelist] 'As a novelist **myself**, I admire Hardy.'
As for C.

E. [Non-writing reader] 'As a novelist **myself**, I admire Hardy.'

Less absurd than A and B, perhaps, but it still won't do.

That 'test', then, will instantly help you to diagnose the accuracy or otherwise of what you're planning to say. And if you do intend the kind of meaning illustrated by C and D, it is good policy to include the reflexive pronoun in your written phrase, if only to dispel suspicious readers' doubts that you really mean what you say!

Finally, remember always to punctuate with absolute precision, especially when you employ **relative** adjectives. Consider the difference in meaning between these two sentences, which follow the pattern first explored on pages 258–9:

1. The book, which is expensive, is essential reading.
2. The book which is expensive is essential reading.

Sentence 1 means that a specific book is expensive but must be read. Sentence 2 means that **any** book that happens to be expensive must be read – a clearly preposterous idea! As we recently found when looking at the definite and indefinite articles, small and apparently inconsequential omissions or inclusions can make a very big difference.

Adverb clauses

Just as there are many types of one-word or phrasal adverbs, so are there many varieties of adverb clauses: nine in all. We all use them every day, naturally and unthinkingly, and becoming fully aware of what they are and how they work is much less difficult than you might imagine. Note that all adverb clauses are subordinate: in each example given below, the clause in bold type either introduces the main statement, or completes it.

1. **Manner**
    As ye sow, so shall ye reap.
2. **Place**
    Fools rush in **where angels fear to tread**.
3. **Time**
    When I've finished this essay, I shall go out.
4. **Degree or comparison**
    Few men worked harder **than did J. P. Morgan**.
5. **Cause**
    I dislike him **because he is arrogant**.
6. **Purpose**
    He took an umbrella **lest it rained**.
7. **Result**
    She took so long to get ready **that he fell asleep**.
8. **Condition**
    All bullies cave in **if you stand up to them**.
9. **Concession**
    Although you have done well, you can do even better.

That concludes this survey of some of the more sophisticated properties of parts of speech. Before moving on to the section on punctuation, try the summarizing exercise that follows.

Exercise 44

A. Identify the following sentences as **simple, double, multiple** or **complex**.

1. The man in the threadbare stained raincoat fell over.
2. As the boy had only just begun his apprenticeship, he did not expect high wages.
3. I love you and I need you.
4. He stood up, stretched vigorously, and then sat down hurriedly, feeling dizzy.

B. Put the following pieces of dialogue into **reported speech**.

1. 'You look very ill,' she told her husband.
2. 'I was just going to call the police,' he said.
3. 'She was here yesterday,' the supervisor admitted.
4. 'I'll be with you in a moment, sir,' the assistant promised.

C. What is the difference in meaning/tone here?

1. I shall be happy just to survive.
2. I should be happy just to survive.

D. Which of these are **count nouns**, and which **noncount nouns**? [N.B.: some might be both.]

1. television. 2. earth. 3. courage. 4. carpet.
5. machine. 6. light. 7. record 8. glass

E. Which of these structures is correct, and which faulty?

1. As a reptile, I find the crocodile uniquely ugly.
2. As a woman, he wanted to sleep with her.
3. As a boss, he was superb; as a friend, he was worthless.
4. As a dish-washer, I think it is poorly marketed.

F. Pick out the adverb clauses in these sentences, and identify their type – **manner, place, time, degree/comparison, cause, purpose, result, condition** or **concession**.

1. Her hair shone as does the sun.
2. You won't survive unless you have immediate treatment.
3. The secretary carefully filed the papers so that they could be easily found.
4. I'll be pleased when it rains.
5. That orange and brown tie is quite fetching, even though at first sight it looks loathsome.
6. Some people are so lazy that they will not even answer urgent letters.
7. Where the bee sucks, there suck I.
8. As you've been under a lot of strain, we'll overlook your error this time.
9. Practise that piece in the way I showed you.

21.4 THE INDIRECT OBJECT

This final item is not a part of speech but a grammatical function, but no matter: it causes trouble to nearly everyone I've ever taught, and is best considered at the close of this 'advanced' section. I hope by this stage that you are clear about the **direct object**; just in case you're not, here are three further examples.

1. The boy passed **the ball**.
2. The inspector questioned **the suspect**.
3. He gave **five pounds**.

In each instance, the highlighted words are on the direct receiving end of the action defined by the verb. Now look at these more complex versions:

1a. The boy passed **me** the ball.
2a. The inspector gave **the suspect** a hard time.
3a. He gave **Oxfam** five pounds.

In these examples the heavy-type words form an **indirect object** that is dependent on the underlined direct object. In each case one could preface that indirect object with the word 'to', which confirms the suggestion of motion or transfer. Notice that in 2a, what was originally the direct object (**the suspect**) has become **in**direct: the direct object is now **a hard time**, given to the suspect.

If ever in doubt about which is the direct and which the indirect object, this simple test will help:

Which one can be left out so that the sentence still makes sense?

Check 1a, 2a and 3a in this way, and you'll quickly establish which is the 'secondary', indirect structure.

PUNCTUATION IN SPEECH AND QUOTATION

22

There is an extensive guide to most punctuation devices and skills in Part Two [pp. 28–49], but nothing on how to punctuate direct speech or its 'cousin', quotation. I have postponed the study of these important skills for one simple reason: they are extremely tricky, even for fully competent writers. Contrary to many students' beliefs and practice, punctuating dialogue or quotation is **not** just a matter of providing inverted commas at appropriate places: all the other 'normal' punctuation skills remain in play as well. This means that at any one time there is a great deal to remember, a great deal to get right; and if those 'normal' skills are not fully assured, any attempt to deal with more sophisticated tasks is very likely to dissolve into chaos.

That's the bad, or forbidding, news; the good news is that

> **Anyone who can punctuate speech and quotation correctly will invariably be entirely competent in all other aspects of punctuation.**

In other words, if you can master this section, any remaining worries you may have about punctuation should come to an end.

Note: this section deals only with the **mechanics** of punctuation when writing speech or quoting. If you are uncertain about the use of quotation in academic essays, reports and articles, please consult pages 178 ff, where you will find advice on lay-out, when to quote and why, and how to ensure that all your quotations work to your maximum advantage.

The rudiments of punctuating speech

1. Practically everyone knows that punctuating speech requires the use of inverted commas. You can use either single or double inverted commas:

1a. 'I'm going out now,' he said.
1b. "I'm going out now," he said.

Both these versions are correct. Most publishing houses use the single version, but you are free to choose whichever one seems most natural to you. However, you should bear these two points in mind:

A. **Never mix single and double inverted commas.**

All drivers will be aware that they should never have a mixture of cross-ply and radial tyres on their car. To mix your inverted commas is a lot less dangerous but no less fundamental an error! So choose one form and stick to it at all times.

That last injunction assumes an added importance when it comes to punctuating quotation:

B. **Whichever form you choose for punctuating speech, you should use the other one for quotation.**

Following that convention will assist clarity anyway, and it is **essential** for those occasions when you need to signify a quotation within a passage of speech. This trickiest of all punctuational skills is covered later*, but you can make a sound start by firmly establishing which form you will use for each mode.

2. Choosing your form of inverted commas and following it consistently is important, but it's also very straightforward. Other rudimentary matters are more problematic, as a return to that first example immediately illustrates:

1a. 'I'm going out now⌞' he said.

Please note the highlighted comma. In my experience as a teacher, at least 90% of learning students fail to insert any punctuation between the passage of speech and the other components of the narrative. **Such punctuation is mandatory at all times**, whether the speech is in the form of a statement –

1a. 'I'm going out now,' he said.

– an exclamation –

1b. 'I'm going out now!' he yelled.

– or a question –

1c. 'May I go out now?' he asked.

In addition, if the overall structure of speech + back-up narrative **ends**

* See below, pp. 321–3.

with the speech component, a full stop will be required if a statement is involved:

1d. He said, 'I'm going out now.'

Of those four examples, it is 1a and 1d that occasion the most frequent errors. A lot of writers comfortably observe the principle behind 1b and 1c: they can 'hear' the exclamation or the question and realize it must be drawn attention to. But those same writers are not aware of any 'break' between 'he said' and the statement itself and punctuate [or **non**-punctuate!] accordingly. I am very sympathetic about this: the need for punctuation is **not** obvious, and including it seems to serve no obvious or clarifying purpose. The fact is that the two components of the complete structure – speech and what I've just termed 'back-up narrative' – **are** separate, and a visual signal is needed to register that separateness. It may not seem to matter much in the case of the short example we've been considering; in longer passages the need to distinguish visually between direct speech and other writing becomes more pressing:

'I'm going out now,' he said, 'and I don't know when I'll be back.' He looked around the room. 'Where are my keys? I thought I left them on that table. Ah! Here they are – in my hand.' Grinning sheepishly, he opened the front door, muttering, 'I must be going ga-ga.'

That is quite a complex little passage. The reader has to absorb various remarks, and also various actions. Yes, they all go together; but I'm sure you can see that if the 'normal' punctuation were omitted – or even just **some** of it – your sense of what's being said and what's being done would quickly get blurred. And in any extended passage of dialogue + action [involving, say, two or three speakers and a lot of accompanying narrative] you would be quite lost within a page or so if those ordinary punctuation conventions were ignored.

3. We'll return to those issues shortly; another rudimentary point needs to be stressed first. Look again at our 'root example':

1a. 'I'm going out now,' he said.

I've already asked you to note the comma; please also note that it is placed **inside** the speech mark. This again is standard unvarying practice, and you should commit it to memory as quickly as possible. Many people mistakenly place such punctuation **outside** the speech marks or, even worse, **directly underneath** them. The latter practice, I always assume, is a simple case of 'bet-hedging': the writer isn't sure where the ordinary punctuation should be placed, so tries to keep all options open! I'm afraid it does not convince: don't do it.

If you think all this is mere pedantry, it isn't: when **quoting**, your 'normal' punctuation will nearly always be placed **outside** the inverted commas. As we'll see, it can sometimes be crucial to distinguish between something that has been said or asked and something which has been quoted: the conventions I've just outlined allow you to do this clearly and with a minimum of fuss.

4. Our final rudimentary point concerns **layout**. Probably the easiest way of determining how to set out exchanges of direct speech is to pick up a novel in which you know there's a lot of dialogue, find an appropriate passage and study its format. You should quickly become aware that

I. **Each new passage of speech is indented**.

And, implicit in that first principle but worth stressing on its own:

II. **Each time the speaker changes, a new line/paragraph is required**.

Two important considerations lie behind these principles, as this little passage, **incorrectly** set out, illustrates:

'Where are you going to, my pretty maid?' 'Mind your own business, you sexist oaf!' 'There's no need to be like that – I was only trying to be friendly.' 'Oh yeah?' 'Yes.' 'Oh well, in that case, I'm off to a meeting of my local "Emma" group.' '"Emma"?' '"Emma", yes: "Extermination of Molesting Males Association".'

That is a bare five lines, but I'd be surprised if you found it easy going. As a single block of prose it is visually taxing: there are a great number of signals to absorb, and it becomes progressively harder to work out who is saying what. As I've stressed throughout, all good writing makes life as comfortable as possible for the reader; that passage does not make comfort a priority – and you can imagine what it might be like to read **several pages** similarly set out.

Happily, it is easily put right.

'Where are you going to, my pretty maid?'
'Mind your own business, you sexist oaf!'
'There's no need to be like that – I was only trying to be friendly.'
'Oh yeah?'
'Yes.'
'Oh well, in that case, I'm off to a meeting of my local "Emma" group.'
'"Emma"?'
'"Emma", yes: "Extermination of Molesting Males Association".'

That is much easier to take in; in addition, in this form the exchanges somehow acquire greater flow and bite. You'll notice that the correct format is not unlike a playscript: perhaps that explains the added **drama** of the amended passage.

You'll also notice that the acronym "Emma" and the final explanation of its meaning are placed within **double** inverted commas. These instances are not quotations as such, but they are analogous to quotations in that they need to be highlighted, and highlighted in a clearly separate way from ordinary speech marks. More on this shortly.

The other great advantage of that correct format, implicit in those exchanges, can be deduced from reading this next passage. What's wrong with it, do you think?

> 'What's going on here?' demanded Susan.
>
> 'Nothing much,' replied Frank.
>
> 'Oh really?' she countered. 'There are three empty gin bottles on the floor, ash all over the carpet, and you seem to have forgotten to put a shirt on.'
>
> 'Can't a man relax after a hard day's work?' he asked.
>
> 'If this is relaxing,' she snapped, 'I'd hate to see what you could manage when really making an effort. And there's another thing,' she added.
>
> 'What?' he enquired.
>
> 'I don't seem to be able to get into our bedroom,' she informed him.
>
> 'Well,' he explained, 'you know how that door's always sticking. Damp, I expect,' he suggested. 'You really need to give it a good shove,' he continued.
>
> 'Don't give me that!' she retorted. 'It's you I need to give a good shove,' she went on, 'out of my house and out of my life!'

This is far from bad writing, but it's **flabby** – and in a precise way:

Apart from the first two remarks, all the 'back-up' identifiers are unnecessary and cumulatively irritating.

Those first two lines establish situation and personnel: it's a row between Susan and Frank. Because only two speakers are involved, and because a new paragraph occurs each time the speaker changes, the reader simply doesn't need the successive **she countered, he asked, she snapped** and so on. Furthermore, they start to get in the way, to interrupt a fast-developing storm: by the time we read the final exchange, the five verbs **he explained, he suggested, he continued, she retorted** and **she went on** are mere annoying hiccups. Susan's last remarks are a scream of rage and frustration, delivered in a single breath: to chop them up like that up seriously reduces their impact.

Be sparing with 'identifiers', therefore. Of course, if your passage of dialogue involves **more** than two speakers, you'll need to make it clear who is saying which lines. This can be done through style alone – establishing a particular 'voice' or idiom for each of several speakers – but that takes a lot of practice [and talent!], and straightforward identification is probably your best course for a while. In addition, there will be times when even if your dialogue is restricted to two speakers, you'll want to include back-up material in the form of qualifiers or narrative information, as in this amended extract from that last passage:

> 'I don't seem to be able to get into our bedroom.' She delivered each word as if biting on a stick of celery.
> 'Well,' he mumbled, not looking at her, 'you know how that door's always sticking.' A thought seemed to strike him. 'Damp, I expect. You really need to give it a good shove . . .'
> 'Don't give me that! It's you I need to give a good shove – out of my house and out of my life!' She flung the car keys at his face, catching him in the left eye, and stormed out of the room.

Even here, however, the additional material is decidedly secondary. None of it is useless; but Frank's explanation is so intrinsically feeble that we can sense without being told that he cannot meet her eye and that he's desperately improvising. Similarly, the last sentence only makes explicit the violence already implicit in Susan's words throughout. So when writing dialogue, give maximum attention to **voice**: you'll be surprised and delighted to find how much unnecessary other work it can save you.

That completes this introductory look at speech punctuation. There are further, subtle things to say about the topic, but first it is time to concentrate on punctuating quotation.

The rudiments of punctuating quotation

1. Quotation is the exact citing of someone else's words. Its most obvious instances are those where the words are famous, and they should be 'clothed' in double inverted commas:*

> 'To be or not to be: that is the question.'
>
> [*Hamlet*]

> 'It is a truth universally acknowledged, that a single man in possession of a good fortune, must be in want of a wife.'
>
> [Jane Austen, *Pride and Prejudice*]

> 'Really quite remarkable.'
>
> [David Coleman]

* Or single, if you prefer: it depends whether you intend to use the single or double form for ordinary speech. The key thing is to keep the two usages absolutely separate.

Figure 47. 'Let them eat cake'.

'Let them eat cake.'

[Marie Antoinette]

2. However, quotation is not **just** a matter of repeating a well-known phrase or saying. Look at these sentences:

1. 'James said, "I'm fed up",' John recalled.
2. 'She said, "Tell the kids I expect their rooms to be tidy when I get back",' their father told them.

These specimens of quotation may be mundane, but they're also pretty complex in terms of mechanics and design – far more so than their famous counterparts above. Let's examine in detail how each one works.

In 1 two speakers are involved – John and James. The latter's words were **I'm fed up**, and John is reporting them. All obvious enough – insultingly so, you might think! But see what a difference in meaning results if we omit those double inverted commas:

1a. 'James said I'm fed up,' John recalled.

Instead of a quotation, we have a form of reported speech. Here John is recalling that James said he, John, is fed up. James's remark has changed from a statement about himself to a deduction about John – a notable difference.

If we wanted to preserve the original meaning but use the reported speech mode, we would need to write:

1b. 'James said that he was fed up,' John recalled.

This is perfectly satisfactory, of course. But the original achieves the same effect simply by the addition of a pair of double inverted commas – clear, compact and stylish.

Sentence 2 is longer and apparently trickier; in fact, it's more straight-forward, because no potential ambiguity can arise. Again, there are two speakers – the father and an unspecified female. This time, however, the audience is implicitly identified – **the kids**, which presumably makes the female speaker their mother. If we omit the double inverted commas –

2a. 'She said, tell the kids I expect their rooms to be tidy when I get back,' their father told them.

– we do not change the meaning: we just end up with something inadequately punctuated. But if you think that doesn't matter much, I hope 1 has shown you that the lazy or incautious omission of quotation marks can make a crucial difference, so be meticulous at all times!

3. When quoting, you need to be especially careful about the accompanying 'ordinary' punctuation. Take another look at that familiar sentence:

'James said, "I'm fed up",' John recalled.

Please note the **order** of the **highlighted** punctuation:

A. The closing quotation marks.
B. The ordinary punctuation. [In this case a comma, but in other instances it could be a full stop, a question mark or an exclamation mark.]
C. The closing speech mark.

Ordinary punctuation is nearly always placed **outside** the quotation marks. The only exception to this is if that ordinary punctuation is itself part of the quotation:

1. 'What is the meaning of "acerbic"?' Simon asked.
2. The teacher commented, 'It's amazing how many people mis-understand the line, "Wherefore art thou, Romeo?"'

In 1 the question mark does not belong to **acerbic**: it signifies that Simon is asking a question about that word. But in 2 the question mark **is** part of the quotation, which is in the form of a question, whereas the teacher is making a statement. Therefore, the question mark belongs **inside** the quotation marks; and since the overall structure ends there, all that is needed thereafter is the closing speech mark.

This is a sophisticated matter, often a question of taste rather than an unvarying rule: I have found that different publishers and editors adopt differing practices, according to their 'house style'.

4. It ought to be obvious that quotation marks **advertise** a quotation neatly and on their own. But many people think it is also necessary to preface any such citation with the phrase **and I quote**. When talking, the phrase is useful [though not essential], because the listener cannot, obviously, hear the quotation marks. But when writing, it is unnecessary and irritating: don't do it.

5. Finally, read this little story – an old joke (somewhat cleaned up!) that illustrates very well the rudimentary principles we've been considering. The scene is a court of law.

> 'Where were you on the night of the 15th June?' asked the prosecution.
> 'At home,' replied the vicious-looking witness.
> 'I see. "At home", you say. Not waiting outside the Midland Bank in a dark blue van with the engine running?'
> 'No way, chief.'
> 'And what were you were doing "at home"?'
> 'Sod-all.'
> 'I'm sorry,' interrupted the judge, 'I didn't catch that last remark.'
> 'He said "Sod-all", m'lud,' the Clerk of the Court supplied.
> 'Oh, really?' said the judge. 'Funny – I thought he said something.'

I hope that amused you, and I'm sorry to descend to an analysis of it – the surest way ever devised of killing a joke. But the confusion here stems from the judge's failure to realize that the Clerk of the Court's use of "sod-all" was a quotation, not a curt statement. The reader **does** realize this, and does so before the judge makes his remark. Hence the laughter – I hope!

Further points and final reminders

Early on I stressed that the inverted commas used for identifying speech or quotation are **additional** to 'normal' punctuation, not replacements for it. You must especially be on your guard when writing passages of conversation, which are likely to require a great deal of 'normal' punctuation. For conversations feature a lot of idiomatic English and interjections or similar phrases, which must all be 'signalled' clearly.

In this example the punctuation isn't all that bad – I've certainly seen worse! It's properly set out, with a new line each time the speaker changes; and the writer has remembered to include a 'normal' punctuation point after each spoken part, correctly placed inside the speech marks. Nevertheless, there are several omissions and at least four choices that could be improved upon. Can you identify them?

> 'Oh hello Mum,' George said nervously. 'Ken and I are just off to the,'
> 'Oh no you're not my lad,' she interrupted. 'There's the little matter of your room to tidy up and then the shoes to clean which you've been promising to do for days.'
> 'But Mum,' he began.
> 'But nothing George. You don't go out till you've done both jobs OK.'

Now study the 'fair copy' version and explanation printed below and see how it compares with what you spotted.

'Fair copy' version

Note: numbers on the right refer to the explanations below.

> 'Oh, hello, Mum,' George said nervously. 'Ken and I   (1)
> are just off to the . . .'   (2)
> 'Oh no, you're not, my lad,' she interrupted. 'There's   (3)
> the little matter of your room to tidy up; and then the   (4)
> shoes to clean which you've been promising to do for days.'
> 'But, Mum . . .' he began.   (5)
> '"But" nothing, George. You don't go out until   (1; 6)
> you've done both jobs, O.K.?'   (7)

1. **Oh, hello** and **Mum** are three separate components and must be punctuated as such. Of course, they are closely related; but they are grammatically distinct – the first two are interjections, the third a name. To be fair, only a pedant would insist on the comma between **oh** and **hello** (though it is correct); but a comma between **hello** and **Mum** is obligatory. The same goes for **nothing** and **George** further down.

2. George's sentence is unfinished: we never find out **where** Ken and he were off to, because he is **interrupted** by his mother. When dialogue is broken into in this way, you should signal it with ellipsis [. . .] – the comma merely confuses and thus won't do.

3. As for 1. Again, the comma after **no** is arguably optional, but the one after **not** is essential.

4. In my view the two chores – room tidying and shoe cleaning – need to be separated; hence the semi-colon, although a comma would do. It

might be your opinion that George's mother is pretty angry and delivers the whole sentence in a breathless rush. If so, fine: keep it as it was. If, however, you think her tone is one of no-nonsense firmness, then that additional signal is necessary.

5. As for 2. Notice that the use of ellipsis means that you can, if you like, scrap **he began**: that information is included in those dots.

6. Putting "But" into quotation marks is perhaps rather pedantic: I wouldn't insist on it. But it is strictly correct: she is 'throwing back' the word at him, and the extra punctuation underlines that fact.

7. Whether you insert a punctuation point between **jobs** and **O.K.** depends entirely on what you think to be the sentence's meaning. If you think **O.K.** is an adverb that goes with **done**, that George's mother is demanding that both jobs be done in a satisfactory manner, then the original version is correct as it stands. But if you take **O.K.** to mean something like 'Do you understand?' or 'Have you got me?', then additional punctuation is required. The comma I've chosen is accurate, but a full-stop would perhaps be better if you think **O.K.** is delivered with a lot of top-spin or menace!

Finally, I must again stress that if you really **listen** to what you're writing, a lot of these subtle, intricate matters will occur to you almost as a matter of course. All those seven points I've listed and discussed are matters of **voice**: once you can hear what's truly being said, everything else should fall naturally into place.

Figure 48. 'Listen to what you're writing'.

Conclusion

As an exemplar of that last point and many others, please read this short extract from P. G. Wodehouse's *The Mating Season*, where Bertie Wooster is talking about Jeeves's uncle, a formidable butler named Silversmith.

> 'Does Silversmith minister to the revellers at the morning meal?'
> 'Yes, sir.'
> 'My God!' I said, paling beneath the tan. 'What a man,
> 5   Jeeves!'
> 'Sir?'
> 'Your Uncle Charlie.'
> 'Ah, yes, sir. A forceful personality.'
> 'Forceful is correct. What's that thing of Shakespeare's about
> 10   someone having an eye like Mother's?'
> '"An eye like Mars, to threaten and command", is possibly the quotation for which you are groping, sir.'

If you've ever found punctuating dialogue and quotation problematic, you could do worse than learn that brief passage off by heart. In its compact dozen lines it exemplifies most of the principles and techniques I've been concerned with; I would draw particular attention to lines 8 and 11, where an incautious writer might have omitted important commas or the quotation marks. As it is, the meticulously correct punctuation helps voice and meaning, thus guaranteeing the lively flow that Wodehouse intended.

There is no more concentrated writing skill than punctuating speech and quotation, especially when they occur together; as I said at the outset, if you can master all its intricacies, you should hardly ever make a mistake in punctuation of any kind.

Now on to the chaotic jungle that is English spelling!

SPELLING AND CONFUSIBLES

23

Introduction

In the various sections on punctuation, I have pointed out that while the skills involved may be intricate and difficult to master, they have the great advantage of being underpinned by 'rules' – rules to which there are no exceptions and which can be trusted. Teachers, or instructional books such as this, are thus able to concentrate on the **principles** of punctuation, knowing that they are watertight and that once their conceptual reasoning is grasped, comfort and accuracy should usually follow.

It goes without saying – or at least I hope it does – that spelling is important. But in my judgment there are serious limits to how far it can be taught, either in a classroom or via a book. Unlike punctuation, English spelling is not systematic in any comfortable sense. There are various 'rules', of course, and only an idiot would say they are not worth bothering with. But there are exceptions to nearly every one yet devised; furthermore, many instances of English spelling are as near to irrational as makes no difference.

Frankly, spelling has to be **learnt** – learnt privately and often one word at a time. I have yet to meet anyone whose spelling is infallible; I know my own certainly isn't! There are still words I have to look up or at any rate check, and there are others I have to think hard about before writing them down. Moreover, ever since I was in junior school, I have found that arriving at the happy state of spelling a word with automatic accuracy is often achieved only by getting it wrong several times first! Such a process of 'trial and error', or of learning from one's mistakes, may be a slow and painful one, but I'm convinced it characterizes the successful speller more than the inculcation of 'rules'.

Naturally, all that is very much a matter of opinion. If you require a detailed guide to the principles and practices of English spelling, there are plenty of useful ones about: I would especially recommend Michael Temple's *Spell It Right* [John Murray, 1985], and others are listed in the bibliography. What I offer instead of a general or comprehensive survey is a focus on **specifics** – words that people very often misspell and words that are frequently confused.

As a taster, here are ten words that in my experience are the most commonly misspelled in everyday usage. If your spelling is at all shaky, a good first step towards improvement would be to learn these ten, noting where the mistake usually occurs and memorizing the correct version.

Correct spelling	Usual mistake
business	s and i reversed
conscious	c omitted
definite	a instead of second i
embarrass	second r omitted
immediately	second e omitted
necessary	2 cs, 1 s [etc. etc.!]
professor/professional	2 fs
receive	i before second e
rhythm	first h omitted; n added
sentence	a instead of second e

Improving your spelling: a strategy

As I've said, I believe that the only way, finally, to become a sound speller is to learn words one at a time – very much as one learns vocabulary when studying a foreign language. 'Rules' are useful, naturally – but as guidelines rather than anything you can fully rely on. Teachers can also help you, of course – partly [if not mainly] by marking your work strictly and drawing attention to any and all mistakes! But in the end it's down to you, to your diligent learning.

That probably sounds rather forbidding, but such an approach should produce an important and pleasing bonus. As you progress you should find that you begin to deduce certain things about how words are put together. You'll see how groups or 'families' of words behave in similar ways, and that the learning of one word will often enable you to spell another dozen or so correctly. As I've warned, there will always be exceptions, to which you must remain constantly alert; nevertheless, because of your developing grasp of how words are formed and how they work, you will find that your command of spelling rapidly increases.

Accordingly, there now follow two large lists, which I recommend you use in the following ways.

1.   Have a reasonably relaxed look at them. Make a rough count of how many you don't know. Be honest about this!
2.   If your 'count' is in single figures, you need neither this book

nor any other spelling guide. Otherwise, take a second look – a fully-concentrated one this time – and commit to memory all those you don't know.

3.   Then read the sub-section that follows the second list, where I go into further detail about the benefits such study should already have brought you.

Spelling list (1)

This first list is straightforward: it contains the 250 words which in my experience are most frequently misspelled. Especially common errors are marked *.

Words marked † can also be spelled with an 's' as in civili<u>s</u>ation and crystalli<u>s</u>e. The important thing is to be consistent throughout your work.

abandon	*beautiful	conjure
abrupt	beginning	*conscience
absorb	behaviour	*conscious
absorption	*believe	consensus
abundant	benefit	contemporary
accelerate	biased	controversy
*accommodate	boisterous	courageous
achieve	bruise	crucial
acquire	bumptious	†crystallize
*across	buoyant	
*address	*business	deceitful
adequate		*definite
*advertisement	calculate	delirious
aggravate	callous	*describe
aggressive	capital	*desperate
agreeable	*caricature	despise
a lot of	casualty	developed
although	catastrophe	diffuse
analysis	ceiling	dilemma
annihilate	changeable	dilettante
anonymous	chaos	*disappear
appalling	character	*disappoint
arrangement	chauvinist	*disastrous
assassin	†civilization	dissatisfy
assessment	collaborate	draught
atmosphere	*committee	
	comparatively	eccentric
	concession	ecstasy
		eliminate

*embarrass

emphasis

enormous

enthusiasm

erratic

et cetera

*exaggerate

excellent

exhilarate

exquisite

extremely

exuberant

facetious

fallible

February

feminist

fiery

focused

forty

fourteen

freight

frivolous

*fulfilment

gaiety

*gauge

gorgeous

government

guarantee

guardian

harass

height

honorary

honourable

*humorous

hygiene

*hypocrisy

in fact

innate

innocent

innovation

instalment

interested

interrupt

intriguing

†jeopardize

judgment

knowledge

laboratory

latitude

liaison

librarian

likelihood

*literature

loneliness

ludicrous

manoeuvre

marriage

marvellous

meagre

meanness

medieval

Mediterranean

mediocre

millionaire

miniature

mischievous

misshapen

mysterious

*naive

*necessary

neighbour

noticeable

nuclear

nuisance

obscene

*occasion

occurred

opportunity

outrageous

overall

*parallel

parliament

particularly

perilous

permissible

persuade

*playwright

*possession

preferred

*privilege

probably

*professor

propaganda

*psychology

publicly

puerile

questionnaire

queue

†realize

recede

*receive

recipe

†recognize

*recommend

referee

relevant

repetition

resistible

restaurant

resuscitate

retrieve

*rhyme

*rhythm

rummage

sacrilegious

salary

sandwich

schedule

scourge

*secretary

*seize

seniority

sentence
*separate
sergeant
simile
skilful
slothful
sluggish
solemn
soliloquy
source
specialist
sublime
subtlety
*success
succinct
succumb
superfluous
supersede
*surprise

technique
theatre
thorough
threshold
traveller
truly

unbelievable
*undoubtedly
*unnecessary
until

vaccinate
vague
*vicious
view
visible

volunteer

weight
weird
whereas
‡whisky
whisper
wiry
*withhold
wholly
woolly
women
writhe

yacht
youthful

zealous

Spelling list (2): confusibles

This second list collects a large number of words that are often confused.
Some are included purely out of spelling considerations, and some for
subtleties of meaning; the majority are significant in both respects.
The list covers a wide range, from elementary 'howlers' to highly
sophisticated distinctions.

N.B. In most cases, the meanings given do not claim to be either exhaustive or definitive: they are designed merely to offer easy identification.

absorb	verb
absorption	noun
accept	to receive
except	not including; to omit
advice	noun
advise	verb
affect	to influence
effect	result; to bring about
allowed	permitted
aloud	out loud, audible

‡ Irish and American spelling is whiskey.

all right	O.K.; completely correct
alright	O.K. – should only be used informally
altogether	completely
all together	as one, all at the same time
allusion	reference
illusion	false image or idea
ascent	upward climb
assent	agreement
associate	to connect
dissociate	to disconnect [N.B. not 'disassociate']
aural	heard
oral	spoken
awesome	inspiring awe
awful	inspiring awe; [colloquial] very bad
bought	past tense of buy
brought	past tense of bring
brake	copse; to stop or slow down
break	interval; to shatter, fracture
bravery	courage
bravado	false or foolish courage
callous	indifferent to others' suffering
cruel	actively enjoying others' suffering
capital	chief, of the head; funds
capitol	building [usually Capitol, as in Washington DC]
cereal	root crop [wheat, barley etc.]
serial	story in parts
check	to restrain; to examine
cheque	money order
climatic	pertaining to the climate
climactic	pertaining to a climax
coarse	rough
course	track; meal; series
complement	a full number; that which completes
compliment	praise
comprehensible	able to be understood
comprehensive	including much or all

contagious	communicating disease by physical contact
infectious	communicating disease by air or water
contemptuous	showing contempt
contemptible	worthy of contempt
council	assembly
counsel	lawyer; advice; to advise
credible	able to be believed
credulous	believing; gullible
curb	to restrain
kerb	edge of the road
currant	berry
current	flow; contemporary, now
dairy	as in milk products
diary	daily record, almanac
decease	death
disease	illness
definite	distinct, precise
definitive	decisive, unconditional, exemplary
dependant	noun – one who depends on someone else
dependent	adjective – depending on
disinterested	impartial, neutral; **not** 'bored'
uninterested	bored
draft	plan, first version; bill
draught	of air, beer; ship's required depth to float
dose	portion of medicine
doze	sleep
dual	of two; double
duel	a fight between two
edible	able to be eaten
eligible	suitable
legible	able to be read
illegible	unable to be read
egoism	theory of self-interest as root of morality
egotism	self-conceit; sustained selfishness
elicit	to bring out
illicit	illegal

eminent	distinguished
imminent	impending
immanent	inherent; [of God] all-pervading
ensure	to make sure
insure	to take out insurance
envelop	to wrap up, surround
envelope	wrapper
excite	to stimulate
exit	to go out, leave
faint	swoon
feint	sham move; pretence
foregoing	preceding
forgoing	doing without
formally	in a formal manner
formerly	previously
genius	spirit; extraordinary talent or intellect
genuine	authentic
gorilla	ape
guerilla	raiding soldier
hangar	huge shed
hanger	for clothes etc.
here	in this place
hear	listen
hoped	aspired
hopped	sprang on one foot
human	of our species
humane	benevolent, compassionate
immoral	knowingly flouting morality
amoral	unconcerned with or not recognizing morality
imply	to suggest
infer	to deduce, interpret
ingenious	imaginative, inventive
ingenuous	naive, artless
disingenuous	pretending to be naive or innocent
irate	angry
irritable	touchy

its	belonging to it
it's	= it is
judicial	pertaining to a judge or court of law
judicious	wise, prudent
lassitude	weariness
latitude	breadth; tolerance
leant	past tense of 'lean'
lent	past tense of 'lend'
licence	noun
license	verb
lightening	becoming lighter
lightning	flash of an electric storm
liqueur	sweet strong drink
liquor	any alcoholic drink
loathe	to detest
loathsome	detestable
lose	to mislay; to be defeated
loose	free; undisciplined
manual	by hand; instructional book
annual	yearly
annal	historical record
anal	of the anus
masterful	dominant, imperious; domineering, self-willed
masterly	very skilful, expert
momentary	lasting a moment*
momentous	highly significant
moral	proper
morale	confidence
official	to do with an officer's duty
officious	abusing that duty; bossy and interfering
opportunity	favourable situation or chance
opportunism	taking every chance one can get
passed	past tense of 'pass'
past	all other uses

---

* It is quite wrong to use the adverb **momentarily** to mean 'in a moment' or 'shortly'.

peace	not war; quiet
piece	part
personal	private, individual
personnel	staff, employees
physician	doctor
physicist	practitioner of physics
plain	flat country; clear; not pretty
plane	level; tool; tree; aircraft
plenty	noun, adjective, adverb
plenteous	adjective only
practice	noun
practise	verb
pray	to worship
prey	hunted creature
prescribe	to order, impose authoritatively
proscribe	to banish, reject, exclude
pressure	[noun **and** verb]
pressurize	to raise to high pressure*
pretension	noun
pretentious	adjective
principal	chief [noun and adjective]
principle	code, ethical tenet
prophecy	noun
prophesy	verb
program	used in computers
programme	all other kinds
racial	pertaining to race
racist	racially prejudiced
rain	precipitation
rein(s)	control; strap(s)
reign	rule
raped	committed rape
rapped	struck; told off
review	critique; to revise, look back on
revue	a theatrical entertainment

* This word should **not** be used to mean 'to put pressure on': use **pressure** instead.

role	actor's part
roll	all other senses
sensual	carnal; depending on the senses, not the mind
sensuous	affecting the senses, especially aesthetically
sceptic	one who doubts
septic	poisoned, infected
sever	to cut
severe	harsh
sew	with a needle
sow	seeds
shear(s)	to shave; [plural] large scissors
sheer	all other senses
shining	luminous
shinning	scrambling [e.g. up a wall]
similar	alike
simile	figure of speech [e.g. 'as light as a feather']
sinewy	muscular
sinuous	serpentine, tortuous
sight	vision; thing seen
site	place, position
sleight	dexterity
slight	slender; meagre
sordid	mean, base, ignoble: a **moral** descriptor
squalid	repulsively filthy: a **physical** descriptor
specific	particular
pacific	peaceful
stationary	not moving
stationery	notepaper, envelopes etc.
story	narrative
storey	floor of a building
straight	not crooked
strait(s)	narrow channel; [plural] difficulties
stupefied	dazed
stupendous	stunningly impressive
suit	of clothes
suite	of rooms or furniture

swinging	swaying from side to side
swingeing	huge, daunting [of damages or taxation]
taught	past tense of 'teach'
taut	tight
temper	mood; to modify, restrain
temperament	disposition, psychic constitution
tenable	able to be argued
tenuous	unconvincing, fragile
there	in that place
their	belonging to them
they're	= they are
there's	= there is
theirs	belonging to them
thorough	complete, conscientious
through	from one end to another
threw	past tense of 'throw'
tier	row
tire	to weary
tyre	on a car, bicycle
to	towards; to do, to run etc.
too	excessive; also
two	2
urban	of a city
urbane	suave, polished in manner
vain	to no avail; physically conceited
vein	blood channel; streak, thin seam
variable	inconsistent
variegated	diversified
venal	financially corrupt, bribable
venial	forgivable [especially of a sin]
vicious	brutal, of vice
viscous	sticky
wave	to gesticulate
waive	to forgo, not claim

weather	climatic conditions
whether	if
were	a past tense form of 'to be'
we're	= we are
who's	= who is
whose	belonging or pertaining to who
your	belonging to you
you're	= you are
yaw	to swing unsteadily [of ships and aircraft]
(of) yore	formerly

Conclusion

If you've just spent a fair time getting thoroughly acquainted with the two preceding lists, you are of course innocent of this next charge – which is that a lot of bad spelling is due to sheer **laziness**. In contrast to such sophisticated matters as sentence structure, paragraphing and the full consideration of parts of speech, or achieving crisp and appropriate syntax, accurate spelling is a simple business. One can see why it takes young writers months, even years, to acquire an authoritative style and an intrinsic understanding of how best to phrase and present their material; there is surely much less excuse for continually misspelling 'necessary', 'definite', 'conscious' and so on. Yet even the brightest and otherwise most professional students are capable of such blemishes. Why?

'Careless' is the descriptor most commonly used by teachers when commenting on poor spelling. It is an admirable diagnostic term – provided it is properly understood. For 'careless' spelling is the result of something more profound than attends such apparently synonymous terms as 'slap-dash' or 'rushed': it denotes a lack of caring. In the majority of instances, people who spell badly don't **mind** enough about getting it right: ultimately, they can't be bothered. They get away with it because, as I pointed out in Part One, a misspelling has to be grotesquely bad for the word to be rendered incomprehensible; another way of putting it is that there is perhaps not enough incentive to be a good speller. Other writing skills seem more important – and these days flawed spelling can easily be attributed to dyslexia!*

* Contrary to claims made by certain 'consultants', dyslexia is a rare and complex condition. It is a term much abused, notably by a growing army of cowboys who charge large sums of money for 'sanitizing' ordinary learning difficulties or unremarkable laziness via seductively remarkable jargon. As I remark in Part Three, euphemism is a handy device for all scoundrels!

So to rephrase a point already made, spelling correctly is your own responsibility: it is a question of how much it matters to you to be good at it. If you're still reading these uncompromising words, it's safe to assume that it does matter to you, and it's time to offer some further constructive advice rather than continue a tirade!

One reason why this section is shorter than most of the others in the Primer is that much previous material has been concerned with spelling issues – plurals, inflections, the use of the apostrophe and so on. Indeed, this whole book has been about how words work, which automatically involves how they are formed and spelled. If you've read this book with care and enjoyment, the chances are very high that a number of things have 'stuck', including a lot of spellings that you might have got wrong before. And that introduces an important point which is my first 'tip':

If you *read* with proper concentration, you will gradually and automatically develop a 'feel' for accurate spelling.

I do not claim that such a 'subliminal' phenomenon will eventually take care of every spelling problem; but there is no doubt that attentive reading is a major help-meet to good spelling, as well as being a virtue in its own right.

Second:

If you know that you regularly tend to make spelling errors, keep a dictionary to hand at all times.

Kingsley Amis has remarked that 'the mark of an educated man is that he's prepared to look things up'; the same goes for properly caring writers. Yes, it's a slow business at first – especially when your sense of how a word might be spelled is so vague that you're not sure precisely where in the dictionary to look! But it will soon reap benefits: the mental discipline it mobilizes should ensure that the word sticks in your memory henceforth.

Third:

Try making a *game* out of difficult spellings.

If you continue to have 'blind spots' or 'memory blanks' about certain words – and nearly everyone does – you need to find a way of making them memorable; this is best done by constructing a mnemonic, preferably one that is amusing. For example, a young pupil of mine learnt how to spell 'necessary' by constructing this mnemonic out of its letters:

never eat chips: eat salad sandwiches and remain young.

I adopted the same principle for 'dilettante' – a word I previously had to look up every time I used it:

don't imagine life exists to take all narcotics to excess.

A bit melodramatic or pompous, maybe, but it works!
   Fourth:

When spelling, *listen* as hard you can.

In an enormous number of instances, the sound of a word offers valuable clues about its spelling. To be fair, maybe that is why so many people misspell 'definite' – normal pronunciation suggests an **a** instead of the second **i**; in keeping with the exceptions that bedevil English spelling, there are other words that are treacherous in the same way! But do not let that put you off: alert 'hearing' will benefit you far more often than not. You will become aware, for instance, of the difference between long and short vowels and the effect this has on spelling, as in this example from Spelling List 2:

hoped is a **long** vowel; **single** consonant follows.
hopped is a **short** vowel; **double** consonant follows.

Fifth, and closely allied to the previous tip:

Try always to be aware of how a word is correctly pronounced.

There is a high correlation between mispronunciation and misspelling. It is true that I have hardly ever seen 'something' written as 'somethink' even though the latter is a common sound in the South of England; but I have often encountered the following misspellings, all of which derive from a mistaken idea of how the word should be spoken:

atherlete	instead of	athlete
secetary	instead of	secretary*
libary	instead of	library
particerlar	instead of	particular*
pacific	instead of	specific*
proberly	instead of	probably*
suprised	instead of	surprised*
primrally	instead of	primarily

Those marked * have already appeared in one or other of my two Spelling Lists, which emphasizes the connection between aural/oral error and written confusion.
   Sixth, and last:

Compile your own dictionary, in which you write down any word you spell wrong or are unsure of.

This idea is a more sophisticated or systematic version of something you may have encounted in junior school – doing 'Corrections'. Unfortunately, young children can associate that admirable practice with

Figure 49. 'Compile your own dictionary'.

punishment for getting things wrong; don't make the same mistake. The very act of writing anything down greatly increases your chances of remembering it: what could be more sensible than to write out [correctly!] and thus focus closely on the words that don't yet come naturally to you? You can create your 'personal spelling dictionary' out of a cheap indexed notebook; peruse and add to it regularly, as you would a French or German vocabulary book, and you'll be pleased how quickly it makes a difference.

As a final word of encouragement: remember that even highly educated and experienced professionals misspell words sometimes. My daughter's recent English report included the rogue spelling 'developped', and two of my colleagues, at the time of writing, think there is a word spelt '**ap**alling'. Since one of them was commenting on a boy's spelling, this was an unfortunate mistake! Accurate spelling involves a lot of care and a lot of work – for all of us. But it's worth it, if only because nothing undermines otherwise impressive writing so obviously as a rash of mistakes that could have been avoided.

APPENDIX: ANSWERS TO EXERCISES

Exercise 1

When feeding the baby with a bottle, the latter must be held at a steep angle with the bottom tilted up and the neck held firmly down, otherwise an air-bubble will form in the neck. Do not allow the baby to drink all the feed at once, but give it a rest sometimes so that it can get the wind up. Finally, when the baby has finished, place the bottle under the tap straight away or soak it in a mild solution of Milton, to prevent infection. If the baby does not thrive on fresh milk, powdered or boiled milk should be used instead.

Exercise 2

1. In the game's very last seconds, McDonald scored with a header.
2. We thought this story superb – very convincing.
3. The Channel Tunnel project seems to be getting under way again.
4. Here we are in the Holy Land of Israel – a major attraction for tourists.
5. She really excited the poolside crowd tonight.
6. No re-write possible, surely. This is a classic example of the need to shut up when there's nothing useful to say!
7. I thought the 2–0 scoreline accurately reflected the play.
8. Tell me, what is your gut feeling?
or
Tell me, how do you feel in your heart of hearts?
9. Obviously you do other things despite dedicating most of your life to ballet.
10. The atmosphere is amazing: you could cut the atmosphere with a knife.*

---

* I've substituted a more than usually stale cliché here; I don't like it, but I'm hampered by the fact that I have no idea what was in Murray Walker's mind when he cited "cricket stump"!

Exercise 4

Prohibition was known as 'The Great Experiment', and it was indeed a remarkable one, occurring in the United States of America in the years 1920–33. During that time the sale and consumption of alcohol was prohibited; the people's liking for alcohol did not disappear, however, and so it was distilled illegally and sold in 'Speakeasies', clubs owned by gangsters. Some of these gangsters became enormously powerful: Al Capone of Chicago was for a time considered to be the most powerful man in the country, and although he was eventually imprisoned for tax evasion, the gangsters' control nevertheless continued. By the time Prohibition came to an end in 1933, the damage had been done: America has had to live with organized crime ever since.

Exercise 5

Counsel maintained that the allegations of some prosecution witnesses concerning the stolen articles were not very reliable; in addition, he revealed that the accused had been subject to temporary lapses of memory as a result of shell-shock sustained during the war.

Exercise 8

There is a stretch of coast in North Norfolk that has a special place in my affections. It lies between Sheringham in the east and the delightful village of Stiffkey in the west, and is especially beautiful because it has not been spoilt by modern developments; indeed, it is much the same as I remember it as a small child twenty years ago and more, when I regularly visited it in the school holidays. I return there most years now, staying in a small cottage in Weybourne which overlooks the sea; however, it may not survive as a safe habitat for very long, as it is close to the cliffs that are rapidly eroding: eventually it may just fall into the sea!

Norfolk is famous for its wild life. From March to October you can see a rich variety of beautiful creatures and flowers, ranging from the hundreds of baby oystercatchers hatched every year on the Blakeney Point Nature Reserve to the very rare bitterns. These shy birds are now found only in certain quiet areas of the Norfolk Broads, and the thriving tourist trade of these waters threatens the bittern with extinction, just as it once drove out the otter and the coypu.

Exercise 9

Cholesterol, a steroid alcohol found in certain fluids and substances stored by the body, is a potentially deadly phenomenon. It promotes arteriosclerosis; this in turn precipitates high blood pressure, which increases the chances of having a heart attack, angina, or a host of similarly dangerous conditions.

Cholesterol's main carriers are foods we eat regularly: butter, cheese, milk and salt. Cream and rich puddings are especially high in cholesterol, as are eggs and anything fried in oil or dripping. If you eat too many such foods, your arteries harden prematurely. Obviously enough, this makes it more difficult for the blood to flow; they also get coated and generally unhealthy, contaminated and weak, so that you run a high risk, at the very least, of premature illness, incapacity or even death.

Exercise 10

1. **He was fed up; the bus had left without him.**
   A colon after **up** would do just as well, as would a comma plus the conjunction **for** or **because**.
2. **His promotion was not due to any particular skill or merit: he had bought his way up.**
   A perfect example of when to use the colon, which 'signals' an intimate, direct link between the two clauses.

3. **Stuck out here in the heart of the Yorkshire moors, in the vicinity of a bog, there is no problem parking the car; a little difficult extricating it may be experienced, though.**
   Some might prefer a full stop after **car**: it depends how <u>long</u> a pause you think the 'speaker' might take. Either device is accurate.
4. **The fridge worked; the food stayed fresh; the milk remained cold; the little light came on when you opened the door.**
   The original commas are not seriously faulty, perhaps, but semi-colons are better: four separate clauses occur, and one should try to avoid the comma where one can, to prevent a profusion which irritates and distracts.
5. **He was caught in a vicious circle: nobody would hire him as a portrait-painter until he was well-known, but he couldn't become well-known until people hired him.**
   The colon sets up the full explanation of the opening statement. The comma is wrong anyway, being too weak to separate two full clauses.

6. **The recent BAFTA awards prove one thing if nothing else: when it comes to excruciating self-indulgence the TV industry has no equals.**
    See explanation to 2. A full stop after **else** would be technically correct but stylistically much inferior.

Exercise 16

1. Throughout the chapter . . .
2. The incident with which the chapter ends . . .
    or
    The chapter's final incident . . .
3. These factors combined to produce . . .
4. It was no more than a passing thought . . .
5. After a while, however, he realized . . .
    or
    But after a while he realized . . .
6. He can do no more than follow blindly . . .

Exercise 29

He escaped by abseiling 60 feet from window to ground, using a waist-attached rope that he had weighted and thrown over a nearby branch.   **25 words**

Exercise 30

Benefits Of Team Games

A movement against inter-school fixtures is gathering momentum and its advocates have mustered some cogent arguments. There is a place for individual sports, but they must remain subordinate to team games for moral and philosophical reasons.

Team sports induce discipline in an individual: initially imposed, it becomes **self**-discipline – co-operation underpinned by regular physical training. In some cases such strength, and its consequent moral uplift, can prevent an otherwise prevalent tendency to delinquency.

Team sports also create pride and a sense of the school as a genuine community; these often blossom into a wider response from the town, which has social and material benefits. Staff–student relationships also benefit through greater mutual involvement and understanding; so as a result does school discipline. And team sports are much cheaper to effect than all individual sports.

139 words including title

Single-sentence Summary

Team sports are superior to solo sports because they inculcate discipline, raise school and social morale, and are cheaper to effect.

21 words

Exercise 31

Test Career Dies As Gatting Flies

This is an obituary: not for a person but for a Test career. Today Mike Gatting will lead fellow-rebels onto a South Africa-bound plane into Test cricket wilderness. He will be 41 when that ends: the finest Middlesex batsman since Compton will never represent England again.

I find that dreadfully sad. For nobody values playing for his country more. He is a proud man and a class player, a master-butcher whose occasional delicacy also delights. At his best he devastates, exemplified by the 79 pillaging runs he enragedly took off Pakistan's previously dominant attack in Faisalabad.

He took 6 years and 52 innings to make his first hundred; when he achieved it in Bombay, the English press rose in applause. Seldom has he given short measure since; but watching him recently decline into premature weariness has been painful. His Australian zenith led to rapid downfall with the infamous Shakoor Rana incident. Team discipline collapsed; performances followed suit. That, and subsequent transgressions in New Zealand, should arguably have cost him the captaincy; instead he was fired for his tabloid-fanned supposed dalliance with a barmaid.

Henceforth Gatting became sour about the Test and County Cricket Board – a condition aggravated by injury, loss of form and bereavement. Yet he could have been won back: he sounded out the TCCB, looking for encouragement. None was forthcoming, so off he goes.

It would be nice if Gatting were remembered for his imperious batsmanship; probably he will be chronicled as a rebellious, ignorant pawn who foundered in games beyond his ken.

Soon to be richer by £200,000, Mike Gatting neither needs nor would seek my sympathy. But he's got it.

278 words

Exercise 32

Language and Politics: Symbiotic Decay

Nowadays political writing is bad writing, unless the writer is unorthodox. In thought and style party lines are robotic, not human, because tyrannies, purges and mass destruction can only be supported by arguments too brutal for the majority to countenance and which undermine parties' pretensions to decency. So political language degenerates into euphemism and distortion: irreducibly abstract, it obliterates mental images instead of promoting them. The enemy of clear language is insincerity. Any gap between real and declared aims is cynically disguised. Everything is politics: politics is characterized by lies and madness, so language follows suit.

95 words

Exercise 33

The Problem of Selfishness

Is ambition a virtue or a vice? In embodying the urge towards excellence, it is good; in evincing the desire to better others, it is bad. Since we are all ambitious, we revert to excusing the former and accusing the latter; and since collectively we are selfish, we tend to excuse ourselves while accusing others. As individuals or as nations, we claim our motives as good while finding the motives of others bad. In fact, our **relative** virtue is only apparent when it coincides with others' interests.

Such sophistry is basic to human nature, wherein good and evil, self-regard and self-giving, and self-obsession and self-forgetfulness are always mixed. And we explain our selfishness in various ways. One is to accept it as innate, and complacently leave it at that; another is to pretend to an interest in others (which is partly genuine) in order to dignify that intrinsic egotism; a third is to attempt to reject the self utterly – which results in a mysticism futile in that it only reveals the self more nakedly. A fourth is to concede that we are selfish but to seek to transcend that state through grace.

Grace is central to Christianity. It is the force that tempers our selfishness, making us most truly ourselves by helping us to forget ourselves through devotion to and immersion in a larger power. And if grace is permanently available, it means that one **can** change one's destiny, alter one's nature. Modern life can thus be made tolerable: our democracies rest on a recognition that we are selfish and that such selfishness is tainted. The humble appraisal of a state both natural and inherently flawed facilitates justice and a proper sense of balance.

288 words

Exercise 34

The Preservation Of True Constitutional Liberty

The belief that civic rebellion is a justified last resort serves, paradoxically, to fuel tyranny. Far from keeping rulers in check, the prospect of tyrannicide invariably makes them more extreme and despotic. It is in everyone's interests to cultivate obedience as the norm. To search at once for exceptions is both absurd and morally precarious, since it fundamentally subverts that central doctrine. However, the **possibility** of exceptions must be allowed if the causes of truth and liberty are to be safeguarded. Furthermore, our British Constitution has now effected a second defence of those causes. A Prince who is above the law but whose ministers are answerable to it may thereby feel personally secure, and thus confidently able to fend off attacks on his sovereignity which, unchallenged, could lead to Civil War. But a Prince who is made to feel defensive in the face of the law may well collapse into catastrophic imprudence, regardless of his goodness and private virtue. Any English sovereign who imagines his power to be absolute gravely misunderstands the nation's Constitution, and can expect nothing less than the removal of his power.   **195 words***

Afterthought
This is the most difficult précis exercise I have ever come across: just understanding the original calls for immense effort and a good deal of skill! For that reason, this particular 'fair copy' is even more 'notional' than usual.

Exercise 35

1. telephoned.	5. became.	9. will be returning.
2. appalled.	6. tasted.	10. will disappoint.
3. was.	7. savaged.	
4. destroyed.	8. has vanquished.	

---

* Obviously, this is considerably shorter than the stipulated maximum of 250. Nevertheless, I do not feel I've omitted anything essential; would you agree?

Exercise 36

	1.	2.	3.	4.
Subject:	The bomb	The dog	The postman	The man
Verb:	destroyed	bit	bit	walked
Object:	the house	the postman	the dog	–

	5.	6.	7.	8.
Subject:	the children	the cheetah	the lecturer	the bulldozer
Verb:	walked	ran	ran over	ran over
Object:	the dog	–	the main ideas	the hedgehog

Exercise 37

A. 1. was shining; intransitive.
   2. burnt; transitive.
   3. exploded; intransitive.
   4. bought; transitive.
   5. hit; transitive.
   6. will be; intransitive.

B. 1. I am going to the shops.
   2. The floods had been devastating.
   3. They were appearing on 'Blind Date'.
   4. He will have passed his driving test.
   5. Julian will be seeing Susan every day.

C. 1. Indicative.
   2. Imperative.
   3. Subjunctive.
   4. Indicative.
   5. Imperative.
   6. Imperative.

Exercise 38

A. 1. The bird was swallowed by the snake.
    2. The slates were blown off the roof by the gale.
    3. The large audience was not satisfied by the band.

B. 1. We would appreciate an early settlement of your account.
    2. The treasurer embezzled the charity's funds.
    3. Your Sunshine Tours representative has taken care of all travel arrangements.

C. 1. brought.
    2. committed (note the *double* t).
    3. gone.
    4. hopped (note the *double* p).
    5. cut.

D. In pair 1a and 1b, there is a change in emphasis: 1a places the primary focus on the organization, 1b on its corruption. The difference is subtle but definite, and determines the use of the passive or active voice, according to which focus is desired.

In pair 2a and 2b, the first is in the indicative mood, the second in the subjunctive. The speaker/writer of 2b sees the proposed action as much less likely than pertains in 2a.

Exercise 39

A. 1. common/concrete.
   2. proper.
   3. collective.
   4. abstract
   5. **either** abstract (state of mind, mood) **or** concrete (a weather front; sunk place, hollow).
   6. collective
   7. common/concrete.
   8. proper.
   9. common/concrete.
   10. **either** abstract (seriousness) **or** concrete (weight, attractive force).

B. Four common/concrete nouns: **man; buses; taxis; hamburger.**
[You could also have **traffic** and **eagles.**]
Three proper nouns: **Big Ben; Parliament Square; McDonald's.**
Two collective nouns: **gathering; fleet.**
Three abstract nouns: **indifference; fascination; interest.**

C. 1. Catching the last train home.
   2. The old man's delight in painting.
   3. the name of that well-dressed woman.
   4. That your writing style is improving **and** how hard you have worked.
   5. that he has the most experience.
   6. what they were looking for.

Exercise 40

1. Between you and **me** . . .
2. She and **I** . . .
3. Pass me **those** socks . . .
4. They think **she** is the only one **who** can do the job.
5. The rich don't care about **us** poor people.

Exercise 41

A. Relative: **which** (line 3); **whom** (1. 6); **who** (1. 8).
Demonstrative: **that** (line 1); **that** (1. 4); **those** (1. 7). **that** (1. 9).
Interrogative: **what** (line 1); **what** (1. 2); **who** (1. 5).

B. Sentence 1 means that students who plan their work sensibly tend to be more successful than other students.
Sentence 2 argues that **all** students plan their work sensibly, and that they are therefore more successful than all other people.
Sentence 2 is, of course, a preposterous claim!

C. 1. all; most.
   2. fewer.
   3. many; much. The second one has to be **much** because the verb is singular; **many** would be correct if the verb were changed to **are**.
   4. is. **Not one** is the controlling subject, and is singular; **of us** is dependent upon it, so a plural verb is wrong.

D. 1. **whose**, not who's.
   2. **you're**, not your.
   3. **they** is inadequate: there is no way of knowing to which team it refers.
   4. **quite** is redundant.
   5. **smaller**, not smallest.

In addition, of course, it is nonsense to talk of one **half** being bigger/smaller than another! The sentence needs to be entirely re-phrased.

Exercise 42

A. 1. panicked.
   2. swollen.
   3. beginning (note the *double* **n**).
   4. lay.
   5. lied.

B. 1. **Once** TV-AM broadcast daily. (The most economical way). **or**
   1. TV-AM broadcast daily **until it lost its franchise in October 1991.** (Much wordier, but more informative!)
   2. **On that occasion** we let them off with a caution.

C. 1. kisses; marches.
   2. (the) Kennedys; verb changes to **were**.
   3. parties; guys.
   4. criteria; verb changes to **are**.

D. 1. **music** must be singular.
2. **those** shears.
3. Spurs'.
4. media's.
5. children's.

E. 1. abnormal.
2. inopportune.
3. misspell.
4. disarray.
5. **dissoc**iate: **disassociate** does not exist, although the noun **disassociation** does. Apologies for the 'trap'!

F. 1. uneasiness.
2. detestation.
3. joyful/joyous.
4. urgently.
5. dependable.

Exercise 44

A. 1. simple.
2. complex. **As . . . apprenticeship**: an adverb clause of **cause**.
3. double.
4. multiple.

B. 1. She told her husband that he looked very ill.
2. He said that he had just been on the point of calling the police.
or 2a. He said that he had merely been going to call the police.
3. The supervisor admitted that the girl had been there yesterday.

Note: this is not entirely satisfactory. We need more context to establish whether the **she** is a girl, a woman or a female animal of some kind. In addition, **there** is very vague in this reported speech version, but there is no better alternative.

4. The assistant promised the man that he would be with him in a moment.

C. Sentence 1 is much the stronger: the speaker is about to embark on a very hazardous mission of some kind, and the remark indicates active worry, if not actual fear.

Sentence 2 is **conditional**: the implication is that the speaker is not going to do something so hazardous, and is assessing the chances of survival in a **theoretical** way.

D. 1. both: (a) May we watch television?   **[noncount]**
              (b) How many televisions have you got?   **[count]**
2. noncount
3. noncount
4. count
5. count
6. both: (a) Light travels at 186,000 mps.   **[noncount]**
              (b) Please turn the lights off.   **[count]**

7. count
8. both: (a) The windows are made of glass.   **[noncount]**
              (b) Have you washed up the glasses?   **[count]**

E. 1. Faulty: suggests the speaker is a reptile.
2. Faulty: suggests the male speaker is a woman.
3. Both structures are correct.
4. Faulty. It **could** be correct if the speaker washes dishes for a living,
    but it's unlikely that this was intended!

F. 1. **as does the sun.**   comparison
2. **unless you have immediate treatment.**   condition
3. **so that they could easily be found.**   purpose
4. **when it rains.**   time
5. **even though at first sight it looks loathsome.**   concession
6. **that they will not even answer urgent letters.**   result
7. **Where the bee sucks.**   place
8. **As you've been under a lot of strain.**   cause
9. **in the way I showed you.**   manner

FURTHER READING

I've subtitled this book 'A guide to good English'; there are many other books which will help you achieve that goal. Indeed, the field is enormous, and considerations of space make a comprehensive bibliography impractical. What follows is a list of the books I have found valuable and instructive while preparing my own text. Titles that are particularly recommended are marked *.

STANDARD DICTIONARIES

* *The Oxford English Dictionary*. Still beyond compare, but the financial outlay is prodigious! The *Concise* and, especially, the *Shorter* editions are excellent, and reasonably priced.
  The Oxford American Dictionary.
  Webster's New Collegiate Dictionary (Merriam-Webster).
  Oxford Dictionary of English Etymology, ed. C. T. Onions.
* *Collins Cobuild English Language Dictionary*. Cobuild denotes the Collins Birmingham University International Language Database, and this dictionary is imaginatively and helpfully put together.
* *Roget's Thesaurus of Words & Phrases* (many publishers).

MAJOR GUIDES

* *Fowler's Modern English Usage*, revised by Sir Ernest Gowers.
* Sir Ernest Gowers, *The Complete Plain Words*.
* *The Right Word At The Right Time*, ed. John Ellison Kahn (Reader's Digest, 1985). An invaluable recent addition.
  The Oxford Guide to the English Language (1985).

SPECIALIST DICTIONARIES

* John Ayto, *The Longman Register of New Words* (1989).
  Ambrose Bierce, *The Enlarged Devil's Dictionary* (Penguin, 1983).
* Bill Bryson, *The Penguin Dictionary of Troublesome Words* (1984).

Mary Edwards, *Dictionary of Key Words* (Macmillan, 1985).

Jonathon Green, *The Cynic's Lexicon* (Sphere, 1986).

Daphne M. Gulland & David G. Hinds-Howell, *The Penguin Dictionary of English Idioms* (1986).

* R. W. Holder, *The Faber Dictionary of Euphemisms* (1989).

Kenneth Hudson, *The Dictionary of Diseased English* (Macmillan, 1977).

* B. A. Phythian, *A Concise Dictionary of English Slang* (Hodder & Stoughton; 3rd edition, 1985).

GRAMMAR, MECHANICS AND USAGE

S. H. Burton, *Mastering English Language*, (Macmillan, 1982).

* G. V. Carey, *Mind The Stop* (Penguin, 1971).

David Crystal, *Who Cares About English Usage?* (Penguin, 1984).

* David Crystal, *Rediscover Grammar* (Longman, 1988).

D. J. Collinson, *Writing English* (Pan, 1982).

Gordon Humphreys, *Teach Yourself English Grammar* (Hodder & Stoughton, 1945).

* Eric Partridge, *Usage & Abusage* (Penguin, 1981).

* Philip Davies Roberts, *Plain English: A User's Guide* (Penguin, 1987).

* Michael Temple, *Spell It Right* (John Murray, 1985).

O. M. Thomson, *Essential Grammar* (Oxford, 1978).

STYLE: GENERAL

Philip Howard, *A Word In Your Ear* (Penguin, 1985).

* Philip Howard, *The State Of The Language* (Penguin, 1986).

* O. M. Thomson, *A Matter Of Style* (Stanley Thorn; 3rd edition, 1992).

John Whale, *Put It In Writing* (Dent, 1984).

STYLE: TECHNICAL, COMMERCIAL AND SCIENTIFIC

Edward P. Bailey Jr., *The Plain English Approach To Business Writing* (Oxford, 1990).

John Kirkman, *Good Style for Scientific and Engineering Writing* (Pitman, 1980).

Walter Shawcross, *English for Professional Examinations* (Pitman; 3rd edition, 1947).

* Christopher Turk & John Kirkman, *Effective Writing* (E & FN Spon, 1982).

MISCELLANEOUS

This final selection has no connecting thread other than my own pleasure. However, each is excellent in its own way and should prove a rich source of both enjoyment and instruction.

Robert Burchfield, *Unlocking The English Language* (Faber, 1989).
* *The Faber Book Of Reportage*, ed. John Carey (1987).
* H. L. Mencken, *The American Language* (1936; 1977 Knopf paperback version, including the two supplements of 1945 & 1948).
* David Lodge, *Write On* (Penguin, 1986).
* David Lodge, *The Art of Fiction* (Penguin 1992).
  Logan Pearsall Smith, *All Trivia* (USA 1945; Penguin, 1986).
  Christopher Ricks & Leonard Michaels, *The State Of The Language: 1990 Edition* (Faber).
  Christopher Turk, *Effective Speaking* (E & FN Spon, 1985).

AUTHORS, SOURCES AND NAMED REFERENCES

Page numbers in **bold** type refer to passages of text; those in roman type refer to simple references or one-line quotations.

SUBJECT INDEX

Page numbers in **bold** type refer to an entire section devoted to that topic.